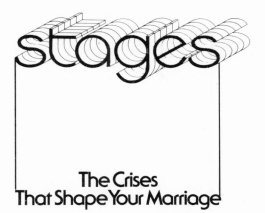

stages

The Crises
That Shape Your Marriage

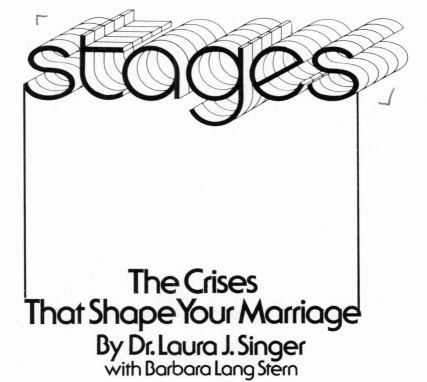

stages

The Crises
That Shape Your Marriage
By Dr. Laura J. Singer
with Barbara Lang Stern

Publishers · GROSSET & DUNLAP · New York
A FILMWAYS COMPANY

To my husband, Sam, and my daughter, JoAnn

———————————

L.J.S.

For my husband, Ernie

———————————

B.L.S.

In every marriage more than two weeks old, there are grounds for divorce. The trick is to find and continue to find, grounds for marriage.

From the play *DOUBLE SOLITAIRE*
by Robert Anderson

Contents

To the Reader

After treating marriages for many years, one begins to see an evolving pattern of critical periods in the relationship between husband and wife. Most marriages go through certain predictable stages that inevitably create unusual stress and build toward a crisis.

The Chinese character for crisis is made up of two symbols: one for despair, the other for opportunity. When physicians speak of a crisis, they're talking about the moment in the course of a disease when a decisive change for better or worse occurs. When I discuss crises in marriage, I'm talking about such turning points when a marriage can go in either direction: it can move toward enrichment, improvement and greater mutual support, or toward dissatisfaction, divisiveness and, sometimes, dissolution.

I don't want to suggest that all marriages are the same. The way in which any crisis is handled will depend on the personalities of the individuals and the nature of their relationship. My professional experience has been largely with middle- or upper-middle-class marriages. One has to be conscious of this limitation to avoid misunderstanding. For example, when I discuss the significance of money for the individual and the couple, it must be recognized that this analysis does not apply to people who are in dire need. To those striving for a modicum of economic security, survival is the crucial issue. On the other hand, within the sizable territory of middle- or upper-middle-class marriages in the United States today, general patterns of crises can be recognized. Therefore, as we approach new stages in our marriage or events in our lives, we can anticipate, understand and prepare for many of the effects we'll be experiencing. I think we should take advantage of this opportunity.

There might not be any crises in marriage if you could capture a relationship at a perfect moment and preserve it, as in a photograph. But individuals and circumstances change. Nothing is static.

As events in your life cause you to adjust to new circumstances, this requirement for change, however slight, produces stress. Most people think of stress as something negative and harmful. Yet, as Hans Selye, M.D., has shown in one of the most remarkable findings in recent years: regardless of its cause, the phenomenon of stress is always the same in terms of the emotional disequilibrium and physiological alterations it produces in the individual. Suppose you receive a telephone call giving you news that affects you greatly. If a doctor were monitoring your emotional and biochemical responses, he'd recognize signs of stress but would be unable to say whether they were present because you were thrilled to learn you'd been given a tremendous raise or shocked to hear you'd been fired. In both instances, your heartbeat would quicken, your blood pressure would rise, your digestive system would slow down and your production of adrenalin and other hormones would alter. At the same time, your intensity and absorption would increase and your emotional equilibrium would be lost. "What am I going to do now? Who am I going to tell?"

Although reactions to stress are predictable, the degree, intensity, and ability to cope with them vary from person to person. Some people perform extraordinarily well under pressure; others feel anxious, disorganized or helpless. Stress may bring out inherent strengths or awaken dormant anxieties. Usually stress throws you back into some emotional and/or behavioral pattern connected with your early childhood. You tend to transfer onto your partner the feelings you had as a child toward your parents. This transference generally causes some of the greatest problems within a marriage. You may unrealistically blame things on or expect things from your partner. Or you may pull back in despair of receiving any help or comfort.

A crisis is an escalation of stress, connected to a fundamental change that is forcing you to make a major adjustment. The change may affect one marriage partner more than the other, but the fact that it's taking place means there is bound to be an adjustment in the existing balance between the two people. Anything that significantly affects one also affects the other. The combination of what is happening emotionally within each person and what is happening between the two partners is at the core of any crisis.

Suppose a husband or wife is having an affair. What are the reasons behind it? What is the emotional effect on that person and on his or her feelings toward the spouse? If the spouse finds out, how will he or she react? Are there ways in which the situation can be examined so the underlying causes behind the affair can be recognized and the needs of each partner might become clearer to the other? An affair is one of the most threatening and devastating crises that couples may ever face. Yet even here, it is possible to achieve greater understanding and perhaps improve some aspects of the marital relationship, rather than precipitate a break in the marriage.

In my experience, the degree to which you and your partner are able to support and empathize with each other is the most significant factor in determining how any crisis will affect your marriage. If you can form a relationship that is of maximum help to each of you, then adjusting to change can be a unifying, strengthening experience. Otherwise, the pressures and stress can be divisive.

As I discuss different crises or stages in marriage, you'll begin to see how each one offers you and your mate the opportunity to improve your methods of dealing with stress. Certainly a crisis is more easily handled if a couple has established a manner of interacting that's open and mutually supportive. Yet even if your history has been unsatisfactory, it's always possible to do something in a fresh way if you are willing to open up, take some risks and, of course, work at it. I sometimes tell couples who think they're locked into an impossible and irreversible trend within their marriage, "Look, you *know* you can always get a divorce, but maybe it would be worthwhile first to see what else you can do that might really change the relationship between you."

I hope that through this book you'll begin to understand the origins of the marital crises you're apt to face and become able to cope with them in more positive ways. As we investigate various problems, you can learn more about the mental processes, developments and experiences that have been important in determining who you are and why you act the way you do. You can discover alternatives for handling problems and developing clearer communication with your partner. You can see ways of continuing to evolve through the stages of your own development that ideally should have been worked through at an earlier time. You can learn not to expect things from a marriage that aren't appropriate, and at the same time, find the strength not to settle for less in the relationship than you might validly expect. And finally, you may discover that your marriage has untapped potential for fulfillment and pleasure.

PART 1: You, Your Partner and Your Marriage

1. Communication

Imagine the following scene:

A husband and wife are sitting together at the dinner table. The husband points his finger at the salt shaker. His wife knows he means he wants her to pass it to him. It's the 300th time she has seen this gesture which she despises. This time she explodes. "What the hell are you pointing at? Don't you have a tongue? Can't you *ask?* Can't you be bothered to talk to me?"

"What do you mean? Are you crazy? All I want is the salt!"

"I'll pass it when you ask for it."

"Don't *bother.*" The husband leans forward and reaches across the table.

They finish the meal either in angry silence, in argument or alone.

It wouldn't be accurate to say there's been no communication here. The husband wanted his wife to pass him the salt and she understood that. The wife wanted her husband to ask for the salt and he understood that. But neither got what he wanted, although it was within their individual abilities to give it. They both ended up angry and frustrated without knowing why.

Most of us are given astonishingly little training or practice in knowing and expressing our own deeper feelings. We're even less accomplished in listening actively and empathizing with another's needs and emotions. Whatever other problems may exist between partners, I find they almost always need to improve their self-understanding and find new ways of communicating. In ongoing therapy, these goals are an integral part of the work of each session. I'm going to devote the next chapter to a discussion and practical demonstration of how you can know yourself better and communicate more effectively with your partner. These skills will be

4

vital to your success in using the rest of the material in this book.

Effective communication is a complex matter. Coming from different families, we each have our own customs, our own ways of being and doing, which may be reflected in both verbal and non-verbal communication. In America, where our parents or grand-parents are likely to have come from other countries, we may echo these cultural differences. It takes time for a husband and wife to learn each other's ways, to accommodate and grow with each other.

Furthermore, not every relationship has to be open and ver-bal in all areas. A touch, a look or a gesture may suffice at times. Couples develop their own individual patterns of communication, their private "shorthand," which is fine as long as it works. What I'd like to explore here, however, are some ways in which partners can open better lines of communication when they're having prob-lems or fights, when they sense that they're not getting through to each other, or they're not getting what they want from one another.

Suppose we replay our dinner table scene. The husband points his finger at the salt and his wife explodes. "I *hate* it when you point like that. It makes me so goddam angry I want to scream."

"What?!" Her husband stares at her. "What's the matter with you? All I want is the salt!"

"I *know*. But when you point like that, it makes me feel . . ." She pauses, angry and baffled. "I think it makes me feel like a goddam servant. It makes me feel demeaned."

" 'Demeaned!' Come on, I don't mean it that way. I just . . ."

Consider the differences between the two scenes. Both times sharp anger was expressed. But in the first exchange, the wife's anger came out as a series of accusations. "What the hell are you pointing at? Don't you . . . . Can't you . . . ." In the second ex-change, she expressed her anger in terms of herself and her feelings. "I hate it when . . . ." And then she was able to reach deeper and come up with an underlying feeling that made her hate the point-ing. "I think it makes me feel like a servant . . . demeaned."

Now the husband has something to consider. His wife feels "demeaned." Does he want her to feel like that? Maybe he still can't understand her reaction.

" . . . I don't mean it that way. I just pointed instead of asking. What's demeaning about that?"

"I'm not sure." She has to think this through. "I guess I was always taught that it's polite to ask and rude to point. I know you're not usually rude, but when you point, I feel as though it must be too much trouble for you to ask—like I'm not worth the bother."

And now, having gotten to the deeper feelings behind what they're arguing about, there's a chance for this couple to really communicate. Maybe the husband *has* been taking short cuts in expressing himself. Maybe his wife is right and he is just not bothering to be polite. How will he react when he understands the distress this is causing her? Possibly he'll apologize and decide that's not what he wants to do at all. If he still insists on pointing, there's probably more to the problem. Why else would he refuse to make a minor change that could please his wife? In that case, they must discuss the situation further.

Maybe the husband's habit has a completely different significance for him. In the husband's family, his father might have had a "code" of pointing when he wanted something rather than asking for it. That behavior was expected and taken for granted. The husband simply acquired his father's habit. If he recognizes this and explains it to his wife, she may acknowledge it and may notice the behavior when she visits his family. (The dinner table, by the way, is a wonderful place to see all kinds of ingrained behavior manifested!)

This knowledge certainly doesn't mean the wife is suddenly going to like or accept her husband's pointing. Coming from a different family background, she may continue to think, "My God, what kind of rudeness is this?" But having identified the real issue, the couple can discuss it. The wife may say, "I understand it was part of your family pattern, but my own training makes me feel you're being thoughtless when you just point. I think a lot of other people might feel that way, too. I know it's hard to break a lifetime habit, but maybe you could give it a try."

How this information is accepted will probably depend on how accommodating the individuals are. The husband may want to do what will please the person he loves. He may think, "Oh, what the hell, I can do that. It's no big deal. She lives with my snoring; I can ask for the salt!"

He may also feel, "Enough already. You're always asking me to do something. I feel like you're closing in on me. Get off my back!"

Ideally the wife will hear this message and respond to it—or to the anger in her husband's voice.

"You mean you're sore because you feel I'm trying to change you too much?"

"Well, aren't you? It happens all the time. I'm too messy in the bathroom, I don't wear the right clothes, I don't buy the right tickets . . ."

Now that the wife has discovered what her husband feels, can she ask herself whether she's been over-controlling? Can she see that occasionally she could be less demanding? Or does she want to say, "I know I want to change some things about you. But isn't that natural when two people live together? There must also be things I do that annoy you. Tell me what they are and I'll try to change, too." Or perhaps she chooses some other approach that's more comfortable for her. The point is, this couple is no longer simply discussing a dining habit but the underlying question of how much freedom or living space they can give each other. In their case, they've uncovered the real point of conflict between them.

In order for two people to communicate as effectively and meaningfully as possible:

1. Each will be aware of what he's feeling.

2. Each will express feelings without blaming or accusing, making it possible for the other to respond positively.

3. Each will listen and genuinely understand what the other is saying.

4. Each will empathize with the other.

Let's consider these points and see how you can practice and apply them.

Getting in Touch with Your Feelings

When I work with individuals or couples in therapy, I encourage them to explore and express their feelings. Each time this happens in a session, it reinforces what may be a new self-awareness that people can practice on their own. Eventually, being in touch with their feelings becomes easier and finally natural—one of the fundamental benefits of therapy.

Being unaware of your feelings is like being unaware of who you are, what you need *or* what you have to offer, why you're doing whatever you're doing *or* what else you might be doing instead. In the extreme, this unawareness creates a kind of alienated, detached non-life.

I don't mean to suggest that it's always necessary to be highly "self-conscious." Living spontaneously can be wonderful. Sometimes your feelings, desires and needs are expressed and fulfilled with no conscious effort at all. You touch your partner, he or she responds, and there's a sense of unity and accord. But life is often more complex, and people are less perfectly in tune with themselves and/or each other. Much of the time you have to be in touch with your feelings both for your own fulfillment and in order to accept, understand and deal with the emotions of someone else.

Tuning in to your own feelings isn't always easy. You probably hide them at times because you're ashamed of them. After all, how can you admit that you're personally relieved to see someone close die after a long illness that drained you emotionally? It sounds too selfish, too awful! You may say instead, "I'm glad, for his sake, that it's over." And this may also be true. But underneath, you may feel guilty about the other, unacknowledged feeling. It may haunt you or torment you with self-doubts and probably prevent you from sharing your emotions with your partner. Yet the feeling of relief is *natural*.

Sometimes you may cover up or deny feelings because they're too threatening, and you may express substitute emotions that you're better able to handle. So instead of saying, "You hurt me," thus acknowledging your pain and vulnerability, you may lash out angrily and say, "You're thoughtless and mean." But the anger seldom relieves the hurt. If expressing anger is difficult for you, you may withdraw and become depressed. But depression seldom relieves the anger. You have to deal with the true, deeper emotion to attain relief.

One of the fundamental concepts of psychology is that people have feelings of all kinds, and this is perfectly natural. Our feelings include love, hate, rage, fear, helplessness, greed, satisfaction, and many others.

If we have the wisdom and compassion to know we're capable of all kinds of feelings and if we can accept them as natural (realizing that there's a vast difference between having feelings and acting upon them), then we'll become less threatened and more comfortable with ourselves and others.

Just how do you get in touch with your feelings? And more importantly, how do you dig down to the deeper ones you may be unconsciously hiding?

1. Sometimes it's helpful to sit quietly alone and think, say, write or even tape record *all the different* words that seem to describe your physical as well as your emotional state. Although you may start with the more obvious ones—angry, for example—you may well progress to others that are more revealing: angry, hot, perspired, shaky, nervous, uncertain. Now stay with the word that seems somewhat unexpected and explore its relevance. "Uncertain. What am I uncertain about? That maybe I'm not right? But I believe I am right. That maybe he doesn't understand? Maybe my being angry put him off? Is there some other way I can explain . . . I never did explain! *His criticism made me feel* unaccepted and putdown . . . ." The deeper feeling that you have uncovered behind your anger is rejection.

2. Whenever you over-react—when your intense reaction is out of proportion to the stimulus—recognize it as a signal that something deeper or more significant is involved. Always try to pause and say, "Wait a minute, what's *really* going on here? Why am I *really* crying over a relatively trivial matter?"

3. You may be able to get at your deeper feelings by "staying with" the emotion you're aware of, thinking of other situations in which you've felt like this or other people who evoked the same feeling in you. What was your position in those other situations? Were you in charge, out of control, ignored, expected to be perfect? How did those other people feel toward you? Were you loved, respected, accepted, judged, criticized, rejected?

4. Sometimes you can get a lot of useful information by asking yourself, "Does this remind me of when I was a child living with my parents? How was I treated then? How did I want to be treated? Am I experiencing feelings I had as a child when I was truly helpless and vulnerable? Are these emotions appropriate for the adult I am today?

5. You may be able to get at your deeper feelings by "trying on" the opposite emotion or at least an emotion that's very different from what you're feeling on the surface. If you're saying, "I'm furious!" try, "I'm hurt." If you're in tears and feel hurt, try on the feelings of anger or hate. Try to stem the tears that may not be tears of sorrow but perhaps tears of rage.

6. If you feel so helpless that you *can't* do something, try saying, "I won't" or "I'm afraid to." "Can't" means you're immobilized, and maybe sometimes you are. But perhaps you can get in touch with what might be operating underneath—"I *won't* do it." If you can get to that stubborn anger, it may offer you a certain amount of tension that you can mobilize for action. If the "can't" means you're scared to do something because you're afraid of what might happen, then examine the fear. "What am I afraid of? What's the worst thing that can happen?"

Expressing Your Own Feelings and Listening to Someone Else

Telling another person how you feel can be very difficult. You may be embarrassed or afraid to say certain things because opening up makes you vulnerable. Are you going to be laughed at?

Rejected? Ignored? Can you trust this other person with your innermost emotions?

I often ask one member of a couple I'm working with, "Do you feel ready to share your feelings with your husband?" Or, "Do you think you can risk telling your wife how that really affected you?" I believe it's tremendously important for couples to realize that this kind of sharing is both a risk taken and a trust given. It deserves an appropriately caring response.

Listening and genuinely understanding what the other person is saying require open-minded concentration, so that you don't project your own thoughts or emotions onto the speaker's words and end up hearing something that was never said. You need the motivation and ability to understand things from the other's point of view. You need to be able to empathize.

Because the ability to empathize is a crucial part of dealing with others, I'm going to discuss that now. In the next chapter we'll consider a roundup of specific techniques which will help you to express yourself, to listen, to draw another person out—to communicate as effectively and meaningfully as possible.

Empathizing

Empathy is the ability to put yourself into somebody's else's skin and feel what the other person is feeling, see the world from the other person's point of view. In order to be able to empathize, you not only need to know your own feelings so you have a frame of reference, but you also need enough emotional "self" left over to want to understand the other individual. The person who's extremely self-involved and sees the world only in terms of how it affects him has difficulty taking this step toward empathy. He must come to realize that other people are also the centers of their own universe. Then he can take the next step and say, "Okay, others do experience things differently from me. Maybe I can try to see it from their position."

Often I'll ask a husband and wife, "Can you imagine how it might feel if you were in your spouse's place? Maybe it would be interesting to see what that might be like." I ask them to switch roles, even to switch the chairs they're sitting in, and try to become the other person as much as possible in order to see how that feels. This technique, which many therapists have found useful, is known as "role reversal." A related technique which can be used by one person alone is "role playing." That means putting yourself in another's place, acting and reacting as he or she would, then becoming yourself and responding as you would. This can be done in a variety of ways: talking out loud, writing things down, tape recording two sides of a conversation, moving physically from one position to another, and so forth.

Both role reversal and role playing can be done successfully outside a therapist's office. Perhaps you'd like to try one or both techniques and see what you discover. Here are a few sample situations you may want to build upon.

1. Think of the next time you're going to see your partner after you've been apart for the day. How do you typically greet him or her? What do you say or do, with what tone or feeling? Now put yourself in your partner's place. You can do this in your imagination or by actually going to the front door or any other appropriate location. Try to "become" your partner, feel the impact of your own greeting. How do you-as-your-partner react?

2. The next time you're angry or upset at something your partner has said or done, go into a room by yourself and say aloud what's bothering you. Now, get up and move to a different place or sit in a different chair and "become" your partner. Listen to what you've just said and try to respond as your partner would. What is he or she feeling? If possible, try to continue this dialogue for a few minutes.

3. Sometime when you're arguing or disagreeing with your partner, suggest that the two of you exchange places and roles. This requires a degree of openness and some explanation, but the idea may sound appealing if you say something like, "What do you think would happen if I could put myself in your place and you could put yourself in mine? How about trying it for a minute?" Often it helps to physically exchange places. Then pursue the discussion with each of you participating as the other person. How do you both feel in your new roles?

Perhaps you'd like to "test"—and at the same time, increase —your degree of empathy with your husband or wife. If you each answer the following questions individually and then compare your answers, you'll have a better sense of how close or far apart you are in understanding what the other feels.

1. What makes you happy in your marriage?
2. What do you think makes your partner happy in your marriage?
3. What do you like to share with your partner?
4. What do you think your partner likes to share with you?
5. What do you prefer *not* to share with your partner?

6. What do you think your partner prefers *not* to share with you?

7. It would make me happier if my partner would ————.

8. It would make my partner happier if I would ————.

9. It would make me happier if my partner would *not* ————.

10. It would make my partner happier if I would *not* ————.

11. Imagine yourself five years from now. Describe the place you'd like to be living, the people you'd like to be with and what you'd like to be doing.

12. Imagine your partner five years from now, and describe the place you think your partner would like to be living, the people he or she would like to be with and what he or she would like to be doing.

2. Applying the Art and Technique of Communication

Communication is a learned art; it involves certain skills that can be acquired or improved. Many of the techniques psychologists use can be understood and tried by couples on their own. Of course, any new method feels a little strange at first. If you learn a foreign language, you're usually self-conscious for quite a while about speaking it. But once you begin to use it, it becomes a part of you. Not all of the following ideas will work in all cases or for all people, but they're here to be considered and tried.

1. Using the "I-message" is almost always the most effective way to say things.

Perhaps you're already familiar with this concept of the "I-message." Quite simply, it's a nonblaming way of saying how you feel. For instance, instead of saying, "You're always criticizing me," an "I-message" might be, "I feel as though I never please you."

"You're always criticizing me" is an accusation. It's apt to provoke a defensive response such as, "What do you mean? I am not." It's a step away from letting the other person know how you feel, helping him to empathize with you.

"You're never around" as an "I-message" might be, "I'd like to be with you more."

"You're not interested in what I'm saying," might be, "I'm afraid that I'm boring you."

"Why don't you *tell* me when you're going to be late?" could be "I have an easier time planning my schedule if I know when to expect you," or, "I get worried when you're unusually late."

2. Try not to blurt out your feelings—however "honest" they may be—without regard for how they'll affect someone else.

Pure honesty may be an ideal, but it's not always possible or

13

even desirable in our society. Adult communication means expressing needs and wishes in a gracious, kind way, not exploding and saying everything that comes to mind. We hope to have developed enough judgment to know what impact our comments will have on another human being and to recognize that we have the choice of what to withhold and what to say, as well as when to say it.

Some people have an uncanny knack of selecting just the wrong moment to be "honest." For a husband to tell a wife that he can't stand the dress she's wearing as they're leaving for a party can be absolutely devastating. Communication can be used negatively as a way of hurting or even destroying another person. Someone may be very proud of his tremendous honesty and say, "I'm the most open person. I tell it like it is all the time." But one has to question that. Is it appropriate all the time? What is the effect of this "honesty?" What's the real motive? What we say may be honest, yet at the same time mask a great deal of hostility and aggression . . . "Maybe you're really angry with me for something else. Maybe you're angry or hurt about another matter entirely, and taking it out on me. There are many other ways you could have said that."

3. Learning how to listen is one of the most crucial aspects of communicating.

We've all seen people who listen with their whole selves, leaning forward in total concentration. Listening is an active art. It's work, not just in terms of the effort to understand, but also in the internal evaluations and reactions being formed. Sometimes the person listening reaches a point of surfeit. He or she can't handle any more information and may say, "I really need some time to think about all this and digest it." And that's fine. It's a very different reaction from that of the listener who hears something and says, "That's ridiculous." Such a comment is a put-down. Maybe the listener really means, "I don't understand how you can feel that way." Then why not say it in those words? Perhaps the listener can't empathize on this issue. But perhaps the individual—or the couple together—can explore what makes it so difficult, why the partner's reaction seems so foreign. At the very least, an effort can be made to accept a partner's emotions or viewpoint as real.

4. One of the most important parts of listening is being able to give "feedback" on what you've just heard.

Giving "feedback" means repeating what you think someone has just said. I sometimes suggest to a couple that they actually assign a time during which they talk things over using this feedback technique. In session I'll take the part of the husband or the wife and suggest, "Let's take one hour. Half of that hour is yours. It's all yours. You can tell me anything. I'll just listen to you and try to feed back to you exactly what I hear you say. And you correct me. Tell me if I'm getting the essence of it. If I'm way off, let me know. Then I'll talk and you listen."

Often people don't realize how easy it is to misinterpret messages. There are all kinds of needless misunderstandings—like the wife who says, "Listen, I really don't feel like going away. The idea of a vacation now raises a lot of questions for me."

Her husband might feed this back as, "You don't want to go on vacation with me."

Her answer might be, "No, that's not what I'm saying at all. I'm worried about spending the money on vacation when we've just decided to get a new car. I'd *love* to go away with you, but I think it might create an awful financial pressure."

"Oh," he says, "really? Maybe we should figure out our budget and see where we stand."

In a different situation one mate might say, "You know, I'm really depressed after visiting your folks."

The other feeds back, "You don't like being around them. They make you unhappy."

"No, *they* don't make me unhappy. I like them. I just feel bad that I can't do more for them. Their friends are dying and moving away, and I feel helpless because I can't change all the heartaches that are coming to them with old age."

One of the advantages of feeding back is that it often helps the speaker as well as the listener to clarify what's on his or her mind.

5. You can help a reticent person tell you how he or she feels.

It's often just a matter of saying, "I'd really like to hear your thoughts about this," or, "Do you think you could share your feelings with me?" Perhaps it's more appropriate to say, "It helps me understand . . . ." or, "It makes me feel good when you tell me what you feel or think . . . ."

Sometimes a spouse responds, "I don't know how I feel." Maybe he or she really doesn't know. It takes learning, doing and time to be able to become introspective, to recognize feelings within you that previously you might have been taught are unacceptable. Frequently you can help by just saying, "I think if I were you I'd be furious!" This gives the person permission to be angry. It's a way of telling him or her, "Look, I, too, have these bad emotions. I, too, am irrational. I, too, run the gamut in my responses . . . ."

6. Introducing a touchy subject means someone has to go first—without launching an attack.

Whether you want to bring up a new issue or reopen an unresolved one, someone has to take the initiative and the risk of going first. If you're so furious about something that the only way you can introduce the subject is with an all-out attack on your partner, it might be wiser to consider postponing a confrontation until you've regained a little self-control. The more you can avoid blaming, accusing or putting your partner on the defensive, the more likely you are to establish an atmosphere that's really conducive to exploring and understanding feelings.

So how do you actually begin?

Perhaps you simply say, "I've been feeling upset about ——
—. Do you think we could discuss it?" With some couples, this is enough. For others, it's not. "We've already been through that and I don't want to start in again," a partner might answer, especially if there's a negative history surrounding the issue.

When you really want to talk about something and the other person doesn't, one natural response is to plead. "Couldn't you just do this for me? Please?" Unfortunately, your plea may strike your partner as a demand, and the reaction might be, "For Pete's sake, will you stop bugging me and drop it?"

If your partner doesn't want to discuss something, one of the most helpful things you can do is to *acknowledge* his or her feeling of reluctance. Perhaps you can also share your own feelings or suggest why a discussion at this time might prove valuable: "I can understand that you don't want to go through another pointless argument about this, and neither do I. It makes me feel awful. But I thought if we took a different approach and just tried to say what we each really feel, we might end up with a clearer picture . . . ." Or you might say, "I know this isn't a problem for you, but it really is for me. If we could talk about it together a little, I think it might help me a lot." Use whatever words are comfortable for you and inviting for your partner.

Sometimes husbands and wives find themselves up against a dead-end communication block. No invitation or request gets through. In this kind of situation, I believe the best thing may be to consider getting professional help.

7. Fights or other emotionally charged scenes can also lead to deeper communication.

When you're angry or distressed, a good fight or confrontation can clear the air, release a lot of built-up tension and end in greater understanding and communication. A good fight doesn't mean denying your anger or hurt. Rather, it involves expressing *your* emotions without hurling accusations or turning a deaf ear to what's being said to you. For instance, "I *hate* it when you call me by somebody else's name. It makes me feel as though you don't see me for who I am, as though I don't exist, as though I'm not important," as opposed to, "If you're too stupid to know the difference between your secretary and your wife, you don't deserve to have either one. You obviously don't give a damn about me or my feelings."

Fights mean different things to different people. Some individuals with volatile personalities flare up easily over small matters, then just as quickly go on to something else. Others fight infrequently, but when they do, it's almost always a sign of real distress. In general, when intense feelings are aroused and remain so for some duration, you can be sure that something vital is at stake. Even if the issue appears trivial, your over-reaction is a message that something significant is involved, although you may not know what it is. Can you acknowledge your own bewilderment? "I hate it when you point without asking for something. It makes me want to scream." Perhaps you're already screaming when you add, "I don't know why this is upsetting me so much . . . ." If you can accept your anger as a clue, go on from there. Take the risk of opening yourself up and admitting there's probably some other reason you're over-reacting. Explore and share your feelings as best you can. The fight may be turned in a direction that's positive and helpful for both people.

8. Body language is part of the dialogue.

Our physical movements are clues to the way we feel. Just as someone may lean forward when trying to make contact, a person often leans back or turns slightly away when he feels like withdrawing or withholding something. Acknowledging this can help the dialogue. "I see you turning away as though you really don't want to discuss this. Are you feeling too much pressure? Do I seem to be coming on too strong?"

The physical movement may contradict what's being said. "Oh, yes, I can understand that," but the head is shaking negatively. Perhaps the head-shaking should be questioned.

Eye-contact is always important, at least in our culture. Looking directly at someone means, "I'm acknowledging your presence, I'm attentive." Maybe you've heard a comment like, "You know, we go out to dinner and he never looks at me. He's just staring all around the restaurant." Few of us feel like talking, especially on a meaningful level, to someone who's gazing about, knitting, or assembling a model engine. We feel—and accurately so—that we don't have that person's caring and attention.

In my office, I often point out certain movements or gestures. I also use television to help couples become more aware of their interaction. When I first set up the camera, people tend to be self-conscious. But after a while, they forget that the lights are on and they become involved with themselves. Then I play back the video tape for a few minutes without any sound, so that the gestures and physical signals stand out. We then can question what it means when someone sits drumming fingers or tapping a foot while the other person talks.

9. Journals and tape recorders can be helpful tools.

Some people enjoy writing down their thoughts and feelings. I've had couples in therapy who kept ongoing logs of their reactions, their hopes and dreams, and the problems they were confronting. Sometimes these are private journals, one individual's way of putting it down on paper to better recognize what's going on inside himself. In other cases, there's a common journal, accessible for both spouses to write in and read. For some people, it's easier to write something down and see it in front of them and then share *that* with the spouse than it is to have a discussion. Articulating on paper may create just enough distance to make them feel comfortable and often it's a bridge to something else.

Tape-recording a discussion about a disputed issue often provides great insights when the tape is played back. Both spouses can listen to what they've said, hear the intensity or urgency in their voices and the kinds of words they used. They have a chance to make corrections and clarifications, to become better attuned to what each of them really means and to hear how they express themselves.

10. Deal with problems as they come up so they don't mount up.

I think the advantages of getting issues clarified and out of the way are fairly obvious. If a problem exists, ignoring it won't make it go away. In fact, it's apt to build up and spill over into other areas of the relationship. Furthermore, what's bothering one spouse may not even have occurred to the other as a problem. We all have a natural tendency to imagine that if someone really loves us and is close to us, he must know how we feel. But, of course, this isn't necessarily so at all. We're all highly individual in our growth, perceptions and reactions—and perhaps that's the best guarantee that a relationship can continue to remain fresh and stimulating for many, many years.

3. I Chose You Because

When you meet someone in a social situation, the first thing you generally notice is whether that person is attractive to you. But then, as you get to know the individual, he or she may either continue to appeal to you or cease to appear desirable. For example, a woman may be attracted to a man who seems to be handsome, strong, loving and protective. But when she spends a little time with him, something seems to be missing and she may or may not be aware of what it is. Perhaps she goes out to dinner with him and he can't make simple decisions, order food or deal with waiters. Or perhaps he defers to her too often and wants her to make all the choices. If this happens repeatedly—when they have to choose a movie, or decide whether to walk, take a bus or cab—she gets the impression that the man is not really in charge. He may act this way out of a wish or need to please her, but very little of his own feelings and desires are revealed and that lack can destroy his appeal for her if she's looking for a stronger man. On the other hand, another woman may select this outwardly strong man because she senses that underneath there's really gentleness and dependency, and something within her responds to this because it makes her feel strong.

When you have a relatively sound understanding of why you selected your mate, it usually means you have a good sense of who you both are. As a result, you're less likely to expect inappropriate things from your partner. For instance, if you marry a gentle, easygoing man who encourages you to express yourself more fully than you've been able to in the past, and if you're *aware* that you value these gentle characteristics in your husband, then you're less likely to blame him for not chastising the person who cuts in front of you in the ticket line at the movies. If a man is aware that he gets satisfaction, pride and support because his wife is a fine business person, then he's probably going to be more accepting of her indifference toward doing some of the things that a full-time homemaker would do.

This isn't to say that a woman will necessarily be happy if her husband lets someone push into line ahead of them, or that a man will necessarily be pleased if he has to take over some domestic chores. In our heart of hearts, we would all really like to have everything, including a partner who does whatever we happen to want the minute we want it, who can be everything we need whenever we need it, and who also leaves us alone when solitude and liberty are our desires. There's nothing unusual or wrong with this all-encompassing wish for perfect fulfillment, *as long as* you realize that you can't possibly have it within the framework of a marriage or any other adult relationship. What you can do, and what you consciously and/or unconsciously tend to do, is select a partner who can give you many of the important things you want and need.

The more you can recognize what these things are—that is, the more you understand about why you chose your mate—the more you can truly value what this person is bringing to the relationship. And you're better able to judge what's possible within the relationship, including how it might realistically be improved. You're also in a better position to understand the effects of changes in your lives. In other words, if you choose a man because he enables you to be supportive and nurturing of him, and then you have a baby who requires this too, you may want something different from your husband. Or if you were drawn to a strong, powerful man and he then becomes seriously ill or loses his job, suddenly he may be unable to meet your needs or follow his own inner drives. Fundamental changes like these require major adjustments. Unless you and your partner understand what your relationship was to begin with, it's difficult to understand the effects of change, or find ways of handling adjustments constructively.

Finally, if you both can recognize and also *accept* your needs, you won't have to hide them or try to fulfill them deceptively. You can talk about them openly, perhaps explain them or at least describe how they make you feel. That way you're apt to become more understanding and supportive of each other.

Perhaps the most helpful, healthful thing we can ever learn is that there's nothing wrong with having needs, acknowledging them, seeking to fulfill them and, as much as we're able, acting in ways that help fulfill someone else's needs. It is important to achieve enough need-gratification so we can develop to a level where our requirements are less urgent.

Finding Out More about Why You Chose Your Partner

You probably can think of many things that attracted you to your partner. But the more you explore the deeper reasons you chose him or her, the more you'll learn about yourself, your partner, the expectations you had of the marriage, and the realistic possibilities of achieving them. Here are some questions that may help you in this exploration.

1. What about your partner initially attracted you? Was it the way he or she looked or acted? Was it where you went, what you did or talked about on your first date?

When you answer, try not to stop at the first response. See if you can ask one more "why?" For example:

What did you like about the way your partner looked on your first date?

He looked attractive. I liked his face and general appearance.

Why?

He had kind eyes. They expressed a warm person. And he was well-dressed. Conservative, but with some style. I liked that.

Why?

I guess I felt he'd gone to some trouble to choose what he wore.

Why did you like that?

It meant he was careful about his appearance. Or maybe he wanted to make a good impression. I don't know.

But you like both those ideas?

Yes. I guess appearance is important to me. And I guess I want somebody to care about the impression he makes on me.

Why?

I don't know.

Could you give it a try?

Maybe because it shows he's thoughtful or considerate? Or because he'll care what I think or how I feel about him? Maybe I need reassurance that someone cares how I feel. I really don't know any more than that!

Okay, good. Go on to the next question!

2. In what ways did you feel you understood or had an immediate or intuitive rapport with your partner? Did you have similar problems, experiences, goals, interests, life-styles, etc.?

A sense of recognition and "alikeness" can sometimes draw two people toward each other. "Birds of a feather *do* flock together." If you're aware of the positive reaction this similarity aroused in you, you may be able to value it more fully. And you may also be better able to handle any feelings of disappointment that might arise in the future when your partner seems to be too much like you with no surprises or excitement. Perhaps you can fulfill your need for excitement and difference through work, friendships, experiences involving people and situations outside your marriage.

3. In what ways did you feel your partner was unlike you?

Often, there is a strong appeal for someone who is exotic and different. Remember another adage, "Opposites attract." If you're aware of this attraction, perhaps you'll be more accepting of differences when they sometimes distress you. Differences can create a lot of anxiety. If you're very conservative and self-controlled, but attracted to someone who is rather flamboyant and expressive, you may try to change that person to conform with your own way of being. But the fact that you were initially attracted by these qualities in your partner probably means that there's a part of you which values them and that would like to be more expansive and expressive. If you can learn how to accept that hidden part of yourself, you may be able to allow yourself some of the joy of experiencing it through another. You may get a kick out of the way the other person does things. There's nothing wrong with vicarious living. One of the most important concepts you can learn is that differences aren't necessarily bad or evil. On the contrary, they can be enhancing and fulfilling. What makes it hard to accept those hidden and/or repressed parts of ourselves are feelings of guilt.

4. If you could design an ideal you, what characteristics would you strengthen?

One's sense of deficiency in certain qualities is often unconsciously the basis of the attraction to another person. "I don't have such-and-such, so I'll find it in my mate. He'll provide it for me or fulfill this part of me that I can't fulfill for myself." So you may choose someone who's strong, tender, generous, decisive, self-assured, adaptable, caring, sociable, optimistic or whatever you may value and want more of in terms of your own idealized self-image, your ego-ideal. By acknowledging that you value such characteristics in your partner, you may find it easier to develop in similar directions yourself. You may also avoid the resentment that can come from feeling you're being "shown up" by someone else.

5. What aspects of yourself that you approve of does your partner allow or encourage you to exercise?

Usually you're drawn toward the person who you sense can help you to be the "self" that you love or like the best.

6. In what ways does your partner remind you of things you like about your mother or father?

Since your parents were your original source of love, your "primary love objects," you're bound to be influenced by the parental love you knew, when you later seek love from a husband or wife. If your childhood experience with your parents was satisfying, what could be more natural than trying to recreate some of the rewarding aspects of that experience by selecting a partner who has some of the same characteristics as your parents? (This may include physical resemblance, although if you're frightened by the strength of your love for a parent, you may choose someone who is the opposite in appearance as a means of denying the forbidden, incestuous attraction.)

The sooner you can see which aspects of your partner reflect those of your parent(s), the sooner you can start recognizing the characteristics that really belong to your spouse, and stop projecting onto him characteristics you wish were his or you assume he possesses because you're unconsciously expecting him in some ways to take the place of a parent. Suppose, for example, you marry a man because, like your father, he's strong and caring, and you feel he'll always be there for you. Your expectations may be for the kind of total caring that a child gets from a parent. If you're aware of this, you may be able to say, "Yes, my husband can give me a lot of the support and help I need, but it's inappropriate for me to expect him to provide the degree of attention that a parent gives his child. It's unrealistic for me to expect my husband to be more caring and 'fatherly' toward me than he is."

Some of the greatest problems between husbands and wives are caused when one of them projects qualities onto the other that belonged in their most complete sense to a parent. You've probably heard someone say, "You know, I'm *not* your father," or "I'm really *not* your mother." What often happens is that the husband or wife not only sees the other as part parent, but reacts to the partner with the same childhood feelings that were felt toward the parent. If a man marries a woman who is understanding and intuitive, qualities his mother also had, he may expect his wife to anticipate and meet his every need the way his mother did in his rosy, fantasy memories. He may feel that his wife should "know" what he wants or should certainly gratify his desire as soon as he expresses it, and he may become angry and upset when she doesn't. He may feel toward his wife the way he once felt toward his mother: if she loved me, she'd *know* what I need and she'd do what I want. While there is usually some degree of parenting within a marital relationship, this other kind of blind transference of childhood feelings is usually very destructive. It sets up expectations that can't be met and are inappropriate within the framework of a marriage. It places a tremendous emotional burden on the partner and creates a one-sided situation that ignores the other person's feelings and needs.

7. *In what ways does your partner remind you of things you*

don't like about your mother or father?

Strangely enough, you may marry someone who has characteristics you disliked in one of your parents. Unconsciously you may be hoping to convert your partner into someone more pleasing and satisfying, perhaps trying to relive an unhappy childhood experience and make it come out right this time. And occasionally, that's possible. Marriage can provide a chance for you to re-experience something from your past and grow in healthy, positive ways through the new experience. But this opportunity is more likely to arise if you choose somebody who already *has* the characteristic you want and need. By choosing someone who is like your parent in some negative way because you unconsciously hope you can convert him, you may be letting yourself in for a futile and heartbreaking experience.

I've seen this happen with both men and women, and I can't help feeling their anguish each time. A woman may have a father who gave her a *taste* of the love and approval she wanted and needed, but who wasn't really available or who was often cold and judgmental. Then she marries someone who tends to be like her father. Unconsciously she feels, "If only I can get through this time to all the love and approval I know is there, it would be the greatest, warmest, most wonderful love in the whole world. If only I can make this person really love me the way I know he can, it will be the most perfect, satisfying thing that could possibly exist." So she keeps trying to please her husband, doing everything she can think of to make him happy. Others may wonder, "How does a bastard like that deserve such a loving woman?" But the wife can't do enough for him, and if he gives her any sign of approval, she thinks, "Now I've reached him, now I'm going to get what I've hoped for." And now she's hooked because there's always just enough of that sweetest milk to convince her that she can eventually tap the source and quench her thirst.

I've had male patients who keep wearing themselves out, buying gifts, providing the best homes and vacations, everything for their wives. Friends may say, "How does that wife of his rate? She's a bitch on wheels." But the husband can't do enough for her, and if she gives him a mere smile, he thinks, "This is it, the appreciation is coming," and he works ten times as hard. He, too, is hooked.

If you realize that you've married someone who has a characteristic you dislike in a parent, then you may be able to examine your fantasy about changing that characteristic. Is it realistic to think that this characteristic can be altered?

In our culture, we place a high value upon individual gratification. When we choose a marriage partner, we expect our main needs—emotional, sexual, social—to be met within the relationship. So a wife or husband has to be friend, lover, companion, nurturer, mother, father, son, daughter, wearing all kinds of masks and taking on all sorts of roles. Marriage is a very complex adventure.

However, there's a paradox inherent in this very idea of marriage. On the one hand, we say that it's terribly important for a person to have his or her individual wishes, needs, expectations and desires met. But then what happens in terms of the couple, where two individuals are each seeking fulfillment? Sometimes your needs may mesh so perfectly with your partner's that both can be gratified at once. But what if there's a conflict? Do you place your own needs first? Does your mate come first? Marriage is an interdependent relationship where a certain amount of exploitation and conflict are built into the situation. How do you recognize and reconcile what's good for you, what's good for your mate and what's good for the marriage? That's what we're exploring in this book.

PART 2:
The Critical First Year

In my practice, I see a number of couples seeking counseling during their first year of marriage, and many more who enter therapy later on, but trace their difficulties back to those initial months together. While I think most people expect marriage to entail a certain period of adjustment, I don't believe that the depth and crucial nature of this adjustment are fully recognized.

The fact is that no matter how well you and your partner know each other, how long you might have lived together before your marriage, or how much you may have in common, you're apt to find that, once married, almost everything about your relationship changes. Some of the changes may be wonderful, positive and fulfilling. A man or woman will tell me, "It wasn't that I really doubted I was loved, but everything seemed so much clearer and more definite once we went through the ceremony. I wasn't just happy, I was relieved." A desire for commitment may be satisfied. There can also be a heightened sense of intimacy, a long-awaited opportunity for more time together, or perhaps a new sexual freedom after the wedding. Marriage can enhance a rich relationship. It can give an added dimension to your own existence, a sense of new possibilities for the future. Marriage tends to create a synergism or interaction that truly produces something larger than just the sum of the two parts.

Yet people often say, "Don't get married. It'll spoil everything." And sometimes this does happen. I hate to say that *any* marriage is doomed, but there are cases where one partner feels trapped and totally negative from the outset. Perhaps this person is unable to make a permanent commitment. In such cases, the marriage usually can't survive. And if it is destructive, dissolving it may be the most positive decision.

The unfortunate thing I see today is the inclination among some couples to think of separating or divorcing before they've really given themselves a chance to confront their problems. One of the reasons may be a new ambivalence about the permanence of marriage. Most people probably still pronounce their wedding vows with at least some hope and belief that their marriage will be "until death us do part." Yet at the same time, divorce is readily available.

It appears that permanence is no longer permanent. Since the marriage doesn't have to be forever, some people feel that they don't have as much of a stake in it. It's not so much a question of working on this marriage and solving these problems as of getting a new partner and a new marriage and starting over. This attitude is destructive to the existing relationship and also to future ones because without a careful understanding of what caused the trouble in the first place, people tend to repeat the same mistake again—and again.

Living with another human being in the intimacy of marriage is an extraordinarily difficult, demanding, fascinating, exciting and rewarding experience. Of course there will be problems. Even couples who have lived together successfully before marriage are going to find themselves having to adjust to a new and different situation. And the adjustments continue throughout life, as various events affect the partners and cause the dynamics of the marriage to constantly shift and evolve. The real challenge is to understand what's happening both to the individuals and to the couple at each developing stage of their relationship.

4. Persons and Partners

In this chapter I want to focus primarily on three issues which surface in the early months of every marriage. The first is how to handle the awareness, and sometimes the shock, of realizing that you and your partner are very different from each other. The second is how to recognize and deal with one of the most common of these differences: dissimilar needs for closeness and intimacy. The third issue concerns togetherness, which often is mistaken for closeness.

In real life, "issues" aren't isolated. When a husband and wife discover they're different in some significant area, one is apt to try to take charge and make the other conform. Maybe both try to have their ways. Who ends up in control? How is the balance of power between partners established? What kinds of personal insight can help individuals to understand and possibly modify their own drives to take control and/or change their partner? These are some other questions we'll be touching on in this and the following chapter.

"Please come in," I said. "This is where we'll be meeting and working together."

Bill Dennis followed his wife, Lisa, into my office. They were young, well-dressed and attractive. She looked around quickly and said, *"Don't* tell me you've read all these books!"

"Most of them—at least once." I smiled and sat in my usual chair.

"Well, I suppose you're going to need them if you're going to do anything with us."

"Lisa," Bill said.

She glanced at him. "Okay." Her tone sounded resigned.

Eyeing the two empty chairs, Lisa looked questioningly at Bill. He waited, impassive. She shrugged and abruptly sank into a black swivel chair matching mine. Bill carefully pulled a smaller chair a few inches back from ours and sat down. If Lisa noticed his move, she didn't comment.

I asked them some initial questions and took notes. Bill was twenty-two years old; Lisa was twenty-one. He worked for his father, who was an accountant, planned to take the exam for his CPA license after completing a three-year apprenticeship and eventually become a partner in the firm. Lisa hadn't decided between working and finishing college, but for the moment was decorating their apartment and taking a cooking course. They'd grown up in the same town in New Jersey, where their families had known each other for years. They started dating the summer after Bill's sophomore year in college. After his junior year they were engaged. The parents on both sides approved of the match, and Bill and Lisa felt confident. Now, after seven months of marriage, they were in my office, frightened and resentful that the relationship that had started out so promisingly was in trouble.

"I think we need some professional advice," Bill said mildly, flushing with the effort of the admission.

"I guess that's a prizewinning understatement." Lisa stopped and studied her nails.

"Why don't you go ahead?" Bill's tone was neutral.

Lisa shook her head. "I'm sorry. Go on."

"Things are like this a lot of the time. Kind of tense and uncomfortable."

"At least we're here together," Lisa offered. Her fingers touched the arm of Bill's chair. Almost imperceptibly he shifted toward the other side of the chair. Lisa withdrew her hand quickly and said to me, "He hates being here." It seemed more of an apology than a criticism.

"Do you hate being here?" I asked Bill.

"I don't like the idea that we haven't been able to work things out by ourselves, but I wouldn't use the word 'hate.'" He continued, still mildly, "Lisa has a way of blowing things out of proportion and getting upset over things someone else would just brush off. I think if she could just get over that . . . ."

"You mean ignore things I don't like." Lisa's voice became hard. "You have a terrific way of doing what *you* want and expecting me to be happy about it."

"We had a disagreement . . ."

"A fight," Lisa interrupted. "Can't you say we had a fight?"

Bill took a deep breath. "We had an argument over a birthday gift that I bought Lisa that she didn't like. I told her she could exchange it . . ."

I said, "Bill, could you tell her now, directly?"

When couples come to see me for an initial interview, I ask them to talk to each other and just let me listen in for a while. My immediate goal is to make them relate in a way that's apt to be new for them. I have them face each other directly which helps to prevent me from being a referee or judge and makes them more aware of their responsibility for any changes they wish to engender. I want them to turn to each other and talk, get reinvolved with eye-contact and, perhaps, even touching.

Bill turned to Lisa. "I told you I was sorry you didn't like the sweater. I wanted to give you something you'd enjoy, but I told you to change it for whatever you liked."

Lisa nodded. "And you said if I liked something that cost more, I should put it on your *mother's* charge account." Her distress showed clearly.

"Because my mother happens to have an account there and we don't."

"Well, you didn't have to buy the sweater there in the first place. Anyway, it looks more like something she'd wear. And I don't *want* to have my gift from you going through on her account."

"For God's sake, Lisa," Bill's voice rose for the first time. "I told you I paid *cash* when I bought it, and I obviously was going to pay back anything extra we charged."

"That's not the point and you know it," she said bitterly. "I wanted you to spend a little time with me. I thought it would be fun if . . . don't you see that it would have been nice if you'd have come with me and we could have gone shopping together for something else." Her voice changed and the hurt came through. "It was my birthday."

"Lisa, I hate shopping. Why do you keep saying it would have been fun? And besides, I was working."

"During lunch? I suppose your father would fire you for taking an extra hour at lunch."

"I don't like to do that. It's taking advantage."

"And you didn't want to change your tennis game on Saturday, so that was out."

"There were three other people involved." He spaced the words slowly as if to help their obvious logic come through more clearly.

"Of course. And I'm just your wife."

Bill's lips closed tightly. There was a tense moment of silence.

I asked, "Bill, do you think you could tell us how you're feeling right now?"

He didn't answer and Lisa plunged in almost desperately. "He's furious. He hates being dragged here and having to talk about any of this."

I tried to interrupt, but she rushed on as though she was trying to imagine the worst things Bill could be thinking and say them first. "He hates arguing. He hates half the things I say and do. And right now—" She stared hard at Bill and her voice trembled as she forced the words, "—right now he wishes he'd never gotten into this marriage."

Bill returned her stare. "Lisa, are you waiting for me to agree or argue with you?"

Her eyes filled with tears. "Argue." It was a whisper and her tears spilled over. She hunched forward in the chair, her crossed arms hugging her chest.

Bill reached over and touched her shoulder. "I'm really *not* sorry I got into this marriage," he said gently.

Lisa moved her hand so her fingers touched his. He squeezed her shoulder once and withdrew his hand.

I said, "Bill, I couldn't help noticing when you touched Lisa just now. How did it feel? Why do you think you did that?"

He shrugged. "To comfort her, I guess."

I nodded. "And then when you took your hand away?"

"I don't know. She seemed better."

"How did it feel to you, Lisa?"

"When he touched me? I liked it. I felt close to him, like he cared. But I understand. He . . . he doesn't like touching in front of people."

"Oh. I wonder why not?"

They exchanged looks.

"It was just something else that upset me on my birthday," she said nervously. "It probably wasn't so important. We were going to a party that friends of ours were giving, and when we were going into the living room, I took Bill's arm—but then he pushed my arm away. It wasn't the first time, but I guess I didn't like it."

"You *guess* you didn't like it," Bill repeated with sarcasm and quiet anger. "You were lovely during the party, then you acted like a sullen baby and wouldn't sit near me in the car when we were going home. And you ended up *ruining* the rest of the evening for both of us." He was as upset as I'd seen him.

"How did Lisa ruin the rest of the evening?"

He flushed. "I thought we'd make love, but she wouldn't."

"How did that make you feel?"

"Angry."

"Do you think it was just anger, or do you suppose it might have been something else?"

"Why wouldn't I be angry?" he countered. "First she wanted to talk about what happened at the party like it was some big thing I'd done to insult her, and then we went into the bedroom and there was the sweater, so she started in on that."

"But she didn't want to make love when you did. Do you think that might have made you feel rejected?"

"Okay, you're right. I felt rejected. *And* angry. There was just no reason to . . . ."

"Bill, how do you think Lisa felt when you pushed her arm away at the party?"

He sighed deeply. "You're going to tell me she felt rejected, too."

I looked at Lisa.

She nodded. "Sometimes it feels as if he doesn't—," she paused, "—as if he doesn't even like me."

"Oh, Lisa, why do you *say* stuff like that?" Bill protested.

"It's how I feel sometimes."

Bill looked at me helplessly.

"Is there something you'd like to tell Lisa about how you feel?"

He thought for a minute. "You're my wife and I love you very much. But sometimes you just keep pushing and pulling at me and putting words in my mouth . . ." he shook his head.

"And how does that make you feel?" I prompted.

"Like I'm being cornered," he said. "Like she wants something from me that I can't give to her."

"Can you think what that something might be?"

"I don't know. Reassurance, maybe, but . . . ." He shook his head again. "It's more than that. She never eases off. It doesn't make sense to say things just so I'll contradict them, but that's what she does. She's got to get to me with *something* all the time."

"Of course," Lisa said excitedly, "because sometimes it's as though you're not there. I don't know what you're thinking or feeling, and then you push me away and I get . . . ." She couldn't find the word.

"Frantic," Bill supplied, and it was clear that the description had been used before.

I looked at them both. "You know, different people have different ways of expressing closeness—and they have different needs for it. It doesn't necessarily reflect on whether or not you love someone. Closeness involves your *own* sense of personal boundaries

—how much you want to open yourself to somebody and incorporate them into your life and emotions. And it also reflects the point at which you may feel you're losing your own identity or becoming engulfed by someone else. It's a very individual matter. But when two people don't realize that they're very different from each other in this respect, then one can start feeling suffocated and encumbered and the other can feel lonely or pushed aside or not loved. I think that's part of what's happening here."

"So what do we *do?*" Lisa asked.

"Well, for one thing, you can each try to realize that you're just experiencing and testing your own different personalities and needs. So if Bill needs the greater distance, you don't have to feel it's because of anything wrong with you or something you did."

"Sure," Lisa muttered. " 'Nothing personal, but stay away from me.' "

"That can be a terribly difficult idea to accept. Sometimes it becomes easier when you start to understand what's in a person's background that might have caused him to need a great deal of distance." I paused. "Does some of this make any sense to you both?"

They nodded. Then Lisa irritably changed the subject. "So what am I supposed to do with the sweater? This week is the last time I can return it."

Bill spoke through clenched teeth. "So *return* it."

"But you won't come with me?"

"That is correct."

Lisa stamped her foot down on the floor. "Why not keep it and *you* can give it to your mother for Christmas."

"If that's what you want."

"What *I* want!"

I interrupted, "Lisa, how did you feel when Bill gave you the sweater?"

"I don't know." She hesitated. "It's too big on me, and I don't have anything that goes with it."

"So you didn't think Bill made a very good choice?"

"Oh, it's not so much that." A note of humor crept into her voice. "He can't pick out anything. Most of the time he asks me to get what he needs." She hesitated again. "I thought maybe it was too expensive. It's cashmere and it must have cost a fortune." Her voice became more certain. "That store charges a fortune for everything. It's one reason we don't shop there. Besides, they've got all this square stuff." She was becoming more and more agitated. "And it's filled with all these matronly types—you feel fifty years older just walking into the place. I'll *probably* meet his mother and half her friends when I go in there."

"Lisa, how do you feel about Bill's mother?"

Lisa's lips tightened. "She's a bitch."

"And how might Bill feel toward you if he thought you were like his mother?"

"*Me?*" She sounded shocked and seemed to hold her breath for a moment. Finally she said quietly, "He'd hate me." Then another answer came, softly, almost despairingly. "He'd be afraid of me," she whispered.

Bill's face was red and he was shaking his head.

"Bill, can you tell us what you're feeling right now?"

He said one word. "Protective."

The unexpected answer brought tears to Lisa's eyes.

"Do you think there are ways in which Lisa does remind you of your mother?"

"My mother can be tough to live with," Bill answered immediately. "Sometimes she really pushes my dad around too much. He's very different in the office. And I guess she used to get on my back a lot, too." He thought for a minute. "But I don't think I let Lisa push me around. And as far as my mother is concerned, Dad and I know that underneath she really loves us a lot. I mean, if anything happened, there's nothing she wouldn't do for us. Maybe —maybe in that way, Lisa does remind me of her."

Lisa absorbed the compliment wide-eyed. "But . . ." she stopped as though reluctant to spoil her good feeling with whatever doubts were still plaguing her.

I thought this was a positive way to leave things. Our time was nearly up and I said, "It's interesting that this all started and ended with a present. Gifts can be complicated social gestures, if you think about it. For the giver, they involve questions such as 'What image do I have of you? How much do I care about you? How much should I spend?' It's a shame that money is so significant in our society. The giver is also thinking, 'What reaction do I want from you?' And the recipient makes similar judgments such as 'That's how he sees me or how much he values me.'

"Sometimes, if there aren't other emotions involved in the gift situation, someone can just say, 'You know, I love you very much, but I really don't love this—whatever it is. We probably don't know that much about each other's taste yet. Do you think we could exchange this and buy something else?' But when the gift itself raises such strong feelings, then you have to get at the underlying message. Is it possible that Bill was unconsciously saying Lisa reminded him of his mother? If so, in what ways might that be positive as well as negative? And what could it mean in terms of rejection or closeness when one person doesn't want to participate in exchanging the present." I paused. "We're just about out of time for today, but I think we've raised some important issues." We agreed to explore some of these question in greater detail.

Sameness, Closeness and Togetherness

In the early stages of marriage, couples inevitably discover certain things that can be very distressing. I often hear the dismayed reactions of people the first time they realize that they and their partners are separate individuals. "We're so different!" they say, "he wants to do this and I want to do that." The issue can be how to spend a vacation or a weekend, or what friends to see socially, or almost anything. But being dissimilar creates anxiety, and it usually stems from the unconscious sense that, "If we *love* each other, we should be the *same*. If he loves me, he should want to do the same thing I want to do, be happy doing what I'm doing. And if we're different, then something's *wrong*. Maybe we *don't* love each other." People even tend to think that, "If he loves me, he should *know* what I'm feeling or thinking, he should *know* what I want or need."

It sometimes takes a lot of work and maturing to get to the point where you can see that the yearning for sameness is really a distorted concept of marriage and the meaning of adult love. To say there's no difference between you and me, and therefore we are one, is actually a yearning for symbiosis. It's like mama and infant all over again. You may project that view or desire onto your partner because it's quite easy for early childhood feelings to be reactivated in the intimacy of the marital situation. So you may be hoping either to relive the wonderful warmth, oneness and well-being of the mother-child relationship, if it was a good one, or else to undo the bad experiences of an early relationship that wasn't fulfilling and make it all come out right this time with your spouse. But either way, your expectations are for something that's usually unrealistic and inappropriate to the marriage. The striving for oneness between husband and wife stifles individuality and creates a sense of being choked, trapped and overwhelmed by too much closeness and togetherness.

Closeness refers to an emotional perception. Togetherness is a physical fact. Depending on your relationship, you can feel close to someone who is miles or continents away from you, and shut out and far from someone who may be lying in the same bed with you.

Marriage usually brings an intensified sense of closeness and also a greater amount of togetherness, especially if you and your partner haven't lived together before. This change raises the issues of how each of you feels about closeness and togetherness, how much of them you need or can tolerate, and how similar your individual needs are. If someone who needs closeness marries a "distanced" person, he or she will be constantly frustrated and distressed while trying to share thoughts and emotions and always feeling rebuffed. And the person who needs the greater emotional (and sometimes even physical) space will experience the other as clinging, suffocating and dependent.

Feelings about closeness can surface in a wide variety of circumstances. Lisa took Bill's arm as they entered a party, but after a few steps, he thrust her arm from him. The closeness and warmth that his wife sought became a burden and a responsibility to him. He experienced it as a clinging demand rather than as affection. The underlying reason probably is that he was having enough difficulty just presenting himself to the social group, and the added "burden" was more than he could tolerate. When we first were starting the session, I also noticed that Bill moved his chair back from ours, and later he retreated from Lisa's gesture toward him. He needed whatever distance he could get within a physically and emotionally intimate situation.

Lisa's reaction to Bill was to feel rejected, insecure and "frantic." The more she felt like this, the harder she tried to break through Bill's reserve. Provoking a fight actually can be a way of seeking intimacy, getting *to* someone when you don't know how else to penetrate his defenses. But attacks usually cause the threatened person to raise his guard, increase the distance around him.

I also suspected that to some degree, Lisa was testing to see who was going to dominate certain aspects of the relationship. When I'd taken her history, she'd voiced reservations about the way her own mother constantly deferred to her father, yet she certainly didn't like the way Bill's mother dominated her husband and son. I thought Lisa had originally been drawn to Bill because he had an easygoing gentleness. However, she also felt that Bill, like his father, wasn't quite the man her own, more domineering father was. We'd have to explore the kind of strength that can accompany gentleness and tolerance.

Meanwhile, Lisa's marriage brought her face to face with the dilemma of how much control she felt comfortable with and how much she wanted Bill to exercise. At the start of the session, she had waited for Bill to select a chair and then, when he declined, she chose the larger one. When Lisa deferred to Bill too much, she may have been afraid that she was becoming a dull, dependent nonentity, which was somewhat the way she viewed her mother. But how strong or demanding can a wife be and still feel feminine, still feel she has a strong husband? Would she get carried away by her aggressive side and force Bill into what she considered a weak and passive position? In other words, would she become like Bill's mother, whom she didn't like, and like her own father, who was, after all, a *man?* The idea of this must have frightened her unconsciously, and the fact that she identified to a considerable degree with a strong parent of the opposite sex raised some interesting questions for me in terms of her conflict over gender identity. These were some of the issues we'd have to examine along with Bill and Lisa's divergent needs for closeness and her apparent expectation that marriage would bring a kind of "togetherness" that Bill didn't want.

I think people must learn to distinguish between closeness and togetherness. Closeness doesn't mean always doing things together. For a period following World War II, there was a "togetherness syndrome" in this country. The ideal family image was one in which nobody ever made a move alone. Kids growing up around that time were affected by the American family as portrayed in the magazines of the period, and many people still go into marriage looking for ways of doing "together things." But a husband and wife can be close without being cemented. And conversely, togetherness isn't necessarily a sign of a good relationship.

I had one married couple as patients who wouldn't do anything individually. If one wanted to take a walk and the other wanted to go to a movie, they'd talk it out until one of them acquiesced. Everything had to be together or not at all. That wasn't closeness; it was symbiosis. They were, in fact, engaged in a power struggle where eventually one would dominate and gradually swallow up the other.

Another couple I counseled were very happy in their marriage except for one thing—each one's parents refused to accept their child's chosen mate. Visiting the parents was always a distressing event, especially for the son- or daughter-in-law who was usually subtly excluded and criticized. "Have you ever considered visiting your families without each other?" I suggested. The idea shocked and dismayed them at first because they were afraid it would "separate" them, and more importantly, it was so far from the way they'd imagined things would—and should—be. But after we discussed it and they'd thought about it, they concluded that they could at least try this approach, and see if it caused them less distress, and possibly even gave them a sense of relief.

As it turned out, the wife's parents finally asked her why they never saw her husband any more. They wanted to know whether there was trouble within the marriage. She told them quite bluntly that he felt unwelcome and excluded by their habit of always directing the conversation to her and dwelling on personal events in the past in which he'd had no part. "I *tell* him about these visits—we're really very close—but neither of us can see why he should keep coming and trying to be part of the family when he's always getting slapped in the face." Her parents finally decided they wanted to get to know their son-in-law, and a fairly comfortable four-way relationship developed.

Doing things separately without jeopardizing the marriage is an important part of establishing one's sense of self. This kind of autonomy can, in fact, enhance a feeling of closeness because both people are secure in themselves, and there's no pressure or resentment involved. They can have their separate activities and then they can also draw together, sharing some of their individual experiences, and feeling free to be truly close and intimate.

One of the times your feelings about closeness are especially apt to emerge is during love-making, which is potentially the most intimate of all experiences. It's the time when you're most able to merge with another and lose your sense of self. That loss is frightening to some people.

A young couple came to see me six months after their wedding, saying everything was fine except that now that they were settled, they both wanted outside sex. On the surface, that's okay. If two consenting adults want other sexual experiences, I think that's their prerogative. Except after only six months of marriage, there's still so much to be mutually explored and discovered. If these newlyweds were turning to outside relationships, I had to question whether that was their way of not being close, whether it indicated a fear of closeness and a desire to escape from the merging. After all, one way of creating distance is to say, "It was stupid to get married; at least let's have sex with other people." This couple had enough reservations about what they were considering to seek professional help, and I told them we might want to explore how completely they'd worked through their own individual identities. We might want to find out whether their extramarital sexual desires were really a defense, a way of saying, "We're frightened of getting lost in each other."

Many people react to the closeness of love-making by clearly showing their need to regain their private self. Some couples regularly fight after intercourse. Sometimes one partner turns his back and goes off to sleep, either feeling totally relaxed and wonderfully content or indicating that he's had as much closeness as he can take and now has to distance himself through sleep.

But perhaps his partner (frequently the woman) isn't ready to give up their contact yet. If she recognizes what's happening, she may be able to tell him that it's important for her to know he's there and that she hasn't been shut out. Maybe if he can just put an arm around her, hold her hand, talk for a moment, or in some way acknowledge that he cherishes her, she won't mind so much if he goes off to sleep. Otherwise she may well begin to feel like a receptacle.

When people have different needs for closeness—*or anything else*—there can be relief in just talking about them—acknowledging and understanding them as causes that make one act in a certain way. I can't think of anything worse than evading this kind of communication and concluding that the person you married simply doesn't care about your needs or feelings.

Suppose one partner says, "I appreciate the fact that you'd like to be closer, but I have difficulty in that area. I don't know why I'm so different from you in this respect, but it's got nothing to do with whether I love you or not. It's something in my own personality. Sometimes I just need to feel separate. There's something within me that makes me need a lot of private time. I think I've been this way since I was a child, although I don't know what happened to cause it. Someone or something must have given me the feeling that I was being invaded. Maybe my rights or emotions weren't respected enough . . . ." This kind of self-awareness and openness can eliminate a great deal of guilt and blame on both sides. The partner who's seeking the greater closeness needn't feel that he or she is unloved, has failed or has done something bad because this is simply the way of the distanced person. And the distanced partner will be more sensitive about giving as much reassurance and comfort as possible. In this manner, two people are much more apt to work out a way of living and loving that provides enough closeness for one and sufficient distance for the other.

We've discussed several predictable issues that arise during a couple's first year of marriage: *the recognition of differences; the balance of power or control between partners; individual needs for closeness; and the question of togetherness.* Yet these are only some of the vital elements that are being stirred into the new marital "mix." Let's go on to see what else there is about the simple fact of getting married that causes fundamental changes in an existing relationship and creates a critical period of adjustment and reevaluation.

5. The Simple Fact of Getting Married

From the moment a man and woman get married, they become in many ways two different people because there is a fundamental role change from single person to husband or wife. Picture yourself and your intended before the wedding. The two of you exist as separate individuals. Then you say "I do," and suddenly you're someone else. You're no longer just your own person—you're also part of a pair. And you're seen as a couple—except perhaps in the context of your work. This new oneness can be a marvelous feeling which allows you to dip into all kinds of love, support and openness with each other. But it also means that as a couple, something different is expected of you by friends, family and society. "Of course, Jane and Jim will spend Thanksgiving together with us now that they're married," or, "Of course, Jane and Jim will redecorate their apartment, stop gadding around the country, start having people over for dinner, dress more conventionally, be more serious about their work, plan a family, etc., now that they're married."

The expectations of others may strike you as more or less comfortable, depending on your own wishes and desires. They may be more or less important to you, depending on your own degree of autonomy. However, they are part of the change that comes about as a result of your simply getting married. If you experience these outside expectations as demands, you may blame or resent your partner or the marriage for the feeling that you're being pressured into doing things you really don't want to do.

I think one of the wisest things couples can do is to stop, question and evaluate their sense of obligation to the expectations of others. If you can ask, "Who says we have to do this? Why do we have to? What will really happen if we choose to do something else that satisfies us?" you may find many more options available to you. Or perhaps when you think about it, you might see that you're going to get something you value by doing what you "should" do. Then you may start feeling, "We want to do this because," rather than, "We have to do it no matter what." Acknowledging that you have a choice is a positive and liberating step. If you say, "Let's visit your mother because, even though she complains a lot, she's really glad to have us and that makes me feel like we've done something nice," then you're much less likely to feel resentful and helplessly at the mercy of outside forces.

If the expectations of others were mainly what affected you, the marital role change might have less power and significance. But the fact is that after marriage, your expectations of your spouse are different, and your expectations of yourself are different, too.

A husband is not the same as a fiance or a lover. For example, a fiance can be dashing, charming and extravagant, and a woman can have a lot of fun with him. Maybe he has some traits of which she doesn't fully approve. Let's say he's a spendthrift. That problem might not seem too serious, especially if he earns a good living. But when he becomes her husband, his extravagance may suddenly begin to matter very much.

"I don't know where this is heading," Sharon said to me. "Kenny spends money so recklessly, it's insane. It's got to stop. At the rate he's going, we'll end up in the poorhouse. But he doesn't even care. I don't think he gives a damn about what happens to us. He's absolutely irresponsible. He certainly doesn't think about our future the way a husband should."

Kenny jumped out of his chair, furious. "You've got a real hang-up about money, and I don't want to discuss it anymore. When you got me to come here, you said we were going to talk about making things better between us. I don't need to sit around while you and a shrink decide what I ought to do with what I earn." He grabbed his jacket from the back of his chair, glared at his wife and then at me. "You sit here listening to her cockeyed version of things and you don't know what's really going on."

"I want to know. That's why I asked you to come in with Sharon—so you could tell us how you feel. Would you be willing to do that now?"

"Why not?" He faced us, still standing. "First of all, I work hard for my money, and I earn good pay. I think I've got a right to get some pleasure out of it now, while I'm still young enough to enjoy it. I thought we could get married and go on having a good time together, like when we were dating only maybe even better. But all of a sudden," he turned to Sharon, "you've got nothing on your mind but the finances. What is it with you? Don't you think I've got any judgment or ability? We've never run out of money yet. But you don't want any fun out of life, and you're trying to stop me from having it, too." He sat on the edge of the chair and looked at me. "She's my wife, for God's sake. Shouldn't she want to help me enjoy things? I mean, she could be enjoying them, too. If you were me, would you figure maybe she got married just to set up a secure future for herself? And what kind of wife is she, if I'm nothing but a meal ticket to her?"

Everybody has expectations, both conscious and unconscious, of what marriage and their partner will be like. These expectations stem from fundamental needs, which at some level you believe will be met.

Sharon, for example, basically needed to feel cared for and dependent. She needed and wanted her husband, the man to whom she felt she had entrusted her whole life, to show that he cherished her and would always protect her by giving her a sense of economic security. When he wouldn't do this, it aroused fears in her that she couldn't tolerate. She saw it as evidence that Kenny didn't really love her or want to be her husband in the sense that she needed him to be.

Kenny had a strong need to spend, to gratify his desires, to make up for things he hadn't been able to have as a child or a young man. Earning money was a sign of success, but putting it in the bank left him unsatisfied. He was hungry for what the money could buy, and he saw Sharon's attempts to save as robbing, cheating and depriving him of what he essentially wanted. His way of showing his love for Sharon was to share "good times" with her. He felt that a wife who expected him to give up all this couldn't really love him or care about his well-being.

The interesting question, of course, is why Sharon and Kenny hadn't recognized their differences before they got married.

The reason this problem had not been foreseen is because there's a tremendous denial that goes on during the whole engagement period. It's a time of denial of differences, displeasing features and troublesome characteristics in the person you love. When you feel an intense need to join and be with somebody, you have a tendency to ignore for the time being things you'd rather not see and say to yourself, "This person's great, and if anything *is* wrong, it will change." The fear is that if you really place a searchlight on the other individual, you'll never be satisfied, or the other person may get angry and walk out, or something else will come into the picture to spoil it. So rather than take such a chance, you deny that anything can be wrong with your partner or the relationship, or you figure you'll cope with it later.

Many people enter marriage with the idea that they're going to change the other person. That's what we call a "hidden agenda" for the marriage. It's a feeling which you may or may not be aware of during courtship, that "This is how things are now, but when we get married and we're alone together, *it will all be different*. He'll become more attentive or closer, or our sex life will improve, or I'll make him feel differently about the way we should live, or how we should spend our money."

Sooner or later, the actuality of the marriage hits you, and this can be a devastating blow if your hopes and dreams have been unrealistic. There's bound to be disappointment, accusation and resentment. The first signs of distress may show up on the heels of the wedding ceremony itself. A woman will say to me, "I should have known we were in trouble when we were sitting in the plane at the start of our honeymoon and he didn't say one solitary word to me."

The husband may counter, "Well, what did you think I was thinking? I was scared out of my wits!" Or he may say, "What do you mean, I didn't say anything? I was reading. What was I supposed to say?"

"Well, you know, we were on our *honeymoon*."

"So why didn't you say something about it?"

Right away I can begin to get a sense of the hopes and fantasies of the people involved, the amount of real communication or detachment between them, the withdrawing and withholding.

Part of the new realism or disillusionment you may feel after marriage comes from the day-to-day quality of living with someone. Flaws, faults and differences which seemed unimportant or acceptable on a part-time basis, or which were denied during the engagement period, can suddenly stand out. Even people who have lived together previously may find that it becomes impossible to tolerate something when they consider living in daily contact with it on a permanent basis.

"What have I let myself in for?" is the shocked question I often hear. "How could I have married someone who's . . . an inconsiderate slob, a neatness fanatic, a bully, a weakling, a cold fish, a clinging vine, an irresponsible spendthrift, a tightwad or a killjoy? What am I going to do now?"

The best thing that you can do now is to explore your original attraction to this person. Usually, if you can delve deeply enough inside yourself, you'll find that to some degree you once were drawn toward the very characteristic you began to detest after you were married. I've already pointed out that you often seek a partner who has a quality or characteristic you lack. Thus you may be attracted to someone because there's an echo within you of certain elements in this individual's personality that you'd like to have more of, but haven't been able to allow in yourself. Therefore unconsciously you reach out toward what you need in order to complement or enlarge yourself. But then you get into trouble when you get what you "need" in this very deepest sense, because all the defenses, which have kept that quality from emerging within yourself, now *attack* it in the other person.

Sharon, for instance, had been delighted by Kenny's liberal way with money when they were dating. Occasionally she'd felt a twinge of worry at his extravagance. But on the whole, it thrilled her to be able to experience vicariously, and sometimes first-hand, the pleasure of buying and enjoying things with such abandon and relish. "I never felt so free, indulged or excited," she said. "We seemed to do exactly what we wanted when we wanted, and it was fun!"

Theoretically, Kenny could have helped Sharon get more in touch with this hungry, eager side of herself that she'd been suppressing and denying. But, in fact, marriage brought Sharon so close to Kenny and to a way of being, which both attracted her and made her extremely anxious, that all of her ingrained controls strengthened and tightened in defense. The buried part of Sharon that would have loved being a spendthrift and buying everything in sight was touched and awakened by its active counterpart in Kenny, and it threatened to break free. Sharon panicked. She was in no way ready to cope with this unconscious aspect of herself, which she feared might actually take control and turn her into a voracious, greedy, demanding child. In her experience, that kind of child was considered bad and would never be given the love and care she needed. Her unconscious projection was that Kenny would reject her, too. So all of Sharon's original defenses against this hidden, hungry urge redoubled, and she started attacking Kenny as a means of reducing the threat within herself.

Kenny actually had liked Sharon's sensible attitude toward money, and even acknowledged that he would like to be able to keep his spending in check a little more. But when Sharon suddenly tried to change his whole way of being, he felt pushed to an intolerable extreme. If he gave in to her, he was afraid that the "sensible" element in *him* would take over and he'd end up leading a rigid, overly controlled life in which he'd be starved for pleasure and gratification.

This feature of human personality is familiar in both psychology and literature. We've all read of the perfectly virtuous, compassionless, and condemning preacher, whose excessive zeal is a defense against the inadmissable fact that he himself has all the same desires and lusts that he considers sinful. There's also the strong, supermasculine male who shuns weaklings and sissies and harasses them with a vengeance, but who is really covering some so-called weakness he fears within himself.

Usually the clue to this kind of defensiveness lies in the intensity of your emotion and your inability to tolerate your partner's showing any evidence of the characteristic that you can't acknowledge or accept in yourself. Perhaps you can compromise about other issues but not about this one; you simply can't accept your partner's different way of being because doing so would make you too anxious.

I worked with a husband, who was a banker, and his wife, an artist. He was a rigid, conservative person, and she was childlike, explosive and very individualistic in the way she dressed. He was attracted to her by the simple fact that she was able to do those things that he couldn't do. He married her, then set about trying to change her into a conformist like himself. Her freedom and self-expression caused him too much anxiety because they were so appealing; they threatened to melt the defenses he had erected to control the part of him that wished to be like that.

This couple came into therapy because the wife was unable to tolerate the changes being demanded of her. And to some degree, the husband recognized that he was trying to "kill the thing he loved" by squelching his wife's uniqueness and spontaneity that originally had attracted him. I worked with him alone for some time, until gradually we began to find out what had caused him to build those defenses in the first place. The marriage survived, but even after many years of therapy, these people still occasionally return when something happens to threaten their equilibrium or test the man's newly acquired flexibility.

What can you do if you're attracted enough to marry someone with a characteristic that you suddenly find intolerable? How can you deal with your unconscious ambivalence about this characteristic and avoid becoming rigidly locked into a position on how things *"must"* be, how your partner *"must"* change?

1. The first step is to *admit the possibility* that deep within you is a hidden part of yourself which wants to be *like* the trait you're condemning. If you can't stand your partner's messiness, consider the possibility that suppressed in you is a wish to be totally messy, like an irresponsible child.

"But *I* don't want to be *messy,"* a patient will object furiously. "I want my *wife* to be *neat*. I can't stand her messiness."

"If having a neat wife is so important to you, why didn't you marry one?" I'll ask. "Isn't it interesting you chose your wife instead?"

2. Sometimes *simply understanding what's happening* enables people to become less frightened and defensive. It usually helps to talk about the ambivalence you feel. "I could never let myself become a slob, but I guess I can imagine something inside me feeling that it might be fun . . . ." Once you begin to recognize and accept the hidden part of yourself, feel reasonably sure that it won't get out of hand, you'll be less and less threatened from within.

3. Perhaps you can start to think of *small, tolerable ways* in which you might try out the quality you've been denying. A husband and wife might agree to try one small change from their usual pattern without committing themselves to anything long-range or overwhelming. Someone extravagant like Kenny might decide to put aside a few dollars one week—maybe not even in a savings account, but just in an envelope at home—to see whether there's any satisfaction in that. Sharon might make up her mind that the next time her husband was eager to go somewhere with her or buy something, she'd try to get in touch with her own sense of pleasure, respond positively and actively join in his enthusiasm to see how that might make her feel. By facing this kind of problem openly and together, couples can offer each other support and approval—and the understanding that change of this nature is difficult. But it can also be exciting and enlarging. Perhaps you can even uncover certain events or relationships from your past that might have caused you to feel unhappy with the part of you that you subsequently suppressed. Sharing these thoughts with your partner may increase your mutual empathy and insight.

In cases where people *won't* try any of the steps I've described, chances are that they're feeling too vulnerable and are unable to take a risk. They may first have to find out a great deal about where their anxieties originated before they can develop new ways of responding that are different from those originally formed during their childhood years.

4. Finally, in exploring your drive to change your partner, make sure that you're *not involved in a power struggle*. Keep in mind that almost any disagreement *may* symbolize a fight for control within the marital relationship. For instance, the question of who controls the purse strings often represents a power struggle over who will control the marriage itself. Since the need to be in control isn't one we easily recognize, a couple can fight on and on about

whether to spend or save (or about another issue) and never get around to discussing the real point of why each of them needs to have his own way.

If you can recognize your need for control, then you can ask yourself why it's so important to you now, and what it might have meant to you in the past to be *out* of control. By sharing your fears about letting someone else take charge, you may be able to reassure and support each other, and become more comfortable with the idea of some giving, taking and sharing the power between you.

6. Expectations

Certain phrases I hear frequently in my office probably play a significant part in your own life. These include, "I should," "I shouldn't," I have to," "I can't," and sometimes, "I want to," or "I can." These tend to be expressions of your self-expectations. "This is how I should be and what I should do."

You may also have certain hopes about the kind of person you'd like to become. This is your ego ideal. But while your ego ideal is something to strive for, your self-expectations apply to the here and now. Your ego ideal tends to remain relatively fixed (i.e. "I'd like never to lie"), whereas your self-expectations may vary under different circumstances.

When you change from being a single person to being a husband or wife, the things that you expect of yourself also tend to change. It's as though a voice within you takes its cue from the marriage ceremony and starts delivering an updated commentary on what you, in this new role, should, shouldn't, can, can't or must do.

Sometimes the inner message you hear is welcome. One woman said to me, "The best thing about being married is that now I feel as though it's okay for me to walk around naked in front of my husband! I never felt right doing that before." The new sense of freedom can be luxurious and exciting. Moreover, if you share these good feelings with your partner, they can be heightened and enhanced.

But sometimes you have self-expectations that make you miserable or that you simply can't fulfill. You may expect yourself to be something you aren't, to do more than you actually can, or to feel things you don't really feel.

"If I were a decent wife, I should be happy to take care of

Larry and do his laundry and cook his meals," Evelyn said.

"Why? Whose definition of a 'decent' wife is that?" I asked.

"It's *my* definition," she admitted.

Often, you accept the demands of your inner voice without question because they're so much a part of you. Yet you weren't born with them. You were born with certain innate characteristics which, combined with your interaction with parents and your identification with other significant people throughout your life, lead you to form self-expectations and an ego ideal. You are, in a sense, a mixture of your inborn traits plus all the values, rules, prejudices and ideals that you've absorbed or formulated.

Nobody can live up to unrealistic self-expectations. You have to face them and then be able to say, "This I can and want to do, and I'm reasonably comfortable and satisfied doing it. This other thing I can't feel or do—at least not now." Then you can start to explore why you can't do it, whether you really want to do it, whether you might be able to gradually develop so it becomes possible for you, and whether it might be more realistic and constructive to modify your expectations.

When you truly expect things of yourself that you can't deliver, you start feeling that you're not measuring up. Your self-esteem drops. You may end up disliking or even hating yourself. One way or another, the destructive effect touches you and your marriage.

You can easily build up resentment and start feeling, "If I were married to someone else, things would be different. Another person would be more understanding, would help me more, or wouldn't expect me to do this." You may project your own inner demands onto your partner—*he's* making me do this—and you may blame him for your predicament. "After all I've done for him, after I've tried so hard, look what's happening. Look what he expects." You may feel hurt and mistreated. You may become caught up in a "poor me" syndrome, or you may find yourself responding with rage.

Maybe you feel, "I've failed. I'm not meeting his expectations or my own. There's nothing I can do about it, so I'll just disengage." You may withdraw emotionally or physically, become silent, retreat and isolate yourself. I've known people who've reached the point of divorce without ever discussing with their partner what was making them miserable. As children, their feelings hadn't been sufficiently considered, their needs or desires weren't effective in changing their circumstances, they found that help or comfort were generally unavailable, "negotiation" was pointless—the child either lived within a situation someone else created, or retreated from it if possible. The adult then sees only those same alternatives—endure or retreat—because under stress, you generally respond in ways you've learned in early childhood.

Unfortunately, most of us simply haven't been trained to say, "This is how I feel, this is what's bothering me. This is where I think I'm failing. Could we sit down and talk about it?" We don't have role models that show us how to do that. We're usually frightened, ashamed or embarrassed at our shortcomings. Unconsciously we think, "Who's going to love me if that's the kind of person I am? How can I expose this side of me to someone else, especially to the one I most want to love me?" When I ask people whether they can take the risk of sharing their feelings, whether they can trust the other person enough to do so, this fear of exposure is exactly what I mean.

To some degree, help and encouragement from someone else can aid you in dealing with your self-expectations. You may get support, relief and sometimes a better perspective if your partner says, "You really are pushing yourself too hard. Why? I'd feel better if you'd ease up on yourself a little." But at some point, outside words of counsel or comfort don't touch you. You yourself must take the basic step of examining and judging your self-expectations.

"I should earn more, give more, take my wife out more, entertain for my husband more, should be happier, make love more often, be more open and free sexually, like my in-laws better, never lose my temper, never be selfish or dependent or a burden, etc." Are your self-expectations encouraging, tormenting or defeating you?

"I have to keep this job . . . I shouldn't be restless staying home . . . I ought to get a gift for . . . I have to clean out the . . ." Can you stop and ask, *"Says who? Why do I have to?" "Is it something I really want to do?"*

It can be terribly difficult to go against your inner sense of what you should do. You're apt to feel guilty or anxious, as though you're being bad and something bad will happen as a result. But can that be true? One of the best questions to ask yourself at a time like this is, "What's the worst thing I can possibly imagine happening if I don't do such-and-such? Is someone going to come and punish me? Slap me? Tell me I'm a bad boy or girl? Is anything really negative actually going to occur?"

When you're trying to modify the things you expect of yourself, it often helps to understand the psychological forces that are pushing and pulling you. As youngsters, we all internalize the harsh demands of parents and other authorities, and they remain a very real part of us when we're grown up. At the same time, we have within us the child of our past who once had to conform to what powerful adults wanted, simply in order to survive. When you, as an adult, are driven by feelings that you have to behave one way or another, it's as though that child is reacting to the parent in you and feeling it has to obey. Thus the child starts dictating what you must do in order to be "good." But the fact is that today you are *more* than just the child. You've got the ability and the right to make your own choices, instead of continuing to perform according to standards set by someone else.

What's satisfying, fulfilling and good for you may be very different from what your inner child says you "have" to do. You wouldn't heed a real child's judgment over your own. If you're to become an autonomous individual, it's time to substitute your own rational self-approval for that of your internalized parent. You can look upon the change you want to make as progress, development or simply a different perspective from what you were once taught.

Sensing your freedom of choice sometimes has an interesting result: when you stop believing you *have* to do certain things, you may decide you *want* to do them! "I *have* to mop the floor" is a demand you may well resent. But suppose you say to yourself, "I don't have to mop the floor. I can let that floor go for weeks or months and nothing drastic is going to happen." There's a pretty good chance that one day during those weeks or months, you may decide, "What the hell, I think I'll do the floor."

Knowing that you're making any decision of your own free will tends to lessen or eliminate your resentment. The reverse is also true. For instance, after marriage self-expectations that you should act one way or another can attach a new sense of obligation or burden to things you previously did willingly. "Before we were married, I bought presents, made love, cooked dinner, visited parents because I wanted to. Now I feel as though I'm doing such-and-such because I have to, and that makes me resentful." The more you can arrange and view your self-expectations to be things you really *want* to do, the more satisfaction and pleasure you'll get from fulfilling them.

We've been talking about setting expectations that are realistic for *you*. This doesn't mean giving up values or goals that you esteem. It does mean differentiating between what you can do now and what you want to work toward as part of your ego ideal.

You may say, "I should be sexually open and free with my partner." You may really mean that you want to be this way, but something is preventing you from letting this side of yourself emerge. Something within you is sending out a warning that it would be wrong, bad, unseemly or dangerous; that this aspect of you might turn you into someone who is unlovable or terribly vulnerable. Perhaps if you think about the important people who influenced your life, you might figure out who could have taught you or shown you that it was necessary to hide, control or deny this part of yourself. If you can clearly and consciously decide that you don't want to continue living according to that person's rules, or if you simply acknowledge that you no longer want to continue the pattern that's existed until now, you've established the groundwork for change.

When the change is too threatening, people may have to get professional help in order to work through their needs and fears to find a new kind of freedom. But it's also possible to encourage yourself to grow and develop. If you can confront your anxieties and goals, and share them with your partner, you may be able to start taking small risks, trying out a different way of being.

Examining Your Relationship

The difference between what you accepted or expected from yourself and your partner before you were married, and what you then expect or can tolerate after you become husband and wife is at the heart of most of the crises that arise during the first year of marriage.

If you and your partner can explore and share your responses to the following questions, you may find it possible to deal in new ways with some of the issues raised during this initial time of adjustment and adaptation.

1. Why did I choose my partner? What did I expect from him or her? What did I expect from the marriage? How realistic were my expectations? What do I feel I can give to my partner and the relationship?

2. How well do we communicate? Do I recognize and express my feelings? Am I able to empathize with my partner's feelings? How open are we with each other?

3. How do I feel about closeness? Togetherness? The ways in which we are different?

4. Did I enter marriage with the idea, conscious or unconscious, that I would change my partner? Can I see ways in which I might want to change or modify myself? Am I attacking something in my partner that on some deeper level I find both threatening and attractive?

5. How do we feel about change? Can we support each other in developing and becoming more flexible?

6. What do we value about our relationship as it is right

now? Can we discuss and enhance the good things?

7. Is there a struggle going on between us for power or control within our relationship? Can we learn to share the power?

8. Am I allowing the expectations of others to rule me? Am I being driven by internal demons? Can I start exploring my own values, free myself from unwanted ties to the past and develop my own sense of autonomy and choice? Can my partner and I encourage each other to do this?

9. What can I do for myself that will give me a sense of fulfillment and self-worth?

10. How do we see the future together?

PART 3:
The Impact of Children on Marriage

For the first time in our society, not having children has become an acceptable choice that isn't scorned and isn't considered a stigma. More and more couples today are choosing this alternative, and one result is that they avoid many major changes, stresses and crises in their lives. As individuals and as couples, they don't have to absorb and adjust to the impact of another incredibly important being entering, disrupting, and at times, taking over their existence.

I don't mean to suggest that childless (or as a friend of mine prefers, "child-free") couples live without stress. They're equally subject to all the changes and adaptations unrelated to children that all couples may have to face. Moreover, the fact that their friends may be preoccupied with their own children, and therefore less available, can make a couple feel somewhat isolated and out of the mainstream. They may turn to each other more, make greater demands on one another, and place a greater burden on their relationship. They're also more available to each other when there's no child around, and have more freedom, time, money, emotional and physical energy for non-child-oriented pursuits.

Psychologically, couples who don't have children may have to find ways to replace the nurturing that parents give their youngsters—the sense of giving and caring for someone, meeting his vital needs, helping him to develop and grow. Non-parents may do this to some degree for each other, older relatives, someone else's child, a pet, a project or a cause. They may have less desire to nurture, and their wish to create may be fulfilled in other ways.

It can be difficult for people who love and want children to understand how anyone can *not* have that same desire. "They're missing all the joy, excitement, pleasure and satisfaction . . . ." I know the feeling. I have a daughter and it's hard for me to talk about her without getting carried away. Some of the most rewarding experiences of my life have been watching her grow and sharing many of her adventures. For me, having a child was a privilege, an added bonus to my life. And now that my daughter is an adult, she's become a special friend with whom I can share ideas, emotions and love. All those things make me enormously happy about my choice.

Yet people are different, sometimes in very fundamental ways. Those who don't want children may be well aware that for *them* the "joys" of parenthood would not be forthcoming. For them, the decision not to have children is a positive and a good one.

Whether or not you want to have children, the important thing to be aware of is that it's *your choice*. Fortunately, more and more couples today are evaluating themselves honestly and consciously deciding whether to have children or not, rather than entering parenthood without thinking about it because it's assumed to be the only natural, normal way of life.

You owe it to yourself, your partner and the children you may have to examine your reasons for wanting or not wanting to be a parent. If you expect that it will be easy, fun all the time, or won't disrupt your life all that much, then you're dreaming.

If you expect that having a child will make you more of a man or a woman, will enable you to live vicariously through your child, or will create a source of love and devotion that will fill your own life, you may be fantasizing and asking for a terrible let-down.

The more *dependent* you are on your child for enrichment, fulfillment or proof of your own value, the more likely you are to be disappointed. The more you're able to view your child as somebody who is separate from you, an individual in his or her own right, the greater the chances are for you to experience the joy, excitement and satisfaction of nurturing and participating in the growth process of a new life.

7. Pregnancy

"I'm pregnant!" I've heard those words said with elation, fear, anger, uncertainty, wonder, contentment and distress. The impact pregnancy has on a woman or couple is a familiar theme in fiction and drama. Pregnancy *is* drama. It's filled with suspense, change, hope and fear, all leading to an overwhelmingly powerful climax. Clearly pregnancy produces stresses, both joyful and upsetting, which deeply affect the expectant parents.

Perhaps in a more primitive culture than ours, most aspects of pregnancy would be taken for granted. Even in our society, some couples try for a "natural" approach, but it tends to be difficult to achieve. First of all, most of us are highly conscious of ourselves— of the way we look, feel and affect others around us. We're also somewhat removed from many of the life processes and taught to deny others. Until recently, a pregnant woman was confined to the home when her belly grew large. Now, our sophistication about prenatal care tends to prevent us from viewing pregnancy as a mere matter of course. We go to the doctor for checkups, watch our diet, our weight, and take vitamin supplements. Our increasing knowledge about genetics, birth defects and ways of testing the health of the unborn baby (amniocentesis) enables us to have safer pregnancies, but they're further removed from naturalness. I think all these reasons, plus the simple fact that we don't become pregnant as frequently as women in many other societies, lead us to view the pregnant woman as someone of special significance and delicacy, someone to be protected and taken care of, because she is now not one but two.

Typically, pregnancy causes the balance of the relationship between husband and wife to change. The woman becomes the "taker," the dependent one. She's having a powerful physical as well as emotional experience. As you know, when something significant is happening to your body, it takes precedence over most external considerations. A pregnant woman has a different way of relating to herself and also sees herself as different in her husband's eyes. He, in turn, has to respond to these changes, which, as we'll see, may exacerbate various feelings of his own. A couple's interaction is constantly in a state of flux, but pregnancy brings something totally new into the picture, and because it so fundamentally alters the existing equilibrium, the marriage enters a crisis or turning point.

The way in which husband and wife handle the pregnancy —the degree to which they're able to turn to each other, be open and honest about their feelings, offer support and participate together in the process—is apt to determine a new direction or pattern for the marriage.

There's no way to forecast how a woman or a man will react to the stresses of the pregnancy period. Even in cases where women suffer from realistic fears, such as a history of abnormality in the family, relatively advanced age, economic worries or an unhappy marriage, the pregnancy may be completely normal and quite easy. In many women, hope seems to be generated during this time. There's a medical theory that the acceleration in hormonal and metabolic processes may sometimes heighten a woman's pleasure in bearing her child by increasing her positive feelings and hopeful fantasies and reducing her anxieties. One woman described her pregnancies this way: "I felt as though something wonderful and almost holy was happening. I felt as though nothing could touch me or go wrong because this was somehow meant to be. I entered both pregnancies feeling calm and content, sure that everything would be fine—and it was."

On the other hand, many women don't experience anything resembling what one mother angrily called "that damn contented cow syndrome." She said, "I couldn't believe what was happening to me and my marriage, especially as I got into the later months. One minute I felt like a crybaby and a louse for what I was doing to my husband, for the demands I was making on him; the next minute I wanted to kill him for being so impatient, detached and unsympathetic."

It seems to me that women are in a double bind when dealing with the problems of being expectant mothers. At the beginning, even though the pregnancy may create difficulties in the marriage, there's generally a feeling of, "Well, this is such a new experience, I'll try to get used to it. It's not going to last forever. And when the baby comes, everything will be different. Let me try to make the best of this." That approach is often supported by a mother or mother-in-law who says, "Don't you know all women get upset during the first pregnancy? Haven't you heard that women are emotional and nervous at this time?" So the pregnant woman may try to ignore or endure some very distressing feelings without questioning or understanding them. At the same time, she may listen to people who have had children looking back on their own pregnancies and denying that they had any negative feelings. They give a glowing report to the pregnant woman who starts thinking, "What's wrong with me? This is supposed to be the happiest time of my life. If I really loved my husband, I would want his baby and I wouldn't feel so upset." She may become ashamed of her emotions and think, "If I make a fuss about this, what does it say about my feelings for John, my marriage, or myself as a woman?"

One of the main advantages of understanding the stresses of pregnancy on a relatively sophisticated level and even seeing some of the possible extreme reactions is that then you won't be as disturbed and confused if some of these problems do arise. Having the knowledge beforehand makes it easier to cope. Then, if you begin to feel terrible uncertainty, resentment, fear, hostility or some other extreme emotion, you can say, "Oh yes, that's understandable," or, "I'm having a lot of trouble with this, but it happens to other people, and I'll get over it." But if you feel, "Oh Lord, I shouldn't have these feelings," the denial, shame and guilt about having them can be destructive. It's much better to recognize and expose them, to examine them and try to do something about them. And, in fact, you usually can.

The "Background" of the Pregnancy

Certain practical considerations that ideally should be taken into account before pregnancy are bound to influence the way in which you respond to it. For instance, when in your marriage is the pregnancy coming? How was the decision to have a child reached? Was it planned and talked through beforehand? Was it arrived at unilaterally and somewhat resented by one partner? Was it an accident? Are you nonetheless content that it happened? Are you dismayed because you haven't had a chance to be with your partner sufficiently to get to know each other as husband and wife? What are your economic circumstances? What reactions can you expect from your partner? What about your families? What kind of "support system" will you have? Does having a baby mean the mother must give up a job or take time out from her career? Does the father feel that this is more responsibility than he wants to take on at the moment? What else is happening in your lives? If you already have a child or children, what will be the effect of a new baby on the whole family?

If some of these questions raise issues you haven't faced, they need to be acknowledged and openly discussed. The attitude that somehow "things will work themselves out" is seldom constructive and never realistic. It generally means you're apt to bring secret burdens or resentments into what is already an intrinsically stressful period.

Besides the practical considerations we've just mentioned, a husband and wife need to become aware of their inner feelings about the concept of pregnancy and parenthood in order to understand their reactions and needs.

Women should ask themselves the following questions to get in touch with their emotions and focus in on what pregnancy means to them:

—Do I think of being pregnant positively or negatively? Do I see it as a joy or a burden? Something that adds to my sense of self and self-esteem, or something that's a further demand and burden on me?

—Do I really want a baby? *Why?* What are my expectations?

—What thoughts and fantasies have I ever had about pregnancy and motherhood?

If you've already borne a child, the kind of experience you had will obviously affect your attitude toward the current pregnancy. If your own mother wanted children and was affirmative about motherhood, especially if she had an easy pregnancy, these influences will make it easier for you. The reverse can also be true if your mother has said, "You should have known what I went through with you. When I found out I was pregnant, I wanted to kill myself. I tried so hard to get rid of you. Then when I finally had you, I was glad, of course, and I love you dearly. But that pregnancy was absolutely the worst . . . ."

Even before there's any swelling or bodily change, sometimes even before the pregnancy has begun, it's *natural* for a woman to experience various fears and fantasies about what will happen. There's usually nothing to be gained from harboring these feelings within you, denying your awareness of them, or hiding them from your partner. By confronting them, you can generally start to minimize their power, put them into a more realistic perspective, separate the truth from myth and yourself from the feelings of others who are negative about pregnancy because of their own problems.

Men are often anxious about the idea of paternity. They

don't know what to expect or how to react, whether they'll live up to their own standards and still be accepted in the same way by their wives and colleagues. A husband may have heard tales about how pregnant women become very self-involved, and he may feel, "My wife is not going to be there for me any more. Here we were just beginning to have a good relationship and look at her. She's already examining her belly and her breasts, spending much more time talking to her mother and her girlfriends . . . ." Both husband and wife may need support from their own friends. Group discussions, where men and women talk about the experiences they're having, can also be very helpful. But above all, it's vital for the couple to share their concerns so they can understand, empathize with and support each other as much as possible.

Pregnancy, of course, is largely the wife's experience. The husband doesn't feel the discomforts his wife may be undergoing or, on the other hand, the pleasurable feelings that may be sustaining her. Of course he may have other emotions such as a sense of pride in his virility. But he won't be as involved in the whole process unless he's brought into it. More and more people today are beginning to realize that this can be done, that the role of father *does* begin during pregnancy, when concerns, feelings *and* activities are shared together. Naturally I'm not suggesting total togetherness! But I do suggest that the husband can go on some of the visits to the doctor, speak with him on the phone, look at charts showing the development of the fetus and know when to expect the baby's first movement. He can read, plan and learn along with his wife. Many couples who don't expect to have natural childbirth go to the classes anyway to learn about what's happening and what to expect during the last part of pregnancy, labor and childbirth. This gives the couple a chance to start a pattern of mutual involvement and to add a new dimension to their relationship. Couples who don't see the pregnancy in this way may subtly lay the groundwork for serious marital problems in the future.

Some women, on becoming pregnant, seek company, advice, reassurance and help from their mothers or other female relatives and friends almost to the exclusion of the husband. Perhaps this is the way they've always seen things handled. While the husband may be informed of what's happening, plans are made, baby furniture and clothes selected, the doctor is visited, without the husband having any real input or participation. His job is to work, pay the bills, and try to be patient and considerate while his wife is "in the family way." When there are problems, anxieties, tears or crises, the women gather round and the husband stands back. To a degree he may feel left out, yet he may also accept this arrangement with genuine relief. It may seem unnatural or embarrassing to him and to his wife to even consider participating in natural child-birth classes, much less to imagine his being in the room when the baby is born. Even today, some people feel that certain things are simply "women's business."

In a sense, this does offer one viable method of dealing with pregnancy. Any way you can cope with a situation and feel comfortable with it is acceptable. Who's to say that it's not? Yet for many people, such an arrangement is unattainable or undesirable. The wife's mother and other support figures may not always be available, or the expectant mother may not feel comfortable turning to them. Furthermore, one should question what it means to want to exclude the husband so completely. How well do the husband and wife really know, see and respond to each other as complex human beings? And what does it suggest for their long-term relationship if they think in terms of being separate during pregnancy, turning elsewhere to share their anxieties as well as their joys? Eventually the problems inherent in this pattern tend to emerge.

Exclusion—or withdrawal—of one partner from a major event within the marriage is generally destructive.

Let's take a closer look at how a couple might attempt to deal with pregnancy more mutually, the stresses they're apt to feel, and the so-called "normal" responses they might foresee. At the same time, we can become alert to signals of more extreme distress, consider what it might mean, and how it might be handled.

8. The Expectant Parents

"I don't know what's going on, Dr. Singer, but he's driving me crazy. We're fighting over everything." Caroline stared unhappily at Steve. "It's as bad as it ever was. Maybe worse."

"You're getting very sensitive, you know," Steve said.

"And you're right back in the old rut of telling me what to do, when to do it and how. Well, I'm the one who's carrying this baby, and I'm perfectly capable of doing what's right for it without your minute-by-minute supervision."

"Oh, really? I suppose the *baby* had a headache and that's why you went for the aspirin."

"I told you Dr. Williams said it wouldn't hurt if I needed just one aspirin occasionally."

"Well, 'need' is a relative word. I just said I thought you should try to relax for a while and you'd probably feel better without needing . . ."

"Thank you, Mother Nature. Thank you for knowing more about my headache than I do, and for telling me not to take something my own obstetrician doesn't think is harmful." Caroline's voice rose sharply. "Thank you for glaring at me if I want a glass of wine at a party, or if I feel like taking a walk in the snow. God knows, I wouldn't want our baby to get frostbite in the womb."

"Oh Jesus, Caroline, that's disgusting!"

"So I'm disgusting. I'm also disgusted." The last point was addressed to me.

I asked, "Can you try to tell Steve . . ."

"Yes, I can." She was amused as she interrupted me. "You were going to ask if I could tell him how it makes me feel when he does this routine, right?" I nodded. They'd been my patients for nearly two years and had made a great deal of progress. They also could anticipate some of my questions. Caroline spoke more seriously. "I've thought a lot about this and I'll tell you how I feel," she said to Steve. "It's as though I really don't count. All that matters to you is how something will affect the baby."

"That's ridiculous. Why do you *say* things like that?"

Caroline glanced at me and back at Steve. "I'm trying to tell you how I feel. Can you try to accept . . ."

"Stop the bullshit, Caroline. I don't believe that's how you really think I . . ."

"Don't tell me to stop the bullshit!" Caroline was genuinely angry and hurt. "You embarrassed me to death last night, then you tossed it off as nothing when I tried to talk about it. I should have said something on the spot, but I was ashamed. I thought, if I started anything in front of the Tompkins, there I'd be, a big fat pregnant woman making a scene—so I just shut up."

I said, "Did something set all this off last night?"

Caroline answered. "We were coming out of a movie with friends of ours and they suggested that we stop for a pizza. I was a little hungry and it sounded great to me, but *he* said, 'Maybe we should go someplace where Caroline can get a glass of milk.' So right away our friends started saying, 'Oh yes, of course, let's go to a luncheonette, or drugstore or something.' And the next thing I know, Steve's thanking them and patting my shoulder and running out in the street looking for a Howard Johnson's sign, or a cow, or God knows what."

Steve gave me a martyred look. "That was what touched her off."

Caroline practically exploded, "But I didn't want a glass of milk, I felt like pizza. I'd had milk with dinner. And vegetables, and I took my vitamins in the morning, just like I do every day so you don't have to worry. Do you understand? The incubator's working *fine*. That's what counts, isn't it? That's all I am, a big fat incubator on legs."

Steve was angry. "Your attitude stinks. You act like you don't want the baby."

"*Of course* I want the baby," Caroline gasped, then recovered. "The problem is that all you ever talk about or think about is the baby. I'm sorry *you* can't be the mother. You'd really be perfect. You wouldn't have to worry about everything I do or don't do that might be good or bad for it."

Steve was still angry, but also bewildered. "Why is it so terrible when I make a suggestion from time to time?"

"Time to time, or again and *again?* You don't trust me." Caroline's voice cracked. "Do you really believe I'd do anything in the world that I thought could hurt our baby?"

Steve shook his head and then asked slowly, almost imploringly, "Do you actually think I care more about the baby than about you?"

Her voice softened at Steve's evident concern. "Sometimes I can't help feeling that way. There's something about hearing you tell me what I should eat, drink, do . . . I get that from the doctor and I get it from myself. I don't need it from you. I don't *want* it from you."

I asked, "Can you tell Steve what you *do* want from him?"

Caroline blurted the answer. "I want him to go along with what I want!" All of us smiled at her immediate response. "I know that sounds crazy," she said, "but it's the way I feel. I can never forget about the baby. I'm always thinking about what's right for it. And that part's okay. But sometimes I want someone to think about what's right for me—not ask questions or make suggestions all the time."

I said, "Most mothers are a little anxious about their first pregnancy. Do you suppose part of your reaction might stem from Steve's echoing your own doubts or concerns?"

She nodded quickly. "He upsets me and makes me twice as nervous."

"But will you consider that your reaction might be so strong because Steve's comments are tying in to things that are already bothering you?"

"You mean I'm over-reacting," Caroline said unhappily. "It shouldn't drive me crazy."

"I don't think I said quite that."

Steve put in, "You know I'm just trying to help."

I looked at him questioningly. "Do you think you *are* helping?"

He was silent. Then he sighed. "You mean I'm being overly protective and not respecting Caroline enough." It was an old problem that had first brought this couple to me.

"I don't know," I answered. "You tell me. How do you feel —really, in your gut—when you think about Caroline and the baby?"

"I . . . I just want everything to be all right. I just feel . . . a little frightened."

"Is it possible that what you're really looking for from Caroline is reassurance?"

He nodded.

"But can you see that this might be a very difficult time for her to always have to be reassuring you? Right now, she probably needs some reassurance herself. So maybe if you want to ask questions or make suggestions, it might be helpful for you to talk to someone else."

"Or just not act as though it's for me," Caroline said. She paused. "You could talk to Dr. Williams. Come in with me to my next checkup."

Steve looked surprised. "Last time I was there you got angry."

"Last time you took over the conversation and gave a calorie-by-calorie report on me. I didn't know it was because . . .I never realized you might be frightened." Caroline shifted in her chair and made a small noise. "It just kicked!" She placed her hand on one side of her stomach."

Pregnancy is one of the unique experiences of a woman's life. No longer a person who solely belongs to herself, she is someone who has total responsibility for another being. While the husband may also sense his new responsibility, it's the woman who lives with it on a daily, hourly, moment-by-moment basis. Whatever she takes into her body will affect the baby. If she bumps into something too hard or falls down, she probably responds less to the pain than to the fear that the baby might have been hurt. Many of her business, social and athletic activities are considered in a new light. Perhaps she has an instinctive sense that all is well with her and the baby. Yet it's just as natural for her to have questions and anxieties about the baby's welfare and her own new responsibilities.

She can scarcely avoid the stress that we all feel whenever we are helpless in some significant way. The fact is that a pregnant woman is at the mercy of her body for a long time. Unless she chooses to terminate her pregnancy, she can't stop or control the process once it starts. There are going to be months of having another being within her, eating, growing and changing her body to satisfy its own needs and demands. Eventually her belly gets larger, she becomes clumsy, has aches and pains, and has to urinate frequently. She lies down to sleep, but the baby starts kicking and keeps her awake. She goes to a play but her physiological needs take over and she falls asleep. She is truly helpless. What could be more natural than for her to sometimes feel resentful, impatient and frustrated?

The kinds of emotions Caroline and Steve were experiencing are apt to be felt to some degree by many expectant parents. There's the woman's awareness of her body being taken over and used as an "incubator" for another being. As much as she wants the baby, this feeling of being used and in someone else's control produces stress. While she shares her husband's concern for the welfare of their infant, the attention he focuses on it may arouse a number of disturbing reactions within her. There's the fear that his primary concern is now the baby—that he no longer loves and values her as a woman and as his wife, but merely as the vessel that's carrying and nurturing the child. Even if she recognizes that his questions and comments stem largely from his own uncertainty, she may resent the implication that she's not a competent mother. Her own inexperience and anxiety may make "outside" questions all the more unsettling because they confirm her uncertainty about her ability (or perhaps her desire) to be a mother.

Regardless of the kind of stress you're under, you'll react in terms of your own personal history, or more specifically, in terms of whatever your own "unsolved problems" are. We all have some because there's no such thing as a perfect childhood. None of us has completely worked through all the developmental tasks of childhood, including dependency, sibling rivalry, gender identity, separation, individuation and autonomy. If, for instance, you once felt pushed aside by a younger sibling or perhaps by a parent, you probably still have deep within you (as Caroline had) an insecurity about being displaced by another. This particularly sensitive and vulnerable point is the one that's touched and aggravated when you're in a stressful situation.

Although you may not consciously rationalize it, you may still sense the connection between what you want or need now as an adult, and what you may have wanted or needed more of as a child. By making this connection, you may find relief simply from understanding why you're reacting in a certain way. You may realize that the situation now is entirely different, and you no longer need to feel threatened or not *as* threatened. You may also be able to share and explain your feelings in such a way that your spouse can reassure you and help you cope more positively with these leftover childhood anxieties.

Pregnancy most often brings out unfulfilled dependency needs in a woman. How strong they are depends on your own personal history. As infants we're all born helpless, completely dependent on our mothers or some other adult for safety, protection and actual survival. All infants *need* a certain period of dependency and the sense of being nurtured. They're not ready to be a "big girl" or a "big boy" yet. However, for one reason or another, we may be rushed into growing up. Perhaps another baby comes along, or the mother may be fed up with babies, eager to have the mothering chores over and done with. In any event, almost all adults have some unresolved dependency needs. You may even recognize times when you consciously want to be babied and cared for, like during an illness. One of the fringe benefits of pregnancy is that a lot of the dependency needs and wishes of the woman can be fulfilled, if she's taken care of and made to feel special.

I once received a relevant letter from a former patient. She and her husband had been in therapy with me, and I'd grown fond of them. Shortly after she became pregnant, the couple had moved to the Midwest, where her husband's company had its headquarters. Many months later, I got a birth announcement and a long "Update" that read in part:

> . . .so as you know, Jerry and I had worked out our arrangement about dinner to fit his office schedule and my working at home. We kept a running marketing list. He'd stop off a couple of times a week with the car and do the shopping on his way home from work, and I'd fix dinner. But as I got more and more pregnant, I started resenting that standard arrangement. I felt, here I am, still working even though I can barely reach the drawing board with this belly sticking out in front of me, and he just walks in, plunks down the groceries and waits for me to get him dinner.
>
> One night when I heard the car pull in, I started to get angrier and angrier. I heard him in the kitchen calling me, putting down bags of food, but I didn't even answer. He came to my workroom and said, "Hi. I'm home. How's everything?"
>
> I pointed to my belly and said grimly, "Everything's getting bigger."
>
> He laughed and said, "Well, the groceries are in the kitchen. I got everything on the list." He was in such a good mood. "What's for dinner?"
>
> "I have no idea what's for dinner," I snapped. "I'm tired of deciding the menu. And I'm tired of making the dinner."
>
> "Okay, I'm sorry." He really looked upset and it actually pleased me. "Look, you just go on with what you're doing. I can get myself dinner."
>
> *Isn't that terrific?*" My voice was dripping with sarcasm. "I don't suppose it occured to you that once, just once, you could get yourself dinner *and* fix me some, too? I suppose as long as you're fed, the important thing has been accomplished." I could hear my voice rising in this incredibly angry desperation. "What about me? Do you ever think about me? Maybe I'd like someone to feed me for a change!" And all of a sudden I was crying, sobbing like a child.
>
> Poor Jerry was absolutely terrified. He came over and held me. He started to rock me and asked me why I was so upset. Had anything happened with the baby? And I just said no, everything was fine. Sud-

denly I realized I wanted him to keep on rocking me. We went and sat in the living room. By that time I was just gulping occasionally and blowing my nose. He kept holding me and started patting my back, and I liked that, too. I finally told him I didn't understand what was wrong with me, but I wanted to be taken care of, and not have to do or decide anything. And even though those are very unusual feelings for me, he said immediately, "Okay, I'm going to take care of you. You just lie here and watch the news. I'm going to make us some dinner." He even switched on the TV for me. I watched for about ten minutes, then I felt like getting up and helping him in the kitchen. We got to talking about something or other, and the incident passed. I wish I could say that was the end of it, but during the last two months of my pregnancy, I started to feel more and more resentful about doing anything I thought of as work. Finally, we had a huge fight when Jerry screamed at me and said that he'd never seen this lazy, selfish side of me. I felt everything he was saying was true and I just started crying. "I've never seen it either," I sobbed. "I hate it. I hate myself."

It was Jerry who said, "No, that's wrong. You mustn't hate yourself."

"But what are we going to do?" I was wailing because I felt so unhappy and helpless. "What am I doing to us? What's happening to me?"

Jerry said uncertainly, "I think maybe you're just having a baby." He pushed the hair back from my forehead and put his cheek against it.

The next night he came home and said, "Ann, why don't we see what happens if you take a complete vacation for the next few weeks?" The baby was due in less than a month. "No more art jobs, no more work around the house—a real vacation."

"But . . . ."

"We can get someone to do the cleaning once a week, and we'll eat out or order food . . . ."

I suspected someone else had given him this idea, but I didn't care. It sounded so wonderful. Just the thought of having to do nothing until the baby came was such a relief that I started grinning and feeling silly.

"Suppose you come home and I haven't even made the bed," I tested. Bending over is a problem when you have no waist!

"I won't tell if you don't."

"If I sit around all day, I might get fat." I was facing him with this huge belly between us. We both put our hands on it and started to laugh.

"Didn't you know I love fat women?" Jerry said, and suddenly I wanted to have this baby so I could hug him and feel my whole body against his. I told him that, and we really kissed each other for the first time in ages.

For two weeks, I watched more TV than I had during my entire life. Then, like flicking a switch, my energy and my usual sense of independence came back. I started cooking, and not just dinners, but things I could freeze for later. I bought furniture wax and polished all the wood in our home, which I'd never done since we'd been married. I'd never felt happier. The day I went into labor, I was just finishing some curtains for the baby's room. I told Jerry I wouldn't go to the hospital until the tie-backs were done. But the baby wouldn't wait, and we ended up using strings on the curtains for the first few weeks.

Clearly, pregnancy is apt to place demands on the husband as well as the wife. If, as we said, the overall relationship shifts so the woman mainly becomes the "taker," *it's vital that she recognize that her husband, too, needs support, appreciation and reassurance.*

But what happens when one partner is unable to give what's needed or cannot tolerate the existing demands? Generally, there's some sort of retreat from the situation and a rift in the relationship occurs. Sometimes family and friends are able to fill in, and the couple manages to cope. Yet when divisive pressures or the pain of feeling overwhelmed become extreme, couples would be wise to consider professional counseling without regarding it as a resignation to weakness or failure on their parts. There's so much room for growth in all of us that it is a shame to close our eyes to our potential and ignore the many kinds of help that are available.

What are some of the signs and underlying causes of situations that might be considered extreme?

1. Complete dependency

The woman who is completely dependent and unable to cope with any of the responsibilities of pregnancy may be unready for motherhood because she doesn't feel like a person in her own right. Her husband cannot give her enough. She may not have had an opportunity to separate from her own parents, and that attachment and dependency is still strong. Now she's being asked to become part of and responsible for another being. The new demands make her even more uncertain about who she is and where she wants to go, and you often find a tearful, pregnant woman who calls momma constantly, wanting to go back home to continue that daughter-mother relationship.

2. Hating or fighting the pregnancy

Sometimes the woman who can't seem to get enough support, or who rejects the support that's offered, at some level may not really want the pregnancy. It might have been an accident, or she might have felt coerced into it, and now she resents it bitterly. Occasionally, if she and her husband can discuss their feelings and explore the question of why they do or don't want a child, they might find ways to adjust to the problem, even consider abortion. But often this may be the woman who goes through with the pregnancy, and then finds her feelings manifesting themselves in excessive nausea or other physical problems. She may try to keep her weight as low as possible and deny the fact that she is even pregnant. She then resents every ounce of weight she gains and every sign or symbol of the pregnancy from the visits to the doctor and the restrictions on what she can do to the need to wear maternity clothes.

In one case, a young woman had dreams during pregnancy about harboring a cancerous growth or an animal that was eating at her insides. Her inner conflicts were considerable. Born out of wedlock, she unconsciously had both self-hate and rage toward her mother, which gave rise to her fantasies.

3. Overwhelming anxiety about the baby

Occasionally parents are unrealistically anxious and overwhelmed with fear over the health and well-being of the baby. This over-reaction often means that the baby is so crucial to one or both of the parents that they fear they'll be devastated and unable to go on should anything happen to the infant. Sometimes a woman believes that having a baby signifies that she's a real woman. Without a child, she may have great doubts about herself and her ability to function and be accepted as a woman. These doubts, however, aren't going to be assuaged by her becoming pregnant. There might be a temporary euphoria, but soon she'll become terribly anxious. If the slightest thing goes wrong, she'll exaggerate it because anything that threatens her ability to carry a child threatens her very identity. Likewise, if a man needs to prove his sexual virility through his wife's pregnancy, his sense of masculinity will be threatened should any problems arise. He may overreact with unjust accusations, "Look what you did! Why weren't you more careful . . . ."

4. An infantile or extremely dependent husband

If a man is terribly threatened by his wife's pregnancy, he may be unable to respond to any of her needs nor tolerate the changes he foresees in their relationship. He may feel consciously or unconsciously that he needs all the mothering, support, attention and love that his wife has to give. He can't cope with the prospect of sharing his wife with a baby—even his own. This kind of infantile male not only makes himself unavailable to meet any of his wife's needs, but also may withdraw from the marriage, seeking solace and support for himself elsewhere.

On a much less drastic scale, husbands can quite easily feel competitive with the unborn child. Maybe a wife's first reaction is annoyance or disdain. But, if she realizes that her husband's behavior really reveals his own fears, she may be more accepting and understanding of this "phase" he's going through. She may choose to put her own needs aside at times and show him in any number of small ways that he's still important to her. She may also be able to reassure him verbally that she'll still love him and will continue to give him support and attention while they give their baby the nurturing it needs.

A final important aspect of pregnancy is the change it causes in a woman's body image and her own sense of attractiveness and sexuality. Some women glory in the pregnancy and say, "Isn't this marvelous! Look what's happening to me. I'm carrying a baby!" They may feel very much at ease with this new image. They've been taught to value pregnancy and motherhood, and they beam. They want to make the most of it, and they show it off with a great deal of pride.

On the other hand, it's perfectly natural for a woman to wonder, "What's this going to do to me? Is it going to make me look horrible? My breasts are going to sag. My body's going to become huge. How will my husband even look at me when I'm going to be like that? And I'll be left with those terrible stretch marks." If she can discuss her anxieties with more knowledgeable and experienced people, she may discover that many of her fears are minor problems. Often, if she shares her feelings with her husband, she finds that he's willing and able to be supportive, reassuring and demonstrative.

Sex during pregnancy differs with each couple. I've known people who've said it was absolutely marvelous. With no worries about contraception and a baby coming, it brings a special sense of joy. However, a man may find his wife completely lovable on one level, but not sexually attractive. He may see her as "forbidden" because she's become a mother figure and evokes feelings in him about his own mother, who, after all, had to be dealt with differently. You may love, nurture and protect your mother, or someone whom you identify with, but you are not to have sexual feelings for her. You just have to deny and resist that aspect of her.

Sometimes a husband who feels excluded by his wife's absorption in herself and competitive with the coming baby punishes his wife by withholding sex.

A man also may say about his wife, "I look at her and visualize that little baby inside her. I have the feeling that if I come in her, I might accidentally hurt—or even kill it!"

The woman herself may have similar anxieties and actually be glad that her husband isn't sexually aggressive. She may even push him away and say, "Gee, I don't feel so well," or, "Honey, please, be careful." Sometimes a little education is needed. Nature has made all kinds of provisions to insulate the baby; therefore intercourse is safe well into pregnancy. Some people maintain that it's safe to continue sexual relations right up until the baby is due. Of course, you have to discuss this and related questions with your own physician. It is important to realize that it's also okay *not* to want sexual intercourse. Just because you're not sexually aroused during pregnancy doesn't mean you won't be later. The more you can share and discuss your feelings, the less rejection or misunderstanding you will feel.

Eventually all couples have to make some kind of sexual accommodation. It's not possible to carry on with the same kind of freedom in your seventh month that you had in your second. Sexual activity can cause a tremendous amount of physical discomfort. But sex is not just intercourse. It's much more than that and includes caressing, feeling and fondling. Whatever is loving and affirming and feels right to the couple is fine and good for them.

One of the painful possibilities that may occur during pregnancy is infidelity. Frequently men say that the first time they had any kind of extramarital sexual encounter was when their wives were pregnant. If the husband is feeling shut out or rejected, as though he's not participating in the process, he may choose to have an affair. He may need the reassurance that he's still sexually desirable. Sometimes he has real concerns about injuring his wife, or he may have sexual needs that are greater than hers, so he'll go out and have sex with someone else. Within this context, that doesn't necessarily have to threaten the marriage. However, it's extremely difficult for two people to sit down and openly discuss this issue. The infidelity comes at a time when a woman feels most vulnerable, least attractive sexually, and perhaps full of doubts and anxieties about her future. I'm not condoning the man's behavior, but at the very least, he has to be as discreet as is humanly possible. If he can't be certain that no one will get hurt in the process, then he should realize that it isn't worth it.

No matter how easy or natural a woman feels about her pregnancy, she always has some anxiety about the birth itself. Will the baby be healthy and normal? Will the delivery be normal? If she's planning on natural childbirth, how will that go? What about the pain? Will she be able to stand it? How will she behave through the whole thing? Attending natural childbirth classes can be beneficial both for learning and meeting others in the same situation, as well as drawing the couple closer in order to share this unique experience.

Sometimes a father who is reluctant to get involved says, "Come on, I don't feel right hearing and seeing all this stuff." He may say he's too busy, or too tired, or make some other excuse. His wife can certainly point out that the notion of pregnancy and childbirth being women's business is quite outmoded. But if he's adamant, she may have to accept that—at least for the moment. Perhaps she can say, "Okay, as much as I want you to come with me, I'll try to understand that it's not where you're at. Maybe later on, you'll feel differently. It would be easier and more helpful for me if you were there, and I wish you were. But I can respect your feelings about it. Maybe you have your own fears and anxieties that prevent you from wanting to become closely engaged in all of this."

The husband may need to have the distance for a lot of reasons. Perhaps he hasn't confronted his own feelings about being a father. He may feel this child is being thrust into his life. "My God, what am I going to do with it? This is an infant that's going to be dependent on me until it becomes an adult. That's 21 years—a long time! How am I going to cope with this? It means diapers and staying up late and then schools and problems . . . ." Perhaps he's trying to postpone the reality of the situation as long as possible. He may also have other doubts about paternity and think, "How am I going to do a good job of this? Look at my own father. He was never around. My mother had to handle all of it, and look what it did to her and to me . . . I'm not sure we should be having this baby!"

The more open the man can be—the more he can recognize and share the cause of his anxiety—the better able his wife will be to understand and ideally empathize. This doesn't mean she'll like being left "alone," but at least she may spare herself the feeling that "he just doesn't care that I want him with me." She may be able to accept his behavior more easily if she realizes that he's having difficulties of his own.

Some men actually cannot participate in childbirth. I remember showing a film on pregnancy and birth at Teachers College at Columbia University. Among a group of doctoral candidates, one man fainted in the classroom and several men and women had to walk out during the birth scene. Such films have become more available in recent years, yet birth is still a frightening thing for some people. What makes it disturbing is the fact that we're neither accustomed to seeing genitals thrust on us that way nor to seeing so much blood. In fact, few of us are accustomed to seeing either birth or death. In the past, more people were born in and died in the home. Many more people had the opportunity to see animals giving birth. Now, however, we're removed from these natural events. Men who have participated in natural childbirth often feel that this is one of the most important experiences in their lives. They eagerly talk about it and even proselytize for it.

One of the most dramatic and fascinating stories couples ever have to tell concerns the period beginning with labor and ending with the birth of their baby. The differences in various deliveries are vast, depending on the hospital, the particular physician, the attitudes of the staff, the presence of the husband in the delivery room, his participation in the birth, the consciousness of the mother, the doctor's decision to give the baby to her immediately after birth, and other factors.

Whatever the individual experience during childbirth, even an unfortunate or horrendous one, it is remarkable how quickly one is able to transcend it and go on—*as long as the baby is all right*. The entire crisis of birth—actually the whole pregnancy period—is fraught with something very positive because the couple is affirming life, and that is a transcendent act.

9. The Early Months of Parenthood

Among the most precious and enchanting experiences I've ever had was having two couples name their babies after me. I can imagine few things as rewarding as knowing you meant enough to people so that they'd want to do that.

Many individuals tell me they're surprised that a psychologist "is so concerned" with her patients. But if you think about it, it's hard to avoid. I don't mean to say that my involvement affects me professionally. But considering all the time I spend with people in therapy, how could I not understand and empathize with their hopes, dreams, difficulties and fears? I become very fond of some of the people I work with.

When I'm in sessions with a pregnant woman who is nearing her due date, I always consider the coming baby a major event in our discussions. "I'll see you next week," a woman will say, "unless, of course, . . ."

I usually get to share their joy when a healthy, normal, wanted baby is born. Suddenly the hopes, fears and anticipations of pregnancy are over, culminating in the wonderful event. Now comes a time of celebration. The mother has gone through a physical and emotional crisis. She rests, recuperates, enjoys the attention of her husband and loved ones and glories in her newborn infant.

Sometimes I hear that the mother has been "down." Probably at some point during these postpartum days, she goes through a brief and maybe mystifying depression. Obstetricians and gynecologists say that it's common to see women who have had good pregnancies and healthy babies feeling tearful and blue. Today we are more sophisticated in recognizing this postpartum depressive reaction, which almost always occurs shortly after the baby's birth. I wouldn't call it postpartum depression per se because that refers to a deep psychosis that's relatively unusual. But general depressive feelings are common, and they have a strong physiological base in the tremendous fatigue the woman is experiencing and the change in her hormonal balance. Also, with the baby born, the mother relinquishes to it the star role that was hers during pregnancy. In addition, there is simply a let-down when the big event is over.

Many obstetricians warn their patients to expect this reaction, and the hospital staff certainly are on hand to reassure both mother and father that it's quite natural. Sometimes the depressive feelings are gone in a matter of hours. In any event, the mother eventually gathers her forces and she starts reacting to the pleasure of knowing that she's successfully gone through an ordeal, had a healthy baby, and that a new challenge awaits her. She's apt to start looking forward to bringing the baby home, being in her own surroundings, and embarking on this new adventure called motherhood. She and her husband are aware of the start of a new life—literally for the baby and figuratively for themselves. Yet seldom, if ever, do they anticipate the extent to which their lives are about to change.

I really don't believe we're ever prepared for the impact of children on a marriage! We may think we are. But no husband and wife can really predict how they themselves, their marriage, their emotions and their routines are going to be shaken up by the arrival of a baby.

Just imagine a brand new being coming into your life. It's totally dependent on you, and you are absolutely responsible for it. It draws your energies and concerns like a magnet. All kinds of new demands are made upon you. There are new skills to be learned, problems to be handled, and naturally, anxieties to be faced. This tiny, helpless, creature requires attention all of the time. Even when it's sleeping, you get worried and go check the baby. Its every act becomes the focus of attention and can evoke all kinds of urgent responses in you.

As responsible parents you find that your lives no longer revolve around your own interests or desires. You must encompass the needs of this new entity: you can't sleep late in the morning; you don't have the spontaneity and freedom to have sex whenever you like, or go to a movie or out to dinner on the spur of the moment. You don't have the time, strength or perhaps the money to do many things you used to enjoy. And you have less time and emotional energy for each other in general.

The transformation in your life is so great that it's even marked with a new vocabulary: no longer are you simply a couple; you're now mother and father. *The presence of a child in the home creates a whole new family constellation, and because it causes such a fundamental readjustment in your relationship, the entrance of a child into the family constitutes another crisis in the marriage.*

Each additional baby entering the family creates a new period of upheaval and adjustment. In a sense, the second child comes into a different family than the first. The parents are older and have had more experiences in life. There may be a new home, a different job, the loss of a grandparent, or some other change in the family situation. The parents are already prepared for living with a baby and can anticipate the impact an infant has on the household. They know more about handling a baby, which may make some things easier. But the fact that they already have a child means they're not going to have all the time to devote to the new baby. The complexity of the situation increases, and there's often the feeling of being torn between the needs and demands of many individuals. Once again, there's a new need and opportunity for establishing a different working relationship between the spouses.

The first two months are especially critical because this is the time when the tone and structure of the new relationship are established. Now the parents must deal with each other in the light of their changed situation, giving each other more or less support, equalizing the responsibility, the workload and the power. The manner of interacting that they develop during this early period tends to establish a pattern which will prevail for a long time to come.

"I want to talk about something today because I've really had it." Louise glanced from her husband to me. She looked tense and exhausted. "I can't go on like this and I don't see why I should have to. I take care of the baby, the house and the cooking all day long and then—every night—*I'm* the one who gets up for the two o'clock feeding. Then I'm up again at six. Do you have any idea what it's like night after night?"

Chuck straightened in his chair. "You talk as though I sit in my office twiddling my thumbs all day. Did it ever occur to you that I work hard when I'm downtown? Don't you think there's a lot of pressure on me, too? Suppose I have a client at 9 A.M. and I don't get enough sleep? How am I going to make good decisions? What's the matter with you anyway? Who's going to pay for all this if anything happens to my job?"

I said, "I hear you both asking for the same thing. 'Help me. Take care of me. Appreciate me. Pay attention to what I'm doing. Recognize how hard I'm working. I feel as though I'm doing it all by myself.' "

They looked at each other, nodded simultaneously, then

smiled a little awkwardly.

"This is a very tough time for both of you. The pressure and adjustments are tremendous." They nodded again, and I saw that they sensed they were facing a common problem—a need for consideration and concern. The accusations and anger were just echoing this need. "I wonder whether you could each share your feelings about whatever seems to be driving you the hardest or draining you the most? Then perhaps you could talk about what you'd like from the other, and what you think you can do to help your partner."

They seemed to agree, and I heard a note of hope in their voices.

I said to Chuck, "You mentioned clients and decisions. How are things going at the office?" I thought I'd begin by exploring his feelings about added pressure to produce at work, now that he was a father. If we could share that, then we could move on and help Louise talk about some of her feelings. Eventually we'd start to work out ways in which they might help each other.

The early months following birth produce extraordinary pressures on *both* parents. Picture the typical circumstances in which mother and infant come home from the hospital. Here's a woman who has just been the focus of great attention and congratulations and has been waited on and supported, both emotionally and physically. Suddenly she's home alone with the baby. Her husband has resumed his regular work routine. Her supports are gone, and she's still fatigued from childbirth, but she's expected to pull herself together and start functioning in a situation that's probably more complicated and demanding than any she handled before the baby came. Possibly she misses a former job or envies her husband's escaping to the office. Perhaps the novelty and excitement of motherhood continue for a brief time, but before long the pressures, responsibility, and ordinary dullness of her daily routine sink in. "It's horrifying in a way because the first thing you're aware of is that you're not your own person anymore," one mother said. "The baby pulls the strings and all you have for yourself are the intervals between cries. That's pretty scary, especially when you're exhausted from breast-feeding the baby around the clock and never get any rest."

There is certainly a different, positive side to this picture, when the woman is suffused with love, fulfillment and pleasure. But although these feelings are a vital part of what is sustaining her, she's often too tired or busy to even be aware of them except during fleeting moments.

Meanwhile the new father, after a brief period of passing out cigars and receiving congratulations, has probably settled down to work. Chances are he is very conscious of the fact that he's the provider (if he's in that position) and that his obligations will continue for most of his life. He may be tired from awakening when the baby cries at night and his wife gets up to feed it. If he's sharing in this activity, which many more fathers are, he may be exhausted. During the course of the day he's probably concerned about his wife and child. Then he comes home to what may be a chaotic situation. Perhaps he wants to tell his wife about something that happened at work, but she hasn't the time or inclination to listen. Instead she blurts out a story about the baby's hiccups, acts as though his return at that moment is just an added burden, or treats him like another pair of hands that she wants to put to work. And suddenly this man is feeling deprived. He's been deprived of his wife's presence and emotional support during the whole period of childbirth and recovery. Also, it's been a while since he's had sexual relations with her, and he still can't have them for some time to come. With couples for whom sex has been a special kind of release and comfort, this is a very difficult loss unless they've found a substitute. In addition, this man has given up his once peaceful refuge, as well as the care and attention of his wife who is now absorbed in the new baby and her own motherhood. Ideally he'll be getting satisfactions and fulfillment from his new experience as a father. But often this doesn't happen.

There are many men who cannot tolerate tiny infants, who see them as "lumps" and can't understand how their wife can spend so much time and energy on them. Such a man is getting all the deprivations and none of the gratifications of fatherhood. He's apt to wonder, "Where's my wife? I don't have her anymore. Are we ever going to get together again? Go out and have some fun? Are we ever going to be close or have a chance to talk about anything but the baby? How long am I going to be stuck supporting everybody and giving without getting anything for myself?" Sometimes the man who feels like this walks out, even if just temporarily. He may have an extramarital affair as an expression of resentment or in an attempt to get the affirmation he needs.

Clearly the pressures on parents can easily become divisive unless they're understood and shared. Perhaps both partners realize that with a new infant, attention and energy are bound to be drained off and directed elsewhere, but that it's not deliberate neglect or lack of concern directed against either one of them. Usually it helps, however, to put this into words.

One woman simply told her husband, "Listen, I'm slightly

crazy now because of the baby, and I know that in a lot of ways I'm neglecting you. It's not because I don't care. It's just that right now I seem to have so little of me left for anything besides the baby. I expect that'll change as soon as I can sleep through a full night, but in the meantime I don't know how tough all this is on you. I really want you to tell me because maybe we need to think about working out a different way of handling things."

All couples need to make time for a respite from parenting. Whether it's a few hours, a day, a weekend, or whatever, they need some chance to be together as husband and wife, to reaffirm that relationship, which preceded the baby and presumably will continue after the child is older and starting to go off on its own.

They also have to evaluate situations and set priorities on how to spend their time, energy and money. Maybe it's more important to hire some household help than to leave the savings account untouched. A wife may have to risk a direct confrontation and ask her husband to help with specific tasks rather than wait for him see what has to be done. If he won't help, then his reasons and needs should be examined. And the wife may have to take a hard look at what can happen if she demands his assistance. Is he so thrown by his new role that she may alienate or lose him? Is she expecting a sudden change in her husband which he isn't able to make? If she married him because she liked taking care of him and having him depend on her, the arrival of a baby may not alter his character, and she may find it difficult or impossible to carry an infantile husband and a real infant as well. Whose needs are going to come first? What arrangements can be made that are best for both? Are efforts to change being made?

The resolution of problems always depends on how the partners can cope individually and how much support, help and understanding they can offer each other. *Each couple has to find a balance of giving and receiving that's congruent with their strengths and tolerances.*

Suppose a husband comes home to a scene of turmoil revolving around the baby. "Dammit," he thinks, "I had a lousy day at the office, and now this. When do I get some peace, quiet and order? When do *I* get some attention around here? How about just a drink and some dinner?"

His wife hears him come in and thinks, "Thank God, he's home. At least he can give the baby its bottle, or get the broken glass out of the kitchen sink, or . . . ."

With conflicting wishes and needs, *they both can't be satisfied right now.* There's got to be some flexibility, some give and take. Otherwise they'll fight for their own demands, "divide" over them (one may even walk out) and neither will gain anything. And so the adapting and balancing proceeds.

Perhaps the husband can shift gears, and give some help and support when he'd really prefer to receive it. How flexible is he? And how does he feel about taking care of the baby or doing some work in the kitchen?

If he pitches in and helps, perhaps his wife will show her appreciation of his efforts. Maybe she can explain tonight's crisis and make a point of arranging her schedule so that her husband will find her more available for him another evening. Is she able to separate from her powerful involvement with the baby at times and make her husband feel welcome, loved and important? How flexible is she?

With all the best intentions in the world, it's still extraordinarily difficult to be supportive, flexible, sensitive and all the other fine things you might like to be while you're also reacting to all kinds of demands and functioning under great stress. One thing that may help the most is to understand on a deeper level why your responses are so intense, and what your baby's presence evokes within you.

10. Connections with Your Baby, Yourself and Your Own Past

The fundamental experience that people go through when they become parents is a reliving of their own childhood anxieties and problems, which are reawakened by the presence of their baby.

Here is this tiny, newborn infant in your home. The baby cries. The baby is frustrated. The baby is helpless. That sparks all kinds of feelings and echoes from your own past. The baby that still exists within us hooks into that baby, and we reexperience all the early fears, frustrations, anxieties and struggles of our *own* childhood.

The intense involvement that parents have with their baby can be a beautiful and very positive thing. A lot of ego gratification and fulfillment comes through identifying with the child. There's delight in watching it change, develop and grow; satisfaction in giving it what it needs for its well-being. Sharing this with someone you love can be especially rewarding.

As the baby is being taken care of and nurtured, there's also the benefit of the nurturing of self as well. It's as though the part of you that still feels like a baby gets cuddled, loved and hugged. The positive effect can enable you to relive some of your own early experiences in a more benign way. You can be helped in terms of your own development, which is one of the great advantages a parent can derive throughout the years of child-rearing.

Sometimes, however, this identification with the baby gets out of control and leads to the exclusion of one partner—usually the father. The baby *is* absorbing, and it's natural to feel, as one mother named Joan described it, "so wonderful because I was in charge of this infant. I could give it everything it needed. I had the milk in me, and I felt this was all so marvelous and exciting—like it was the first thing I could do all by myself."

But Joan's feelings were carried to such extremes that her husband was pushed out of the picture. She never asked or encouraged Burt to help care for the baby and never shared her dreams for the baby's future with him. She confided her feelings in me, as she had in a couple of close friends, but never in Burt. "When I look at Nina, I feel that here is this wonderful little being that I don't want to spoil," she told me. I want to allow all the potential that's in her to come out. I think this is a totally different attitude than the one my parents had about me. My younger sister and I were brought up in a strict, proper household. We were expected to be good and do well. We were always told we shouldn't touch this or that, and we were supposed to be restrained. I remember my mother constantly telling me I must never speak too much because people would think ill of me. I want to do things differently with Nina. I want to watch her carefully and provide her with all the things she'll need to be happy, to grow, to be interested in the world."

Certainly it gives you a sense of productivity and enrichment to be able to meet the needs of a child, but that doesn't mean you derive your sense of self-worth or identity from what you can give the baby. Furthermore, being able to fulfill *all* the baby's needs is a very questionable and unrealistic goal. Nobody in the world can meet every single need of an infant, or be there instantly to provide total fulfillment at all times. And is this desirable, even if it were possible? I, like most psychologists, believe that a child has to have a certain amount of anxiety and *un*fulfilled desires in order to want to continue developing to the next stage. After all, if someone is there to hand it whatever it wants the minute it starts wanting it, what incentive does the baby have to try to reach out? Wouldn't it prefer to remain a contented "blob?"

What's needed by the baby isn't total satisfaction but an environment with enough love and caring during the time when that's necessary, and then, less than total attention or response at other times. The child needs to feel that the world isn't a hostile place. He needs to know that there are warm and loving hands to support him, and that if he takes a step forward, he can also take a step backward and there'll be somebody there to receive him. But he also needs the opportunity for exploration and a little anxiety, for struggling and working things out, for eventually going off on his own. He must be allowed to make errors, fall, hurt himself, get up and go on. That's all part of the growth.

Joan, however, had needs of another kind. Partly because of her childhood with very rigid, demanding, performance-oriented parents, she needed to give her baby a sense of being totally gratified. On one level, the ability to supply everything to her child made Joan feel she was worthwhile for the first time. Suddenly her self-esteem was enhanced. Joan's answer to the self-doubts she'd grown up with was to be a "perfect" mother. At the same time she was feeding and giving to her infant, she was also nourishing herself on a deeper level through her identification with the baby. Her absolute control was a kind of insurance: as long as she was in complete charge of feeding and gratifying the baby as well as herself through identification, she didn't risk having anyone else do an imperfect job and thus withhold the nurturance and gratification she felt was denied her in childhood.

Joan's relationship with her baby had many benefits, enabling her to grow and giving the child a great deal as well, but it affected her marriage adversely. It reinforced the parallel lives she and Burt had already been leading, enhanced the power struggle going on between them, and did nothing to reduce their fear of intimacy with each other.

For some women, the assumption of control is clearly a way of saying, "This is my bailiwick and I don't want you to be in it." And they send out those messages. If the husband himself has needs which make him refuse or resist, if he's a "workaholic" or must be distanced from the family situation, then it may turn out that both of them are in collusion to maintain their separate roles and lives. Parents who adopt this approach, however, should know that there will be a skewed input into the marriage and the raising of the child. There are certain things that can be shared, but there'll be a great many others that can't. While surely not every aspect of any marriage must be communal, I think the rearing of a baby is such a crucial experience for a couple that it demands mutual participation in both the problems and the joys.

You and Your Baby's Crying

For God's sake, pick that baby up, give him a bottle or do something, but *make him stop crying*," a husband yells at his wife.

"What do you mean, make him stop crying?" she reacts furiously. "What do you think I've been trying to do for an hour? And where the hell do you come off yelling at me? He's had his bottle and I changed him two minutes ago, so you pick him up for once instead of sitting there glued to football." And a fight gets started over watching sports, who's a good or bad parent, or some other issue that really isn't connected to the cause of such intense emotions.

There's probably no sound that pierces to a parent's core like the wailing or sobbing of the baby. A part of you hears, identi-

fies and responds. In a sense, the baby that exists within you silently screams in concert with the real infant, and you reexperience
intense "baby" emotions of your own. On top of that, the adult
part of you reacts, "My God, what's wrong? Why is my baby
crying? What should I do for it?" Then, "I'm a bad mother, I'm a
bad father, I'm not taking proper care of the baby, it might choke
—or even die!"

So the baby's crying is a source of enormous stress. It's not
just an irritation because of the noise, but because of what the
sound symbolizes and evokes in you. I remember one mother who
said, "There was my baby crying and I didn't know what to do
about it, so I started to cry, and the two of us were there together,
bawling!" It was endearing in a way and perfectly understandable.

Hearing your baby, the most helpless of all creatures, cry
may touch off feelings of acute and intolerable helplessness within
you.

If you have no idea about what's making you feel so miserable, you may become frightened or overwhelmed by a sense of
inadequacy. But if you start to make some connections between
what you're seeing in the real baby and how that's causing the
"baby" part of you to respond, you often can get some perspective
on the situation. You may think, "Of course, that's the baby in me
that still feels helpless. But there's also an adult side that can provide help or seek aid from someone with more knowledge and experience." Then you can begin consciously to support and encourage
your feelings of competence, recognize the many times you succeed
in satisfying the baby, and remind yourself that no parent can keep
an infant content at all times—and this doesn't mean anything terrible is happening to it. Perhaps you can even begin to realize that
the baby's crying may sometimes be harder on you than it is on the
baby itself!

Rona and Gary

Rona and Gary's four-week-old infant girl was sleeping
soundly in a portable carrier on the floor of my office.

"I wasn't sure if it was all right to bring her, but the babysitter canceled at the last minute and I had no choice," Rona said.

"I'm delighted I had a chance to see her. Nobody's brought
any babies in recently," I said.

Gary whispered, "As long as she stays asleep, I guess it's
okay."

"You don't have to whisper," Rona said. "At this age they
sleep through anything."

"Except through the night." Gary still spoke in an undertone.

"A lot you know about that. I get up. You roll over and go back to sleep."

"Shhh."

"Please don't tell me to 'shh.' I'm not going to sit here whispering for an hour, and she's not going to wake up!"

"Sure. Like last night when she was going to go right off to sleep."

"I thought that was still bothering you." Rona stared at her husband. "You think I don't know how to take care of her, right?" Gary looked away. "Well, if you know so much, why do you have to drag me out of the shower every time she starts crying?" She turned to me. "I was washing my hair last night and all of a sudden he's banging on the bathroom door telling me the baby's screaming and something's the matter. So I come running out terrified, dripping suds all over, and she was just crying because she had a diaperful."

"She was *screaming*."

"Okay! She was angry and uncomfortable, but I told you to change her yourself or else I'd be back to do it in a minute."

"And then you walked out and left her screaming!"

"For God's sake, Gary, I wasn't sailing for Africa. I was going to the bathroom to wash the soap off me and get into a robe."

"But how can you let a baby lie there crying like that?"

"It's *okay* for a couple of minutes."

"Well, I don't agree. I don't think it's good for her."

"What the hell do you know about it anyway? You can't even handle a diaper that has anything but pee in it."

"That's got nothing to do with this!"

"Of course, it has. If you could change a shitty diaper, you could have gotten her quiet in no time."

"All I'm trying to say is you shouldn't just let her cry. I've heard it or even read it somewhere. You pick them up and they feel . . . they get . . . ." He stopped, trying to remember.

Rona shook her head. "I can find you books that will say just the opposite. The real point is I *don't* just let her cry. You make it sound like I leave her screaming for hours, and all we're talking about is a couple of minutes."

I said, "It seems as though each of you feels differently about the crying of a baby. I wonder what's really going on when you have such a strong reaction."

"It was a strong noise," Gary said. "Desperate and helpless."

"That sounds as though it might echo something of your own from earlier on. Do you recall any feelings like that, that *you* might have had? Were all of your needs as a child attended to immediately? Did you have to wait? How do you feel about waiting?"

He glanced at Rona. "I guess I don't like waiting."

"He hates to wait," she affirmed.

"Do you remember having to wait for things when you were very young?"

"I don't know. You're asking about what went on so long ago." Gary sounded sullen. "I guess maybe I got a lot of things because we could afford it and I was an only child." Suddenly he stared at me resentfully. "Look, you know a lot more about this than I do, so if you say I'm trying to spoil the baby because I was spoiled myself, I don't know how I can argue."

"I didn't think I said that, but the idea seems to bother you."

"Because I don't feel like I *got* all that much. I mean, things —sure. But not attention." Gary was agitated. "Let me tell you, in some ways I was the *least* spoiled kid I knew. I remember how there were always promises about what the three of us—my folks and me —were going to do together, but they never happened. I'd just be left waiting and hoping."

"Waiting and hoping," I repeated.

He looked surprised and moved at the way his own words sounded.

"Gary, what do you think it would be like if a very young child cried or wanted something, and his mother just kept saying, 'Yes, dear, I'll be right there, just a minute, I'm coming, be patient, I'll be there . . .' "

"Horrible!" Gary exclaimed. "Empty promises."

"Do you think a child who has experiences like that might begin to believe that the world is a hostile place and he can't afford to wait?"

Gary made an abrupt sound of agreement.

"How do you suppose he might feel then, if he were a man and he saw his own baby having to wait?"

Gary's eyes widened as he stared at me and then looked thoughtfully at his sleeping child.

As adults, we all learn to tolerate a certain amount of discomfort, but frequently a parent envisions the baby's discomfort as being more intense than it actually is. Moreover, the *parent* may not be able to tolerate any kind of frustration. Perhaps at one time he was always given everything immediately, or perhaps he never was given to at all. Either way, he may grow up needing immediate gratification. He can't wait or cope with such things as not having a meal ready for him, or not getting the kind of attention he wants the minute he wants it. If a person has never learned how to postpone gratification, and if he then identifies with the baby's frustration, the infant's crying may become intolerable to him. (We tend to have low frustration levels in our country, and value instant gratification. That's something we have to check in ourselves and our progeny because the ability to postpone gratification is an important part of growing up.)

I don't mean to suggest that parents might not be convinced that there are proper ways to tend an infant (how often to pick it up, how quickly to run when it cries) and later rear the child. However, strong opinions may be based on vague knowledge. And even where there has been study and a serious intellectual commitment to a school of thought, you have to explore the personal reasons that attracted you to this theory. Why does someone else who is equally intelligent, perceptive and eager to do the right thing for the child choose an entirely different approach? Is your belief objectively based on the welfare of the child? Or is it possible that you feel drawn to a theory because it fits in with *your* history, character structure and needs? I think we always have to question our real motives when we're adamant or highly emotional about a position and unable to see another point of view.

In general, if you can view your intense reactions to your baby as perfectly natural, *and as stemming from within you,* then a lot of the anxiety, anger and blaming between spouses will diminish. For instance, when the baby starts crying, instead of panicking, yelling or accusing, you might say, "It makes me feel *awful* when the baby cries."

Perhaps your partner answers, "Of course. It's terribly hard not to get upset. But sometimes babies just cry, and it can sound a lot worse than it really is."

You may be reassured. However, if you continue to be distressed or to urgently feel that the baby's plight is intolerable, you really should ask, "What does this crying awaken in me that makes it so terribly painful? Am I feeling frustrated, powerless, out of control, thoroughly inadequate? Am I being realistic about what the baby needs or feels, or am I experiencing my own needs and emotions? How can I begin to separate the two and try to deal with each in appropriate ways?"

Angry Feelings toward the Baby

While you identify with your baby on the one hand, another

part of you sees and reacts to the child as a separate, outside entity —a new star that has entered the family constellation. Its presence is almost bound to evoke some feelings of competition, displacement anxiety or dependency needs which are left over from your own childhood. You may react as if you are the baby's sibling.

Let's briefly review the origin of these emotions.

When, as a child, you're the center of the universe to your parents, a certain relationship is established. If a younger brother or sister enters the scene, then of course, you're pushed aside. There is jealousy toward the new sibling and/or a fear of being displaced by the new baby. In the same way, if you have a need for your mother's total attention but she turns to your father, you feel rejected, ignored, and again you may become competitive or anxious about being displaced. And if your desire to be dependent, totally taken care of and solely loved has not been sufficiently satisfied, then you have an unresolved dependency need.

In early infancy during the symbiotic period it's difficult to make the transition to sharing love. A baby doesn't have any judgment, only wants and needs. He doesn't know that it's right for his mother's attention sometimes to be elsewhere, and that this needn't be a threat to him. But when this child becomes an adult and has a baby of his own, these early anxieties are awakened and reexperienced by the adult. So, for example, a father may say, "Dammit, you pay more attention to that little brat than you do to me." Or a mother who's been devoting so much time and energy to the baby may suddenly feel an overwhelming rage: "I'm fed up. I can't stand it another minute. This brat is ruining my life."

If the anger at or rejection of the baby is taken at face value, the parent who has these emotions can become terribly guilty or frightened. "What's happening? Am I starting to hate this baby?" The partner who hears such fury may be shocked. "For God's sake, what's the matter with you? You wanted a baby, didn't you? You wanted to be a parent—so *be* one." And the conflict erupts, fed by unrecognized or misunderstood emotions.

What's needed is an understanding on a more basic level of what's actually going on. In this case, a part of the parent is asking, "Who's taking care of *me?* Where do I come in with all of this? I need. I want. It's my turn." There may be a lot of rage because these needs haven't been tended to in your formative years. And it's perfectly understandable to have these feelings. Children are hungry little mouths. They keep on demanding and demanding, and it's right for them to demand. But what about the parents? They also need some time to be away from these hungry little beasts or else they feel they're being sucked dry.

Understanding where your anger or resentment stems from

can relieve a lot of the pressure and guilt. You may realize that this baby is not the sibling or parent who originally took away some of the love and attention you wanted. You're likely to feel better about giving yourself some of the things you need now: perhaps some individual time alone to replenish yourself, or time with your partner away from the baby. Clearly, sharing your feelings and needs with your spouse is crucial to dealing with your new role of parent.

Making connections between present reality and your own childhood needs or anxieties often provides relief and sometimes, revelation. I worked briefly with a husband who was very unhappy that his wife was nursing their son. He'd urged her to bottle-feed. But since she'd chosen to breast-feed, he wanted her to do it when he wasn't around. It became apparent that this man resented the baby nursing at his wife's breast because he was reliving the early experience of being displaced by a younger brother. "Oh my God," he said, "of course, that's true. I never realized how much it affected me." And a moment later, "It suddenly doesn't seem necessary to feel that way about my own baby!"

"I suppose you were over at your mother's again." Norman's tone was accusing.

Maria nodded.

"Well, I think you're too dependent on her." Norman's annoyance was clear. "It's one thing in an emergency, but you're always calling her or running over there with the baby." His voice rose. "I don't think it's good. I've told you before, it's time you learned to be more independent."

A great deal of friction can arise if a woman keeps turning to her mother. She remains a child, and her husband feels as though he's being pushed out and his authority is questioned. He may feel that he married a child who isn't grown up enough to be there for him and give him the support he desires or needs. Yet I knew Maria well enough to know that in this case, the problem wasn't her immaturity.

I asked, "Norman, how do you feel when you imagine Maria spending time with her mother?"

"I told you. Like she's not very grown-up."

"Do you suppose it's possible that there may be some advantages to not being grown-up? That maybe an adult can get something valuable from a parent."

Based on what I knew of Norman's past, I wanted to help him explore the possibility that what he really resented was Maria's getting something that he wasn't. A husband may feel toward his wife, "Sure, you can go home to Momma. Momma's going to help you and give to you. But who am *I* going to get all this from? *I* can't go home to Momma. I'm supposed to be grown-up and strong and able to shoulder all these new responsibilities . . . ." The father is really experiencing the child's cry—"I want. I need. Who's taking care of me?"

If Norman could get in touch with this feeling and bring it out in the open, Maria would be able to encompass his need for more attention than she had been giving him. In a sense, she could also share her mother with him once they both understood and got past his apparent resentment of the older woman.

Here are a few questions that may help you to "make connections" and evaluate how you wish to act:

—Do I want more of what my partner is receiving?
—Do I resent my role compared to my partners?
—Do I want more of what my baby is receiving?
—Am I trying to give my baby things I didn't get enough of?

The Involvement of Fathers with Their Infants

The more fully we each can accept the varied aspects of our own being, the more comfortable we'll feel with our baby and the better we'll be able to participate in all the different aspects of parenthood. Because men often have particular difficulty in handling certain feelings that the baby evokes, one of the common problems couples face is the withdrawal of the father from involvement with the infant.

You've probably heard someone—usually a man—say, "Newborn babies are boring. Until they start to talk, there's really nothing interesting about them" This may be a man who doesn't know how to relate to a child. He's having difficulty seeing that the infant is a living, vital, growing being. Since the mother is more involved and intently looks for every sign of progress, she's going to be able to notice and delight in all the small changes. If the husband takes part in physically caring for the baby, he may become more attuned to the infant's many responses, sounds of pleasure, motions, and growth, and thus become more involved.

But if a father adamantly refuses to get involved because the baby is "boring," then one has to ask what it means to be bored. I might say to someone who reacted like that, "Let's see what's involved when we talk about boredom. What do you see when you look at this baby that's so uninteresting?"

"A little blob that just lies there. You don't even know if it's smiling or just has gas. As long as you feed it and change it, that's all that matters. It can't respond to you."

"Okay, granted there's not all that much responsiveness in an infant. But why do you think you need responsiveness? Maybe we can figure out why that's so essential. Why isn't it possible just to enjoy the viewing, the experience of watching and helping an entity evolve, develop, and respond to a few things in the external environment? Why do you suppose that the lack of response creates this feeling we're calling boredom?"

This father has to make some sort of connection between the baby's unresponsiveness and some crucial factor in his own early years. For instance, if we're accustomed to being stimulated constantly and need that stimulation, or if we need a response to our own efforts to stimulate and that response doesn't come the way we want it to, we feel cheated. We become anxious. So we retreat from this baby which can't respond, and we explain our defensive action by saying the baby is boring. Much of the concept of boredom involves some sort of anxiety.

Perhaps a "bored" man is actually reacting to the infant's essential passiveness, helplessness or absolute lack of control. If a person has a problem with his effectiveness, his power or control over his own life, then he may be unable to tolerate being near this helpless infant because it evokes too much anxiety within him. He can't face that part of himself that still exists and sometimes feels like a little baby, helpless in this big world. It's easier to distance himself and say, "Oh, it's boring, it's dull," than to try to explore his own emotions and ask, "Well, what is it about helplessness that makes me so anxious?"

A wife may be able to articulate some of her husband's feelings, or help him say certain things he hasn't already expressed. Reassurance is often useful: "Of course, the baby *is* helpless, but look, right now it's so contented. All of its needs are being met and it must feel so surfeited and secure . . . ."

Many fathers are reluctant or unwilling to change diapers. Possibly the task, undeniable evidence of the baby's helplessness and lack of self-control, makes the father too anxious over these elements within himself. Yet what about the father who'll change a diaper that's only wet, but hands the baby over to Mother if there's a bowel movement to be cleaned up, saying, "How can you stand that diaper? It stinks. It really makes me sick to smell it."

I've asked men who say this, "Did you ever smell yourself? Did you ever play with your feces? Were you ever curious about your own bowel movements?"

They usually say "no."

"Well, that's *very* unusual. Most children are very interested in exploring and examining everything that comes out of their bodies. We're all curious about every part of ourself. We feel funny about it, embarrassed and ashamed, because we're made to feel that way. But most of us, left to our own devices, would still be fascinated. We'd examine everything—between our toes, under the nails, everything."

The man may shrug. "Yeah, but come on, it stinks."

"Well, we're taught that certain smells aren't nice, and we're taught that we have to deny them absolutely and categorically. And to be sure, it's the baby's feces, not your own, and sometimes it does smell. But you can transcend that if you want to. If you think, 'Isn't that curious and interesting, how it differs from mine.' But if you still have to deny that you yourself have feces, or that you smell at times, then you're not going to be able to relate to a baby's natural functions."

If a man is detached from the physical part of himself because he thinks it "isn't nice," this defense is threatened by confrontation with the infant's physical nature. He can't face the reality that the child is essentially a little animal. The father needs to deny it in the child just as he denies it in himself.

Children really show you all kinds of things which you may or may not be prepared to face. They rip the masks off and say, "Here, this is what's real, this is primary and basic; this is what *is*."

Part of the complexity of "sharing" parenthood stems from the fact that we live in a culture which has traditionally divided and separated the man and woman vis-a-vis their responsibilities within the family. Today our values are starting to change, but this view of the woman as a servile or at least a servicing creature is still very much ingrained in our whole culture. I think men resist any basic change partly in defense against the woman's essential power as the figure at the center of the household. She has the say about a great many things. There are basic decisions that are considered the mother's jurisdiction, like who'll eat what and when, how the baby's schedule will be handled. I think there's an unconscious rebellion by men against this feminine power, and a putting-down of the woman's traditional role in an attempt to make the man feel strong and powerful.

Yet some men reared in the "macho" tradition are—and always have been—able to break with it. There are men who have deep feelings of warmth and can give in a spontaneous, easy way. They value and are very much involved in their relationships, especially with their own families, and they find few if any aspects of these relationships unnatural or debasing. They're not threatened about their masculinity and are thus able to transcend the male supremacy attitude. They can participate in housework, hold babies and diaper them. They support their wives and respect what they do and therefore feel comfortable doing it themselves.

Whatever our cultural conditioning, I believe that psychological insights often encourage us to reassess our patterns of behavior. When the underlying reasons for our negative reactions become clearer, we're often able to deal with them in new ways. We may feel free to break with a habit and begin to try out other ways of being, start exploring our inner resources and test how we feel when we get in touch with the parts of ourselves that we may have kept buried or hidden.

11. The Start of the School Years

As children develop and mature, parents find themselves reacting to various stages a youngster goes through—the first separation from Mommy which provokes wails of anxiety and unhappiness, the "terrible two's" when the child's communication consists largely of a vigorously stated "NO" and so forth. The changes often seem rapid, exciting, and challenging. Yet as long as the child is young and remains at home encompassed within the household, there's a certain regularity and constancy to the family unit. A general living pattern develops. In a traditionally structured household, the wife cares for the youngster(s) and the home while the husband works. Evenings and weekends he reenters the domestic situation and participates to one degree or another, depending on his own character and the family relationship. After four or five years, however, a major change occurs: the child starts school. Suddenly the dynamics of the household are different, and there has to be an adjustment in terms of tasks, roles and the way parents view themselves.

"She doesn't give the child room to breathe," Len said. "Wendy's our youngest, and Jill's at her all the time. 'What were you and Cathy playing? Then what did you do? Tell me everything that happened at school today. Is that all? What about recess?' She just won't leave the kid alone."

"What do you mean, leave her alone?" Jill demanded indignantly. "I'm her mother. Why aren't *you* more interested. You're her father."

"I am interested. But I don't feel she has to report to me about every game she played at whosit's house."

"Ha," Jill snorted. " 'Whosit's house!' You don't even know the names of her friends."

"Cathy Rockland, the little one with the blonde braids down to her waist. Her parents are adding on to their garage." He stopped. "What's that prove?"

"I still don't think you really give a damn. How could you send your own child off for three hours on a Saturday and not want to know what she did? You should *want* to know what goes on at school."

I said, "It's awfully hard to see your child going off to school and having a whole bunch of other new experiences in which you don't participate. I wonder whether you might be feeling what many people do: here's your child who's been so close to you and so much a part of your life, and now she's going away from you. It can be very hard not to want to hold on, to keep experiencing with her and through her. The letting go can be wrenching."

"But it's not a question of letting go." Jill objected. "This is my child, and I'm still responsible. Can you believe they're talking about letting the children watch kittens being born! What are they going to be teaching next?"

"Nobody is saying that you shouldn't be interested in what goes on with your youngster. All parents are. And you *are* responsible. This is the first time that she's away from you. It's very hard to develop trust in other people's caring for your child, so it's natural that you would want to know a great deal more. But it's also not possible for you to know everything."

Jill sat silently.

"How does it make you feel when I say that you have to trust other people?"

"Not very good."

"It's not easy to develop that kind of trust, and to be able to let go."

"How do I even know she's ready?"

"Does she seem to be keeping up with the other children? Is she relatively happy being with them?"

"I . . . I guess so. But I just don't think I like any of this."

"I don't blame you, because this is a *hard* time. It does mean that you're sharing your child with strangers, and that you're not going to be that preoccupied with every detail of her development. That's no longer possible. But I wonder—is there anything that you might have wanted to do and haven't done for yourself? Might this be a good time to start doing it? What do you think about that?"

The adjustments that couples have to make when their youngest child goes off to school are more significant than many people realize. You may be delighted with the additional freedom you have now. Yet despite your sense of liberation, it's perfectly natural for you to experience some anxieties. It's understandable that many parents feel deeply unsettled.

Until the youngster goes off to kindergarten or is out of the home for a good part of the day, the parents have had total control over that child. This power is typically focused in the mother. She decides when the child does what and with whom. She knows exactly what's happening at almost every moment and is in charge of all the child's experiences.

Then, suddenly, the child is going away to school, having experiences the mother no longer regulates and doesn't even know about. Both parents start to realize that control over their child is not in their hands alone. Teachers and school authorities begin to have a say. The child's peers start to play a role. "So-and-so can watch TV whenever she wants to . . . so-and-so gets an allowance!" There's the first impact upon the child and the family of experiences outside the household.

"What's going on here?" parents often say to me. "What are they doing? It's *my* child." But the fact is, this is no longer solely your child. This period marks the onset of diminishing parental authority, and it's never really the same again.

Now is the time for you to confront some key questions:

—Are you ready to start letting go of your child?

—Do you accept the idea that your youngster is a total individual and separate from you?

—Are you content to relinquish absolute authority and start trusting "outsiders" with your child?

—Are there other arenas in which you can operate and find an affirmation of your strength, power, judgment and effectiveness?

These are difficult questions for both parents.

Sometimes a man sees his family as a small, primary unit which belongs to him. He may feel he can safely invest a great deal of himself here because it's a secure little group totally under his guardianship and control. But he can become anxious about his value and importance when he sees this unit dispersing. The children are in school, he's not sure what his wife is doing during the day—everybody is going off in different directions. The household he saw as the focal point of his life is being disrupted and changed. He misses the security of everybody in a manageable, orderly unit under him. Often he tries to get everyone back into formation by exerting extra control over his wife or demanding unusual obedience from the kids. He may also turn elsewhere—to another woman, to business, politics, sports, or some other area to regain his feeling of being *centrally important and powerful*.

For a woman, the change within the household can be even more threatening because she may have fewer outside interests than her husband. Her sphere of authority may be limited to the home. Her sense of importance, power and identity may be intimately tied to her supervision of her children, and she may have invested a huge portion of herself in them. Therefore she's particularly vulnerable to anxiety, resentment, a sense of loss or a sense of being lost when the last child starts moving beyond her dominion.

Perhaps, like Jill, she tries to maintain an unrealistically close liaison with the child. Some women will postpone enrolling the youngster in school. Others involve themselves in school activities, "following the child to class" as a way of holding on. Some women choose to have another baby.

Sometimes the mother who has been intensely involved with her youngster may undergo a separation anxiety and a feeling of abandonment. "My child's left me? Gone off to school. I'm *alone*. What am I going to do now?" The event may awaken in her an echo of an earlier anxiety: she may experience the separation as abandonment by her own mother. Her feelings of disequilibrium and diminished authority are compounded by an additional hurt and sense of loss.

At the same time their control is decreasing, father and mother are bound to realize that while their youngster is far from self-sufficient, they are no longer the "needed parents" they once were. To the degree that their self-esteem was enhanced by their being vitally necessary to their child, they now feel a loss of importance and identity.

Again, this loss is apt to affect the woman more severely since in our culture the man traditionally feels needed and important through a variety of outside activities. But for the woman who has viewed rearing her children as her purpose in life, the realization that she's now not as necessary—and will in the future become increasingly less so—can be a blow.

Even the mother who's initially thrilled with the thought of having some time to herself may become anxious and go through an identity crisis. She may start out feeling, "How wonderful! I'm going to be free. I'll have several hours a day when I don't have to watch that child and constantly worry about what he's doing. I'm going to have time to do what I want. I'm going to become my own person for a change!"

But eventually, either consciously or subconsciously, she's going to think, "If I'm to become my own person, who is that person? I have some time now. What is that time going to be devoted to? Who am I and what do I want to do with my life?''

Couples seeing each stage their children enter are made aware of the passing years and the fact that as the kids are growing older, they are, too. This is something that doesn't happen in a childless marriage, where the periods of time are less defined. A mother tends to think, "Yesterday I was the mother of an infant, now suddenly I'm the mother of a school-age child! What have I accomplished? What's my life all about?''

The husband, as well as the wife who works outside the home, may experience the passing of time as an increased pressure to achieve professionally. There's apt to be a reevaluation of goals and an urge "to show 'em what I'm made of. Is it enough to be involved with an advertising agency, or do I want to try to become a 'real' artist or writer? Is it time for me to stop working for someone else and set up my own business?'' There are decisions about how much of yourself to devote to each task and responsibility; how to spend evenings, weekends, vacations. Added pressure sometimes comes from your own children. Now that they're in school, they see or hear what the other children's parents are doing, where they go on vacation, and what they give their kids. Your children will bring home reports and make comparisons.

In sum, you now find a household in which the previous structure has been greatly altered, where new needs and anxieties are surfacing. The parents feel a loss of control, power and authority. They are less vital in the child/home microcosm. There may be an identity crisis and/or increased pressure to achieve something meaningful with their lives.

On the one hand, this can be a time of self-discovery, individual development and accomplishment, as well as an opportunity for deeper understanding and appreciation between partners. On the other hand, any potential conflicts between partners occur more easily because of the emotional edginess of the individuals. When your own sense of self is threatened, you often turn to outside sources for support and reassurance, while at the same time you feel unable to give these very things to your partner. The higher incidence of extramarital sex among both men and women at this point in marriage generally reflects a search for someone who can reassure them and supply some of the things that seem to be missing in their lives.

A man who sees his wife continuing to cling to the children may feel excluded and wonder, "How long is she going to be a Mommy? Why isn't she thinking more about me? Supporting and encouraging me? I'm working harder than ever before, and she doesn't seem to care.''

A woman who sees her husband throwing himself into his work may feel, "He doesn't think I'm attractive. Business always comes first. He'd rather stay at the office than come home to me and the children. Well, I'm not chained to the house any more. I don't have to be neglected and taken for granted."

As always, the couple need to share their deeper feelings and explore their priorities in life. They have to question what they're offering to their partner, and their mutual expectations.

Tanya and Phil

"I didn't say you were having an affair," Tanya corrected nervously, "I just said it wouldn't surprise me *if* . . ." She let the sentence dangle.

"You keep talking like that and I'll go out and do something about it." Phil's threat was quietly angry.

"And I know who you'd like to do it with."

"You're not going to start that again."

They sat staring at each other. Finally Tanya said, "Yes, I am—because I think it's at the bottom of everything." She turned to me. "We have these friends—a couple we've known for a while —and whenever we go out, Phil insists that they come along. Whatever we're doing, we do it as a foursome. It's never just the two of us, or even us with anybody else." She was upset.

I said, "Tanya, how does it make you feel to spend so much time with this other couple?"

"Uncomfortable. Angry. I know Phil has a thing for Lois, but he won't admit it."

I glanced at Phil.

He shrugged. "That's her imagination."

I'd already talked to them both in private sessions, and Phil had said that so far he'd been faithful to his wife.

Tanya said, "Are you really going to sit there and pretend you don't enjoy being with Lois?"

"Sure I enjoy being with her. And with Al. They're good company."

"Better company than I am." This came as half question, half statement.

Phil took a deep breath. "Sometimes."

"See." Her voice quavered.

"Okay, they're interesting people. They're fun. They do a lot of things."

"And I don't."

"Well . . ." For the first time, he sounded uncertain. "You do a lot of things but . . . they don't seem to mean much to you."

"The children and the house don't *mean* much to me?" Her voice reached a high, trembling tone. "They're all I've got. They're everything to me. All I need is a little appreciation instead of criticism about everything."

"I don't criticize you."

"Maybe not in so many words, but you don't like what I do. You don't like the way I am. When you come home from work, you don't want to talk to me. You spend a little time with the kids and ask them about school, but you'll never keep me company while I'm getting dinner. You never ask me about my day."

"I can't believe I'm hearing this." Phil turned an incredulous look from Tanya to me. "Last time I asked her what she'd done all day, she got furious and said, 'I did plenty.' And then she told me not to cross-examine her."

Tanya was staring at her hands clasped in her lap. When she looked up, there were tears in her eyes. She said in a small, desperate voice, "He wouldn't talk to me when I called him at the office today."

"I was in a *meeting*." Phil's exasperation overrode his concern at Tanya's distress. "My secretary told you that, and you said it was nothing important. That's what was written on the message slip. 'Mrs. Barton says it's nothing important.'"

I said, "Isn't it curious how both of you seem to feel the same way—that Tanya doesn't have much to contribute." I thought, "Tanya's self-esteem is at such a low point that she's actually begun to feel this horror about herself." I looked at her. "You feel that way about yourself, and it seems as though Phil is reinforcing that feeling. Why is that going on between the two of you?"

There was silence.

"Is it possible there might be some form of collusion? I think you certainly wouldn't want it to continue. It wouldn't be a conscious, deliberate thing, but it sounds as though you both are convinced that Tanya's not very interesting, so almost anything that happens reinforces it." I looked at Tanya. "Maybe what's at the bottom of things is not so much that Phil necessarily enjoys somebody else's company more than yours, but that you both hold this view of yourself."

Still they were silent.

"Okay, let's try to see what all this means. Let's see if we can explore what may be happening in your lives right now to make what once was very good become less good."

Neither one of them indicated a wish to speak. Phil shifted his briefcase in a slightly different position against the legs of his chair.

"Phil, how are you feeling right now?" I asked him.

He looked up, startled, then averted his eyes. "Maybe it's wrong when I'm supposed to be concentrating on this, but I was thinking about the agency." He glanced at me. "I've got a meeting there this afternoon and it could be . . . important. It could affect my whole career."

"Oh? Is this something new? I don't think I remember you mentioning it before." I'd only been working with Tanya and Phil for two weeks.

"Well, it's just that the agency's been doing very well, billings are up about fifty percent over last year, and I've been bringing in a lot of business." He broke off and looked at me skeptically. "Do you understand anything about business?"

"I deal with quite a few businessmen," I said quietly. "Why don't you try me?"

"Okay. I've got a conference with the president today and I'm going to ask for an equity position in the company. I think I've got a pretty good case to make, but if he responds with a flat 'no,' I'm not sure what position I'm going to take."

Tanya exclaimed, "You never said a word to me about this!"

"I wanted to wait and see how things turned out."

"But I always ask about work . . ."

Phil sighed. "Tanya, you ask too much. Sometimes I don't want to be pumped."

Tanya's face fell. "I don't mean to pump. I'm just interested." Her eyes looked moist. "You used to like to tell me about work."

I asked them, "Is that so? Has there been a change in the amount you share with Tanya about your business concerns?"

"I don't know, maybe," Phil said.

"I wonder what could be going on inside of you that would cause you to pull back now?"

Phil sounded annoyed. "Look, it's no big deal. I can tell her more if that'll help."

"I'm not sure I know what you mean by 'help.' "

Phil's annoyance increased. "Help her feel like she's a part of things."

"Do you want her to be part of things?"

"Oh, for God's sake." Phil ran his hand across his brow. Then he sighed. "I don't know any more. When the kids were little, she used to say I was her link to the outside world. I understood that. And besides, it wasn't all one way. We'd talk about the kids and work and stuff. But now . . ."

"Now something's changed? Can you try to explore what the change might be?"

"It's not just me. She's got no sense of . . . proportion." Suddenly he turned angrily to Tanya. "How the hell do you think I feel when you call me at the office to tell me I shouldn't have something or other for lunch because you're making it for dinner? I'm in the middle of work and I hear that—or I get it in a message from my secretary. I've told you I'd rather eat the same thing six times over than have that going on."

I said, "Phil, how *do* you feel when Tanya calls you at the office for something like that?"

He thought very carefully. "It's almost as though she's trying to control me, monopolize me—like wanting me to stop seeing Lois and Al. But it's also . . ." His voice dropped and became reluctant, then determined, "It's as though she's trying to live through me. I sometimes feel as though she's sucking me dry."

Tanya started to cry.

Phil looked at Tanya, then said angrily to me, "I don't see what the hell good any of this is doing. It just hurts her . . ."

"Yes, it does. But do you think it's better to leave things unsaid and maintain a distance that adds to Tanya's sense of being left out and unimportant?" I spoke to Tanya. "What Phil said hurt you, and I can understand why you would feel so awful. Apparently life was exciting and stimulating when the kids were young, you shared a great deal, but now what is there to share?"

Tanya reached for a tissue.

"Is it that you feel there's nothing in your own day that interests you?"

"The kids are gone a lot now."

"It sounds as though you need to have somebody to take care of, and if there's not a child around, you want somebody to be a substitute. Is that what's going on between the two of you?"

She took a fresh tissue and pressed it against her eyes. Finally she said, "All this makes it sound as though I never want to do anything, but last fall when Joey was starting first grade, I told Phil I wanted to go back to school and he was so much against it . . ." Her voice trailed off.

"Oh!?" My surprise was clear. "I don't think that's been mentioned here before."

"I wanted to take some graduate courses in French. I majored in it in college, and I thought I could brush up and maybe do some translating at home or even teach . . ." Again her voice trailed off.

I looked at Phil.

"I just thought it was the wrong time," he said uneasily. "I mean, the kids aren't that grown-up. She'd have been gone two afternoons a week and right at a time when they were coming in from school. And it was pretty expensive as I remember." He shifted in his chair. "Besides," he said to Tanya, "you didn't seem that serious about it."

"I told you I wanted to." She turned to me and said softly, "I think I have a hard time doing things Phil doesn't approve of. Maybe partly because it's his money. I don't know."

I said, "Perhaps at some time we ought to explore the ways in which you each view the money that comes in and the different contributions you both make toward the household. But in the time we have left today, can we go a little further with some of the issues we're already discussing?" I faced Tanya. "When you were talking to Phil earlier, you said the house and children were all you had. I thought it might mean there was hardly room for Phil. But now some other things seem to have emerged. Could you be feeling that in order to get Phil's approval, you have to limit your activities to that sphere?"

She nodded quickly.

"But do you think it's wise or even possible in the long run to look to someone else as a source for your own satisfaction and ego gratification? Do you think perhaps that makes your own self-esteem too dependent on someone else's opinion?"

"I guess so. But I never felt this way before."

"Things are different now than they were before. You sensed it yourself. You have more free time, and there's less to do for your children."

"Well, there's still quite a lot."

"But is it enough? Maybe you want to think about that. Even try to imagine what things might be like when both the children are older."

"But if Phil is against it . . . ."

I turned to him. "I wonder why your first reaction to Tanya's doing something outside the household was negative."

"I told you, she'd have been gone when the kids came home. I don't think that's right."

"Oh? Right for whom?"

"For our children. You're not trying to tell me they shouldn't come first?"

"What I'm trying to say right now is that your needs and Tanya's are certainly just as important. For Tanya to be able to do something that gives her a sense of fulfillment and enables her to become a full partner in your relationship is much more crucial than her being home every afternoon when the children return from school. Certainly it would mean that some other arrangements would have to be made. In a way, it's very convenient to have a wife who's always there taking care of things. But it limits her, and it limits what she might be able to contribute to you, your marriage and the children as well."

"Okay. I get the point."

"How do you feel about it? About Tanya now doing something outside the home?"

Phil sighed. "Like it's a lot of changes all at once. First the children, then Tanya, plus everything at the office."

"It *is* a lot of changes, and they take a lot of adjustment."

"You know, there's a lot more pressure on me than she realizes. It's not easy to handle the clients and the office politics and everything else. She has no idea."

"Yet for some reason you haven't felt like sharing that with Tanya."

"Because she bugs me too much." Phil's annoyance was sudden. "Those damn phone calls during the day . . ."

"Phil, what are you feeling right now?"

"Frankly, I think you're both trying to butt into my business life."

"And you'd like to keep that separate?"

"Yeah. I would like to."

"Then perhaps it's not just a question of the phone calls. Is it possible that you take all Tanya's questions or interest as an intrusion?"

He shrugged.

"Is it possible that you'd like to have a world of your own where you have control and can show your prowess?"

"Damn right." He glared at me.

"And it's satisfying to you, it makes you feel good to be able to do that."

"Of course."

"Do you suppose that maybe Tanya needs to have an area in which she also can feel some of the same sense of control and importance?"

Phil jumped to his feet, suddenly furious. "I already said it," he practically shouted. "How many times do you want to hear it? She can go back to school. She can do whatever she damn well wants to, and right now I'm going to get back to the agency."

"Come on, Phil, let's see if we can't do something else about this." He stopped. "That way is always possible. It's too bad this happened so late in the session when we're out of time. Obviously you're disturbed and angry about what was brought up. It touched a sensitive nerve. How do you feel about coming back next week to see whether we can make some sense out of all this?"

He stared from Tanya, who looked almost paralyzed, to me. "I'll see."

"Okay," I nodded. "Think about it."

He strode out. Tanya started after him, then turned to me. Her face was white.

"I think it'll be all right." I walked her to the door. "I think he'll decide to come back."

I dictated some notes before my next appointment. It was clear that there was a power play going on here, and Phil was using various means to maintain a distance from Tanya and keep her in a role with which he felt comfortable. We hadn't explored their involvement with Lois and Al, but by keeping them always around, Phil could set up a barrier against real intimacy with his wife. He arranged it so he and Tanya had little time to confront each other or discuss matters. Also, Lois provided him with an emotional sword to hold over Tanya's head. Phil probably felt totally accepted by this other couple, and Lois made him feel desirable as a man without making any demands on him. Phil and Tanya had been reluctant to discuss their sexual relationship, and I wondered about that. After ten years of marriage, many couples find it less interesting to be with the same person all the time either socially or sexually. Many people like variety. Lois's company enabled Phil to have an illicit yet safe fantasy, which was intolerable to Tanya, enhancing her self-doubts even more. This was such a complex case that intensive individual as well as marital psychotherapy would be required. A great deal would depend on Phil's motivation to continue to explore his needs for control and distance.

We each need to derive our primary sense of value and meaningfulness from within. We have to discover who we are, then accept and like that person, or else find ways of changing and developing to become acceptable to ourselves. A husband and wife can help each other enormously. But in the end, we have to be able to fill our own lives and feel good about ourselves; otherwise all the support in the world won't be good enough to fill the hollow, doubting emptiness inside us.

The search for "self" is always difficult, and for women it can present unique problems and challenges. The following story was told to me by an attractive, articulate mother of three.

I always wanted children. I *wanted* to be a wife and mother, to make a warm, nurturing home for my husband and our kids. And for fourteen years, that's what I did—and I loved it. Then, when our youngest was six, I told my husband I wanted another baby. He got very upset, saying we'd agreed that our third would be our last. He'd really only wanted two, and had already given in to me about the third.

It was a terribly sensitive issue between us. I even thought of letting myself get pregnant without telling him, then presenting him with a *fait accompli*. But somehow I couldn't do that. I just kept trying to persuade him, and we had many arguments about it. Then one evening he got angrier than he'd even been before. He yelled at me and said that just because I wanted to be a mother forever didn't mean I could do it. "You can't be a baby machine for the rest of your life," he shouted. "For one thing, we can't afford it. It's irresponsible to keep having children if you can't do the right things for them. And I don't want to go through the diapers and night feedings again. I don't want to be living in a nursery for the rest of my life. I want to go on to other things, and I'd like you to go on with me."

The way he said that last thing frightened me. I couldn't imagine living without my husband, and I certainly didn't want to have children with anyone else. But what was I going to do? I went to bed feeling very depressed and frightened.

The next morning I got up, and suddenly my position was as clear to me as a message taped on the wall. The message was in the form of a pink slip from an employer: I was fired. Maybe the reason I thought in those terms was that my husband had just received a promotion at his job, and I suppose in some way I was envious. The contrast was so great. My "job," which I loved, found satisfying and *was very good at,* was simply becoming obsolescent. I was *furious* and terrified for quite a long time.

I don't know why anyone is surprised when a woman starts reacting "badly" when this happens to her. Look at how men react—and are expected to react—when they're fired or forced to retire. You go to the movies and see a story about a policeman whose entire life was built around his work, then he's forced to retire so he commits suicide. Everyone understands what drove him to it. You read about a man who gets laid-off from work and suddenly he's impossible to live with. He feels inadequate, maybe becomes sexually impotent for a while, but everyone understands why *he's* having such problems. But then you see a woman who's going through the same kind of situation and somehow her problems are considered a peculiar feminine weakness. Well, the only peculiar part about it is that when she first signed up for the career of mother, no one warned her that it was essentially a temporary situation! And she didn't acknowledge the fact herself. Maybe we avoid that knowledge—it would be difficult for us to give so much of ourselves if we were also thinking about the day it would be all over.

I remember I really used to pity the female "libber"-types who were always harping about the importance of women 'finding themselves as people.' I never felt lost in the first place. I never wanted to go out and compete in the world. I used to think that nothing anyone did could be more important or fulfilling than what I was doing—raising happy, healthy children. And I still think that's true. But it's not much consolation when you see your chosen career gradually coming to an end. It's not much help when there's nothing else you *want* to do, much less are qualified for.

I stewed in my own anger and self-pity for months, getting more and more difficult to live with every day. Finally I asked my husband if he and I could go away together for a weekend. I wanted a chance to be alone with him and really talk. His first reaction was totally negative; he thought I was going to start a new campaign to have a baby. When I explained that I needed his help in just the opposite direction, he eagerly agreed.

So we went and I told him how I felt: I wasn't talented in any particular field, and I didn't think I had a unique contribution to make to the world. In fact, there was nothing I really wanted to do.

His reaction surprised me in many ways. The first thing he said was, "I think I know how you feel."

My disbelief must have been evident. My husband is an administrator in a large corporation where he's been working since we got married. But he said, "I felt the same way you do now when I was in college. Some of the guys seemed to know where they were going, and I envied the hell out of them. I didn't know what I wanted. Finally I took some courses in economics and business administration because they sounded like they might lead to something. But I never had a plan beyond finishing school and getting a job that would pay me some money. When I look back to the very beginning, I can tell you my career was ninety-nine percent luck. If either of my first jobs had turned out differently, you might have seen me as a completely different person."

We talked a lot more during the weekend. At one point, Larry said, "Listen, how many people do you think have a real vocation for something? You certainly don't believe that there are young men all over the country dreaming of the day they're going to become salesmen, or computer programmers, or God knows what. Most people work because they have to and because they'd rather do something productive than take a handout. In a way you were *lucky*. You did something you really wanted to do for a long time."

Larry also said, "I can tell you from experience—if you go out and try some different things, you'll probably find that a lot of the 'interest' in a job comes from getting involved or seeing you can do it pretty well." He even pointed out some of the things I did well but took for granted, like organizing the household, arranging large dinner parties, handling and teaching children, even dealing with contractors. His words and support helped me tremendously, but they still didn't solve anything. When I came back, I was still at a loss about what to do. I was also afraid to go out and apply for a job because I was sure I'd get turned down. The only real improvement was that now that the problem was out in the open, it didn't seem quite as terrible.

It took me another half a year before I got the courage to actually do anything about my life. I started volunteer work at a day-care center. Helping with children satisfied a lot of my motherly instincts and was something I was good at. But I still remember my thoughts when I first went to the center: "I can try this because I'm only a volunteer. How much do they expect? Besides, they're so desperate, they'll take anyone. And after all, I can always quit." Two years later, with experience and some college courses, I went on staff with a salary.

It's vital for every woman to find ways of developing her own autonomy. She needs to have a sense of doing and being, of activity and productivity. All my experience leads me to conclude that once a woman's children are in school, she should start laying a foundation for her own future and cultivating some private interests. Perhaps this means going back to school. More and more women are doing this, and they've become an accepted part of the campus population. It may mean doing whatever is necessary to develop some skills while she's still young.

Does this mean I believe all women, regardless of financial need, eventually should get paying jobs? Not necessarily. There are many opportunities for unpaid but vitally important, useful, nurturing activities within one's family or in the community. But in our culture, money is closely connected to status, success and esteem. We pay for certain skills and to have certain work done. And there's a hierarchy of labor in our society that is translated into an individual's feeling about himself or herself. It becomes extremely difficult to divorce the one from the other. For instance, the woman who takes over the care of an infirm relative may at first receive praise and support for doing something valuable, yet eventually her "work" may be taken for granted and she herself may begin doubting its value, wondering whether it's enough. I tend to think she wouldn't have these doubts if she were doing exactly the same work as a "paid companion."

I think it takes a great amount of inner strength to fight our cultural conditioning and reshape our personal value systems. Certainly some people are able to do so. They get all the reward they need by doing things which are worthwhile according to their own standards. On the other hand, when a woman considers how she's going to spend the rest of her productive life, I think she should be tough-minded about how she can best fulfill her own needs. She should consider what she might get from knowing that she can command a salary; from attaining whatever self-sufficiency, autonomy, pride, respect and other positive benefits she may derive from a paying job. She can then realistically make her decision on the basis of long-term fulfillments because, in the end, what women (and men) need is to *do something* that gives them the opportunity for self-expression, nourishment and growth. Eventually we *all* need to do things—separate from and independent of our spouses or our children—that enhance our self-esteem and give us a sense of self-respect, productivity and gratification as individual human beings.

12. Fighting over the Children

"If it were up to you," Gail said coldly, "Bobby would be a savage for the rest of his life. He'd never learn to be considerate. You'd just spoil him and let him do whatever he wanted."

Tony answered in equally cold tones. "You don't know what you're talking about. He's a responsible kid with a good head on his shoulders. What do you know about little boys anyway?"

"Enough to know they need some discipline, which is apparently more than you realize."

Tony's eyes narrowed. "Maybe I just never thought a responsible mother handled her child by screaming at him like a wild banshee. How can you be so harsh? Did you *hear* yourself yelling?"

Gail's voice rose. "How many times do you think I've *told* him to *wash his hands* before he flops down on the living room furniture. Did you see the stains he put on the couch? And it had to be oil from his baseball glove. *You* were showing him how to oil it. *You* could have reminded him to wash up afterward."

"Maybe you should appreciate the fact that he takes care of his things, instead of threatening him with something stupid like forbidding him to use his glove again this season."

"Don't you call me stupid. And don't you dare refuse to back me up next time." Gail turned to me, unhappiness mixed with the anger in her voice. "He won't help teach Bobby any kind of consideration. He never backs me up. I just had that couch recovered. I thought we could do that now that the kids were a little older." She quickly turned back to Tony. "I hope you're going to enjoy paying the cleaning bill because this is one time I'm not going to clean up the mess myself."

"Screw the cleaning bill," Tony said nastily. "Why don't you put a plastic bag over your precious couch if nobody's supposed to use it?"

I asked Gail, "When Tony doesn't back you up, do you feel your authority is being questioned?" The reinforcement issue is a terribly important one.

"It's not just being questioned. He's completely under-cutting me. The boy turns to him knowing he's got an easy touch in his Daddy."

"Well, if that's so, perhaps we ought to explore whether or not it might be valuable for the two of you to make decisions *together* about how issues should be treated." I turned to Tony. "If you really feel that Gail is being overly harsh, maybe you could say, 'Look, I know you don't want to sound that way, but I feel very uncomfortable because that's how your voice comes across—and maybe that's what triggers my feeling that I *can't* back you up, and I have to take Bobby's side.' "

Tony was starting to nod when Gail said, "Are you trying to tell me that I can't yell at my own kid when I'm angry and want to impress something on him?"

"There's no question that you have a right to say what you want to your own child. But sometimes it can become coun-terproductive. I wonder what feelings the yelling evokes in both of you."

Tony answered firmly. "I don't like her yelling in the first place. On top of that, I think she's just plain wrong. Bobby was taking care of his glove the way he ought to. That's more important than the crummy couch. I mean, after all, there's a child in the house."

"Which may be a point we want to talk about—what's best in terms of the child's well-being and relative freedom. But first, let's see what your own deeper feelings are because a baseball glove or a couch isn't really the crucial issue here.

"The crucial issue," Gail said cuttingly, "is that 'Daddy' just doesn't believe in discipline."

"He doesn't believe in discipline," I repeated thoughtfully. "Is that so? What do you each mean by discipline? Is it pun-ishment? Is it guidance? Is it learning?"

Tony said, "I guess it's guidance and learning. He was learning to take care of a new glove. If there's definitely a disregard for what you know you should do, maybe discipline is punishment. But it's *not* yelling all the time, and it's not setting up a household where there's no freedom for the kid."

"That may be your impression of the household, but you don't have to live in it all day with a seven-year-old," Gail retorted. "You don't keep straightening up, then seeing things turn into a mess the minute you turn around."

"Is it possible that there *is* less freedom?" I asked. "Let's try to focus on that question for a minute." I was trying to get them to listen to each other, to see whether there was some validity in what the other was saying.

Gail took a deep breath. "If you mean there's less freedom the way we live than there would be if I just let the house be a pigsty, okay, that's true. Maybe I'm crazy, but I never thought a child had to have complete freedom, or that a home had to revolve entirely around him. If you talk about learning, how is he supposed to learn to live with other people if we don't teach him?"

"Tony, do you think there's something to what Gail is saying? Is teaching your child how to be a social human being and live comfortably in a household one of the goals that you also have?"

"Sure, it's one of the goals. . ."

I interrupted before the argument became circular again. "Then if I understand what each of you is saying, you each think there's some value in teaching a child to live with others, and you both agree that there's a little less freedom in the way you live than there could be if you lived differently. What I'm suggesting now is that those are issues most parents have to deal with, and of course, you do, too. It's certainly not easy to make wise decisions, but when the two of you have such intense reactions to the events you've described, then I must wonder what all this means to each of you on a deeper level. Something pretty powerful must be going on inside you to prevent you from sitting down together and discussing how to handle these practical issues. I wonder what could be evoking such strong emotions?"

For the first time in that session they looked at each other with what might have been puzzlement or curiosity rather than sheer hostility.

"Tony, do you think you could try to share with us what you really feel when you hear Gail shouting?"

He ran his hand across his face. "I don't know. Maybe . . . embarrassed."

"Embarrassed?"

He hesitated, avoiding Gail's eyes. "Yeah, I guess so. Like I don't want to be a part of it because I don't like it."

"Why don't you like it?"

"Because I wouldn't want it to be me." He seemed surprised at the ease with which the answer had come. "I mean, I'd feel lousy if someone yelled at me like that."

"I wonder if a part of you *actually does feel* lousy along with Bobby? I mean, does a part of you identify with him and almost feel as though *you're* the one being yelled at?"

A look of recognition crossed his face. "That's what you meant before about my feeling I had to take Bobby's side."

"Do you think that's what could have been happening?"

"Yeah. You know, it was as though I sort of cringed inside." He glanced at Gail. "Then I got mad." There was a hint of regret.

We then talked about Tony's childhood in a family where there was very little yelling or emotional display, but a lot of quiet, tense undercurrents. Tony said he didn't really think he'd prefer to live that way, but he wasn't comfortable with wild outbursts either.

"I'm glad you usually don't yell," Gail said. "My mother did all the time, especially at me. I never thought I'd end up doing that to my own children."

I nodded in sympathy. "It's terribly hard not to repeat patterns you grew up with. It takes an enormous effort to substitute something different for the role model you saw when you were a child. Sometimes you need to learn quite a lot about what's really happening inside you so that you can develop a new approach."

Gail gave a barely perceptible nod as she fingered the pleat in her skirt.

"Do you think you can start to explore the deeper source of your rage at Bobby? What do you think it really might mean to you when he dirties up your furniture?"

"It's so . . . frustrating." Gail looked up. "I guess in a way I know he isn't doing it on purpose to upset me. But then it happens and I think, 'Oh no, not again. How can I win?' "

"That almost sounds like you're in some sort of battle."

"It is a battle in a way, isn't it?" She looked from me to Tony. "I don't mean against the children. Maybe 'battle' isn't the right word. But it is a struggle." I nodded and she continued. "At first the kids are young, and you sort of know things have to be geared toward them. But after a while, it seems like I should be able to go on to something else. It seems like it should be possible now to fix the place up and live a little more . . . graciously."

"How do you picture things if you could arrange your life the way you'd really like it to be? Can you share that wish or fantasy with us?"

Her expression softened. "Well, I'd like to do the living room. We're still using some of Tony's bachelor furniture! And I'd like to entertain more. I like to cook and try new recipes, you know, challenging things. Sometimes I picture us giving a terrific dinner party in a place that really looks nice. I'd even like to do some business entertaining for Tony. But the way things are . . . ." She shrugged.

"How do you feel about what Gail has been saying?" I asked Tony.

"It sounds nice. But not if it means getting into the kinds of hassles we've been having. Nothing's worth that."

Gail slumped in her chair.

"What are you feeling right now?" I asked.

"Depressed. Like I'm going to be trapped in this kindergarten forever. And I'm getting angry again."

"I wonder if part of your anger might stem from a sense of your own identity not being sufficiently respected. Is it possible that in a way, you feel your home is an extension of yourself? Do you feel you'd get a sense of value and satisfaction from doing the things you talked about, but those wishes and your identity are really going by the board?"

Gail sat straight up. "That's exactly right. What I want comes last. Nothing changes until everybody else is ready for the change, and I'm supposed to wait it out or . . . ." She shook her head. "I just can't do it all alone."

"Of course not. There has to be some sort of consensus, first between you and Tony, then within the family as a whole. Sometimes there are going to be conflicting needs. Maybe you and Tony have to discuss what it would take to fulfill your wishes and whether it's advisable to do what you want now or whether it might be better to wait until Bobby's a year or two older. On the other hand, that may not be necessary if he can understand why this is important to you. Maybe he has some thoughts about that, and you could ask him. Perhaps the three of you can set certain realistic goals together. How do you feel about that?" They both nodded, and I asked Tony, "Do you feel as though you understand more of what's been going on inside Gail? How do you think you'll feel about backing her up at some point on some of the goals or rules you set together?"

Tony touched Gail's hand. "It sounds reasonable."

I looked at Gail. "It isn't easy to wait for something that's important to you. But if that's the situation, maybe you also want to consider whether there are any other ways in which some of your own needs could be met now. Is there some way in which you can start planning or preparing—something you might want to learn more about if you're going to be in this waiting period a little longer?"

Of all the problems that cause parents to seek help at this stage in their marriage, one of the most recurrent is the battling that goes on over how to handle their youngsters.

While the subject of child-rearing is fascinating, it's not within the scope of this book. Unquestionably there are differences in ideology—permissiveness vs. authoritarianism, and so forth. If you and your partner have dissimilar values, or come from dissimilar backgrounds, disputes can arise from genuine concern over what's really best for the child. Ideally you'll be able to agree on how you want to raise your children. Otherwise, not only will there be continual conflicts between the two of you, but the youngster will get very confused when faced with different values in his parents. It can be harmful for him to sense that he has the power to divide his mother and father. Occasionally, when agreement in principle isn't possible, the only option may be to explain that to the youngster, and together face each issue as it arises.

More often than not, however, conflicts over the child usually *can* be resolved if the parents are sufficiently aware of their own motivations so that they can find a way of negotiating openly. But they first need to explore why a particular issue is so important to *them*. What are they really getting out of the enforcement or relaxation of the child's discipline?

For instance, if a man teaches his son "masculine" values, while his wife identifies with the home, there's going to be trouble if she keeps trying to be the perfect housewife, which is where *she* gets her sense of self-value. She'll have unrealistic expectations about how a child is going to behave at home, and she won't be able to fulfill her perfectionist goals—unless she puts up red velvet ropes which mark those areas that are out-of-bounds for the children.

By the same token, if the father identifies with the child to the point that he's unable to exercise any control or help the youngster learn to take responsibility for his own actions, the whole family will lose out in the long run. Because the father can't see or empathize with his wife's needs, the marital relationship may well be endangered.

Once partners understand what their own stake is in any dispute, they can view the situation more objectively, see more alternatives, and explore what the issue really means in terms of their own well-being and the development of their child.

One of the most common settings for family "scenes" is the dinner table. Since dinner is one of the few regular occasions when everybody gets together, it provides an opportunity for interaction between people. (Too frequently it becomes a time for airing problems which would be better handled at family conferences arranged for that purpose.) Moreover, some of our earliest, most fundamental needs involve hunger and feeding, so it's small wonder that food often becomes the object around which many battles take place.

A great deal about relationships is revealed if you watch what goes on at the dinner table. A whole pecking order may be established; authority and control may be tested for their own sake. There's also the matter of who is allowed to say what, which parent sides with which child and why, whose needs are attended to in what priority, and so forth.

The "magic" word, as one of my patients described it, is "*Why?*" Why does someone need to do whatever he's doing? What is he getting out of it? Why is it so difficult for someone else to accept? What kind of threat or loss might it represent?

Suppose a father demands good manners, and the mother protests that the child is only five and that "he gets excited, he forgets."

"Now's the time for him to learn," the father might say. "If you keep spoiling him like that, he'll end up being a grade-A slob."

Why does the father believe that, while the mother does not?

Has one of these parents clear-mindedly found the key to what's best for the youngster, while the other parent is so blind or stupid that he or she can't recognize it? Or might we assume that each parent's opinion is inevitably based on his own personality and development?

Perhaps deep inside, this father would really like to be a slob or a little boy himself. Perhaps he was never able to let that side of himself out. When he sees his son behaving that way, it causes him anxiety because it touches so closely to a part of himself that he can't accept. For the mother, this may not be an area of concern. She may feel that children will grow and learn in time, and she herself is more comfortable with that messy, greedy, childlike part of herself.

One should always consider what is realistic to expect at any given level of a child's development. If the child is, in fact, behaving like an infant and throwing food around, why is he doing that? If the mother won't help discipline him, perhaps she's identifying with the rebellious infant, in some way enjoying that part of it, even rebelling against her husband through the child. She may be feeling, "I hear my own father telling me how to behave, and if you tell me what to do with my child, I'm just not going to do it."

Again, we are talking about making more connections with our own past, so we can separate ourselves, our experiences and our needs from those of our children. Doing this is difficult.

Our every instinct is to avoid looking so deeply at what we need, at pains we may once have felt. Yet if you can make this kind of self-exploration, bring out the buried anxieties, uncover the old wounds, then the light of understanding can often be a healing one.

I worked with one couple who were experiencing increasing difficulties over their opposing views on how to raise their son. The husband accused his wife of trying to make the child into a "mother's boy." One of the regular areas of conflict was the dinner table.

"She'll never say, 'Stop fooling around, sit down and eat your food.' As soon as he gets restless, she just says, 'Willie, have you eaten enough? Do you want to play now?' The boy's old enough to sit at the table and eat properly."

"Oh, Barry, he does eat quite nicely," Alice protested. "He's really very good for a seven-year-old, but it's hard for him to sit still and listen while we go on talking and eating."

"It wouldn't be so hard if he were finishing what was put in front of him. How can you leave it up to a child to decide. . . ."

"Hold it!" Alice protested. "One minute he's old enough to sit at the table and the next minute he's too young to know if he's full. Will you listen to yourself?"

"Look, he's not the biggest kid in his class by a long shot, and encouraging him not to finish his food sure as hell isn't going to help him grow."

I said, "I wonder how you feel about him not being the biggest kid in the class."

"What's that got to do with it?" Barry demanded. "He's got several more years to grow. I'm talking about the right way to bring him up and *help* him grow."

"But why don't we stay with your feelings. Maybe that would be more fruitful than discussing child-rearing practices because this clearly evokes something within you."

"It's not 'evoking' a damn thing in me—to use your jargon."

"Yet you seem very angry and upset. Are you?"

"Sure I am. All these words and questions. The real question is, what kind of a mother is she?"

"What kind of mother *are* you?" I asked Alice.

"A good one, I think. I don't try to push Willie into doing things, but he's quite outgoing and . . . and happy. His pediatrician says he's fine, and he does well at school. I don't know what's the matter with Barry. Sometimes he seems to get hold of an idea . . ."

"Let's see whether we can sort out what's real from what's not," I suggested. "If Willie has been getting good checkups, and he's functioning according to his age level, then maybe there's something in your expectations for him." I faced Barry. "How would you want him to be? What would you wish for your son?"

"Well, you know. For him to be happy and strong. Grow up and be able to take care of himself."

"The idea of size and strength seems important to you."

"They're important for any boy."

I looked at Barry thoughtfully. He was of average size and had a good build. "Can you remember how you felt about your own size when you were a child? Did you feel powerful and self-sufficient?"

"Sure. At least most of the time. A kid can't always feel powerful. He knows he's smaller than all the grown-ups around him."

"Of course. But is it possible that there were times when you'd have liked to be bigger and stronger?"

"Well . . ." Barry seemed reluctant.

"Is it difficult to talk about those occasions?"

"No, it's not difficult," he bristled. "I had an older brother and he pushed me around a lot. Probably all older brothers act like that. I finally stopped him though." There was satisfaction in his voice. "He was chasing me one day—I don't even remember what I had that he wanted—but I do remember turning around and all of a sudden I was slugging him. I was scared to death. I'd never done that before. It stopped him cold. I remember thinking, 'He can't push me around any more. Now he won't dare try.' "

"And you felt good about that. It's hard to be younger and smaller, and many brothers and sisters feel the difference. Sometimes an older sibling can be a hard act to follow. And it's not always just a difference in size, sometimes it's in performance of various kinds. I wonder. Is it possible you'd like to spare your child the difficulty you went through? When you see his size and his reluctance to eat, does it make you remember that part of your childhood that's not a welcome recollection?"

Judy and Max

I was looking forward to seeing Judy and Max. They'd been "up" emotionally for quite a while, and we'd been talking about terminating their therapy. They felt—and I agreed—that they were about ready. They had all the tools that were necessary to function effectively on their own. They'd come to grips with how they felt about themselves and each other, with Judy's wanting to work and not wanting to have more than one child. They had a deeper knowledge of what it means to be parents as well as to be a couple living together. They'd been increasingly free about sharing their feelings with each other and they were sensitive, empathic, secure within themselves, able to afford taking a risk and not having to be defensive because they didn't feel vulnerable. We'd set a tentative date for their last session at the end of April. That would mark the end of three years of work together.

It was early February when they came in for their appointment, and I could see that something was troubling them.

"We're going through a new phase that we haven't figured out," Judy said. "It's about Jenny's bedtime. The problem's been going on this whole past week, but it really started the week before. She's staying up later and later, and Max is going along with it. She'll say she wants to see the end of a TV program, and he'll say, 'Okay, sweetheart, but right after that.' " Only then it's 'Tell me a story, Daddy,' and the last few nights, the child has ended up going to bed at ten o'clock. That just isn't enough sleep for a seven-year-old."

"I don't think it's so terrible," Max said. "If she's tired, she'll go to sleep earlier on her own, or she'll take a nap in the afternoon. She seems to get such a kick out of staying up. It's *fun* for her."

Judy bristled. "Of course she's having fun—at *night*. But when she gets up in the morning, you don't see the result." Judy's voice became concerned. "You leave for work, but I'm the one who gets her ready for school. I see her sleepy, squinched-up little eyes, and I have to drag her out of bed. I can promise you she isn't having fun then. You know, it also makes me the nagging shrew, and I really don't like that. I feel awful in the mornings, pulling and pushing her off to school."

Max said, "I guess I can understand it if you feel like I'm making you the bad guy. I didn't realize that part of it."

Judy nodded and waited a minute. "So how do you feel about going back to her regular bedtime and enforcing it with me?"

"I don't think we have to be so rigid about it." Max sounded firm.

"I don't mean to be rigid." Judy glanced at me. We'd talked before about the fact that life would be a lot easier for parents if they could turn kids off and on when they pleased. Of course that's just not possible, nor is it desirable. In fact, breaking the rules from time to time is a good thing. "I know I'm more comfortable when things have some sort of schedule. I tend to be the timetable-type. I *know*." Judy smiled deprecatingly. "And it's true that Jenny naps in the afternoon if she's tired.

"I'm not saying she's going to drop of exhaustion. But something in me says it isn't *right* for a child to make up for sleep she didn't get at night by napping during the day. The idea seems crazy, and it bugs me. So it's not just what happens in the mornings." Judy sighed. "There must be something else to all of this." She looked almost comically from Max to me. "Is there *always* something else?"

"Is the sky blue?" Max intoned.

We laughed. Then they were silent a moment, thinking.

Finally Judy said, "What I don't understand is why this has started all of a sudden. What's changed? What's caused this change?"

Max shook his head.

Judy tried again. "What do you feel while Jenny's up with us?"

"Well, I guess . . . I guess I feel good. Like those are precious hours for me."

"Have you wanted to spend more time with her than you've been able to?"

"Maybe. But you know, there's a lot of time when she's around on weekends, and I don't make a point of being with her. I'm not sure that's it."

I asked, "What are the two of you doing while Jenny is up? What effect does it have on your relationship?"

There was a silence. Then Max said quietly, "We're not together as much. We don't talk or act the same way together while she's there."

They looked at each other.

Max pursued it. "So the question is, why am I arranging that?" He thought for a minute. "Dammit, I don't know. I can't think of anything that's been happening to me *or* between us."

"What about something that's going to happen?" I asked.

"Our vacation!" They spoke simultaneously.

"Oh brother," Judy groaned. "After all the talking and work we had to do to figure out a vacation we both wanted, now it's coming and we're still not that sure it'll turn out as good as we hope. . . ."

". . . so I'm just not giving us a chance to think too much more about it, and we'll be leaving in four days!"

Judy looked questioningly at me. "If we're nervous about being away together for two weeks, would we want to be more separate now?"

"Some people tend to distance before going away together. It's not universal, but it can happen. What do you think?"

"I suppose," Max said grudgingly, "we'd better go into this vacation thing some more while we're still here."

Judy looked at him. "Do you really want to?"

"No. I think we've been over it enough. And I think we can afford to be a little optimistic—or at least know we'll be able to handle things."

"Me too!"

"Then let's declare a moratorium before we worry the thing to death!" He looked at me. "Okay?"

I smiled. "How do the two of you feel about the way you just handled that situation, about Jenny and bedtime and so forth?"

They glanced at each other. "Pretty good," Max said for both of them.

"I think you should feel pretty good about it, too."

One reason it's important for couples to come to a mutual understanding as early as possible in their relationship is that, as you and the children mature, unresolved problems tend to grow as well. In the adolescent years, they often become more dramatic and more divisive for the parents. Past disagreements can suddenly re-emerge in a new round of blaming and vilification. "If only you'd made him do his homework and respect authority years ago, he wouldn't be a dropout today, bumming around the country stoned on grass." "What do you mean? If *you* hadn't been so harsh, he wouldn't have wanted to strike back and rebel. He ran from the kind of life you showed him."

There are different ways to bring youngsters up to be relatively healthy, whole, positive individuals. But usually this is accomplished within the context of a home where parents avoid unconsciously acting out their own inner conflicts through their children.

13. A New Sexuality in the Household

I've never met a couple who breezed through their children's adolescence! It's only natural that as your youngsters enter these years of development and change, you'll be drawn with them into a time of emotional turbulence and tension. You're bound to be affected by day-to-day living with a child who's undergoing tremendous mood swings, rebelliousness, sexual exploration, physical awkwardness, self-doubting, questioning and searching. This is a difficult, exciting and worrisome time for everyone in the household. Homes that have any degree of instability to start with are apt to face serious trouble.

On a deeper level, your child's passage into adulthood tends to awaken or add urgency to all kinds of feelings of your own:

1. You yourself may have had a stormy adolescence (most of us did), and now you may be reliving many of your own experiences.

2. The new element of your adolescent's emerging sexuality must be confronted. Few of us have worked through our own feelings about sexuality, so living with a youngster who is burgeoning and experimenting and exploring is bound to evoke strong (though possibly unconscious) emotions.

3. The moment comes when almost every parent thinks, "Look at this, my child is starting to date! I must be getting old! What have I done with my life? Where has it gone?"

4. At some point, you're going to see your child having experiences that were denied you or doing things you don't condone. Sometimes you'll be worried because an activity seems risky or dangerous. And you'll discover that you have less control than ever over your adolescent's behavior.

If you and your partner still haven't come to terms with who you are, both individually and as a couple, and with the idea that your children are separate individuals, then the adolescent years will be filled with anguish and rage for all of you.

While the stresses and emotional upheavals of this period have the potential for throwing the relationship between parents into chaos and conflict, this is also a time when many couples come to grips with their lives. The very pressures they feel and the intensity of the experience they're going through can be a positive impetus to make them decide to confront the changes that are affecting them and to consolidate their relationship as parents *and as husband and wife*.

The Need to Be a Team

More than at any previous time in the marriage, it's now crucial for couples to operate as a team. They need to recognize the adjustments they're facing, come to mutual decisions about their own values and their expectations for their adolescent, and take steps to avoid being divided or sucked into some kind of collusion with the youngster *against* each other. This is quite a job.

Roberta, a close friend of mine, was telling me about her daughter's thirteenth birthday. Beth had invited several girlfriends for dinner on Saturday and ice-skating afterward.

Roberta said, "It was all planned, I thought. Then the evening before, I mentioned to Beth that I hoped dinner would be finished in time so that we could make the early evening session at the rink. She turned, looked at me and said, '*We*? What do you mean? *You're* not taking us, we're going with Daddy.' I was so startled—and I guess I felt angry. Rejected." Roberta smiled faintly, but her voice revealed hurt.

"I had no idea when this had been decided. Jay hadn't said a word to me. So I asked Beth, 'Does Daddy know about this?' 'Of course he does,' she said. 'We talked about it last night when you stayed at the office late.' There was this kind of smug tone in her voice, and she was sizing me up. I really wanted to shake her, I wanted to slap her face. All I did was smile and say, 'That sounds nice.' But by the time Jay came home, I was madder than hell at *him*."

I nodded sympathetically.

"Anyway," Roberta continued, "I guess when Jay walked in I jumped on him—so of course, he got angry, too. He said that if I didn't put in such long hours at work, we'd talk about things more. That made me furious. To begin with, I wasn't that late on Thursday, and it was the first time I'd worked late in *months*. There was plenty of time before bed for Jay to have said something to me, and I told him so. You know, he never did explain why he didn't mention the arrangements with Beth. He just said I was blowing it up out of proportion and he didn't understand why I was so upset. And I couldn't really explain it to him." Roberta paused. "Sometimes I can't help wondering if Beth resents my working and turns to Jay because of it. Maybe *he* resents it, too. I have one friend who says that if you work, the kids blame you for not being there; if you don't work, they resent you for being around."

I asked, "Do *you* feel your job has been taking more—or enough—of your time and emotional energy away from the family to make you want to question it? Question your priorities?"

"I . . . I don't think so. It's pretty unusual for me to work late, and I never bring office work home with me. But I just wonder if maybe my working itself is causing trouble now. I guess I've been dreading that."

"It doesn't seem to me that that's the issue, although you might want to discuss it with Jay and Beth. I'd say you're providing a good role-model for Beth and enabling her to eventually grow up to be her own person, which is very important. But it sounds to me like this might be a time when you and Jay would want to be closely allied. Beth may be testing you two out, seeing whether you can be divided—you know, an acting out of her Oedipal wishes. You and Jay might want to think about that a little."

Roberta sighed. "You know, all this Oedipus stuff—the whole father-daughter and mother-son bit—it's just kind of hard for me to take all that seriously or literally. I'm sure I'll run into a lot of hostility at some point with Beth. Evidently it's already begun. And I think I can understand that. My mother and I went through a hell of a siege when I was growing up. But that's not quite the same as the thought of this thirteen-year-old brat of mine lusting after her father."

I smiled. " 'Lusting' makes it sound a lot more conscious than it is. Maybe what she's unconsciously seeking is a chance to test or assert her own womanliness. But how did it make *you* feel when Beth changed the ice-skating plans without consulting you?"

"Left out. And angry."

"Sure. It's hard to accept someone else being preferred over you for whatever reason. But do you sense a little competition over 'who got to be with Daddy' mixed in? Do you think you'd have reacted the same way if Beth were your son who'd arranged it so Daddy took him and his friends to a hockey game?"

Roberta looked at me for a minute and finally shook her head. "I guess . . . maybe not. But still—feeling like I'm in competition with my own child. That's *awful*."

"Awful?"

"Well, isn't it? Come on, Laura, talk to me!"

"You see, it's complicated. We're talking about feelings that are so unacceptable to us—because they're so far from the ideal image we have of ourselves—that we can't bear them. But in every family with adolescent children there are sexual feelings, however fleeting they may be. We just deny them, push them aside, bury them so deeply that we're totally unconscious of them. A mother can't let herself acknowledge a sense of competition with her daughter any more than she can look at her maturing son and allow herself to think, 'Oh my, isn't he gorgeous—too bad he's my son!' By the same token, a father who sees his daughter wearing a revealing dress for a date doesn't permit himself to recognize his own feelings of arousal or jealousy. He's got to convince his conscious mind that because she's his daughter, this emerging young woman has absolutely no sexuality for him. But she has. And sometimes I'll get a father who's scared to death of his own feelings when he sees his daughter bouncing around the house in her cute little shorts and bulging halter."

Roberta smiled wryly.

"Seriously, what's this fellow supposed to do? Here he is, attracted to his own daughter. Just for a minute set aside all the taboos we have—and we *want* to have—about what's acceptable between a parent and child, and just look at the situation itself. Here's this man living with an adolescent who's becoming a sexual being right in his own home. Why wouldn't he see this beautiful young woman and be attracted? Why wouldn't a mother feel attracted to her son or competitive with her daughter? In a sense, what could be more natural? Of course, in our society and in most societies, it's unacceptable, sinful and forbidden to act upon these feelings and for good reason. The trouble is, we make it sinful even to *have* these feelings. But how are you going to control your feelings?

"What we've discovered is that the unconscious is unbridled and irrational, and we all run the gamut of emotions. The question is how do you handle your feelings. If we can simply realize and accept that we all have these feelings, and that there's a vast difference between having them and acting on them, then we can begin to be more comfortable with ourselves. We'll also be able to *deal* with various emotions better, if we can talk about them and see how they may be affecting us.

"Look at this father I was just describing. The possibility that he could have sexual fantasies about his own daughter creates overwhelming anxiety in this poor man. If he can't admit the cause of the anxiety, he's got to deny it. The more threatened he is by the existence of these forbidden feelings, the more violently and completely he's got to deny them. Many times, the denial comes out as tremendous rage.''

"Rage at whom?" Roberta questioned.

"It depends on the circumstances and the personalities. Say a father sees his adolescent daughter walking around the house in her bra and panties. Maybe he yells at her about modesty or something. Maybe he yells at his wife about teaching their daughter how to conduct herself and 'what the hell is the kid doing on dates, if this is how she acts at home?' Maybe the guy is too anxious to approach the subject directly so he takes his anger out at some other time or in some other way. For instance, he attacks the girl about her grades in school or her messy room, or he picks a fight with his wife about something or other. Maybe this man is sexually stimulated and chooses to take those feelings *out* of the household, turning to some other woman for a release. You can't predict exactly what the behavior will be, but you can be pretty certain that any time you're denying strong feelings, they're going to manifest themselves in some way or another.''

"I feel like I'm hearing a preview," Roberta said. "What do you do with a teenager who wants to walk around naked?''

"I think the parents have to talk about the behavior, what it means and how it affects them. But first they have to recognize it as sexual. Then, if they decide they don't want the girl going around the house undressed, they can say, 'We think you've got a lovely figure and you're an attractive young woman, but it seems to us that you're showing your sexuality inappropriately. When you walk around the house like that, it tends to sexualize the relationships within the family—and that's something we just don't feel is suitable.' That way, the daughter's emerging womanhood has been supported rather than attacked or ignored. And since it's been rechanneled, the familial relationships are reaffirmed.

"And there's something else that sometimes happens. If couples can acknowledge the echoes within themselves of the sexual blossoming of their children, they may decide to take some opportunities for more or different sexual activity with each other. Sometimes they see the kids are having the life experiences that were never available to them, and they decide to expand their own boundaries—take trips, start tennis or golf lessons, subscribe to the theater. It can be a very exciting and positive time for a couple.''

"Fascinating." Roberta sounded enthusiastic. "So you talk about the real—the 'primitive'—feelings instead of letting a lot of dark undercurrents swirl below the surface, making waves in your marriage!''

"Not bad," I acknowledged Roberta's image.

"And once you realize your feelings are natural and not freaky, you can figure out how you want to handle them." Roberta stopped and stared at me. "Okay, we can say that it's normal for me not just to love my child and be proud of her, but also to feel jealous or competitive with her. She's really turning into another woman in *my* home, right?"

"Right."

"In fact, it's like when my mother used to prance around and act girlish in front of my dates, and I wanted to kill her, right?"

"Right."

"Okay." Roberta leaned back in her chair. "Now, do you want to tell me how I go home and say to Jay, 'Honey, Laura told me at lunch today there's a pretty good chance that you're going to be sexually stimulated by Beth.' He'll think I've lost my mind!"

"He probably will!" I was laughing. "But you could raise it a little more indirectly. Maybe some evening when Beth has looked or acted particularly mature, you could say, 'Beth is really blossoming into a very lovely young woman. I don't know what kind of a reaction you're going to have, but I think it's natural for you to be more aware of her physically and to know that she's certainly becoming much more aware of you, too.' "

Roberta was shaking her head. "That sounds like you, not me. I think I'll be better off telling Jay right out that we had lunch and talked about this."

"Why not? Try him out. He seems to be fairly open. What's the worst thing that can happen? He can say, 'What? You're crazy! That friend of yours is really a kook.' Possibly he will be uncomfortable about pursuing the discussion for the moment, but just you bringing it up can be a relief. The feelings don't have to be totally denied now. And maybe later on, it can be discussed more comfortably. Anyway, acknowledging the fact that these emotions *can* exist sometimes makes them dissipate. There's no longer that secret, hidden quality."

"Can I ask you one more thing?"

"You know you can."

"It's about Beth and Jay spending time together. I remember I practically never had any time alone with my father, and I wish I had. It seems to me it's good for both of them in a way."

"I agree. I think it's great for a father and daughter—or for that matter, a mother and son—to go off on walks and talk. When it becomes excessive or exclusive—or when it's handled the way this

ice-skating episode was in which one parent is simply pushed aside
—then you get into trouble. You have to put a stop to that. But a
great deal depends on the nature of the total relationship that the
three of you have."

"I bet it can be damn hard for the parent who's being
pursued to really want to put a stop to it."

"Sure. It's great to be wanted, but it can get to a point
where the child is setting up a rivalry between the parents. And
that's devastating. Parents have to stand together at this time. They
must declare, "We're of a different generation, we're a team, we're
your parents. We have ways of being and doing that are based on
many years of growth and thought. We love you and want what's
good for you, but we will not be manipulated and divided by you
because that will be to everyone's disadvantage.' "

14. Parenting Adolescents

Adolescence is a prelude to leaving the home. It's a time when your youngster is struggling to separate from you, often rejecting you as a means of testing himself. Your adolescent is in the process of maturing and establishing personal identity, and developing sexually and emotionally to be able to have an intimate relationship with somebody else. An adolescent thrusting toward maturity is also afraid of what it means to be grown-up, and experiences a regressive pull toward childhood dependency. Anger at the need to be a child struggles with the need to be independent, and is complicated by the need to deny and disown any dependency wishes.

One way you mark the start of your child's adolescence is the first time your youngster says, "Oh, *Muh-ther*," or challenges Dad instead of looking up to him with adoration. Your child no longer sees you as omniscient and perfect. You are being judged and found wanting. That's hard to take. On top of that you now see your marvelous, even angelic, little one suddenly turning into someone you can hardly recognize, someone who looks and acts like a stranger, who answers back, takes stands, criticizes, disobeys, behaves incorrigibly and is a disruptive element in the family setting.

What does all of this summon in you? In your partner? What impact does it have on your relationship with each other?

Parents Picking On Each Other

When parents become emotionally edgy or anxious or threatened about their control, self-worth, significance and so forth, they often panic and vent their feelings by picking on each other. "I thought you were going to try to lose some weight? Is that how you

do it—with a second helping of . . . ?" or "Don't you have any
sense of style? How long are you going to wear that same suit
. . . ?" or "Do you know, I've never seen you wash your hands
before you sat down to dinner. *Never.*"

But now is when these issues get raised.

Frequently the children are used as a justification. "Look at
you," a wife will lash out at her husband, "you leave your shoes in
the living room and your stuff all over the place. What kind of example is that for Marty? How do you expect your son to be neat
and take care of his things when you're such a slob? But you don't
give a damn. You just take it for granted that I'll pick up after you."

Before a couple can resolve this kind of bickering, they have
to find out what they're really saying to one another. In this case,
is it actually a question of setting an example for the child? If so,
how significant or successful will that be at this stage in his development? After all, by the time kids are adolescents, they've already
picked up many of the characteristics of the family. If the mother
feels the child is inexcusably messy, why hasn't she discussed it
directly with the youngster? Or with her husband? Why the angry
attack on her husband instead?

Chances are that something else is going on here. I think it
has to be understood that it takes two people to maintain this kind
of interaction over the years. You can't have a household in which
the husband doesn't pick up, if his wife absolutely will not tolerate
it. If she says, "I put my clothes away and I expect you to do the
same," and backs up her position *one hundred percent*, then some resolution will be reached. Either the wife will agree to keep picking up
or else she will let her husband's clothes pile up until he gets the
message.

This situation is quite different from one where the wife is
constantly complaining that her husband expects her to pick up after him, which she ultimately *does*. As long as she cooperates or
colludes, no matter how much she objects, he doesn't believe her
because she isn't concrete and absolute in what she's saying. Somehow what gets conveyed to him, perhaps by something in her voice,
is that she doesn't really mean it. And she may not! As much as she
resents the servant role on one level, it may give her a sense of being
useful and needed on another.

In order to discover what is really going on between them,
this husband and wife have to communicate openly in the ways we
described at the beginning of the book. They need to explore their
deeper feelings and consider the possible motives for their behavior,
*especially in the light of the pressures they're currently experiencing within the
family situation.*

Did the husband just recently develop these sloppy habits? If so, then why now? What does he feel as he drops his garments about? What is he expressing? What wishes, needs, anxieties or resentments might be coming out in this behavior?

The answers to these questions will depend on the individual, but here are some possibilities:

—If this man is angry with his wife, he may be getting back at her by acting in a way he knows will upset her.

—Occasionally during their children's adolescence, parents find themselves jealous of the freedom their youngsters have—the freedom to be sloppy, to be carefree, to be sexual, to lose control, to rebel. Sometimes adults who have been restrained in some of these areas may suddenly feel, "Well, the kids can do it and so can I." The parent may act out a wish that's been reawakened by the experience of living with an adolescent. Often the adult has feelings of anger, defiance or rebellion not unlike the adolescent's own rebellion and defiance.

—There are times when a new behavior represents a wish to be noticed and taken care of. The parent may be reaching out and saying, "Gee, you're paying so much attention to the kids, but where do I come in? How do I get some attention?" A very young child isn't expected to be neat or self-sufficient; he's picked-up after by a loving parent. The adult who longs for attention, reassurance and a sense of being cared for may unconsciously choose this early form of behavior in the hopes of evoking these responses from a husband or wife.

I've known wives who reacted with indignation or outrage at suddenly being "treated like a maid" by a "thoughtless" husband. And I've known husbands who were furious about being "nagged to death" in their own homes. Yet when they began to understand and empathize with each other's deeper feelings, the hostility generally diminished or vanished. Usually the partners became eager to negotiate, be supportive and more openly ask for and give what was needed or desired.

Let's go on and consider what it might mean if a husband has always behaved in a sloppy manner, but his wife has just now begun to resent it:

—A woman may be angry with her husband about something else, and therefore refuses to "do" for him in the usual manner.

—Sometimes she starts feeling that her adolescents are using or abusing her. "They come home when they need something, but vanish when I need anything," one mother said. With this feeling building, a husband's long-time behavior may suddenly make her aware that she has been "taken advantage of for years," and she may lash out at husband and/or kids.

—A woman may become resentful because she'd like to have *her* dependency needs and wishes fulfilled, but she sees her husband's behavior as an act against her: "Who's going to pick up after me?" she wonders. "*I* never get a chance to throw things all over the damn place. . ."

—If a woman feels that her destiny and worth are closely tied to her home and family but now sees her children about to depart and her domain shrinking, she may become more rigid about the area she feels she still controls. "My home is all I have left and this man is showing disrespect for it—and for me."

—It's also possible that a woman may be changing her view of who she is and what her role within the household should be. Her children are striking out on their own, and she, too, may be redefining her identity. She may be saying in effect, "I no longer consider it my job to be picking up after you or anybody else." But since this represents a major change in how she thinks of herself and how she wants others to view her, she may be anxious and unable to say it openly in a non-blaming way. So she attacks her husband without explanation.

Again, the more the underlying feelings, fears and anxieties are recognized and shared, the greater the couple's chance for drawing closer together and supporting each other.

Fights Involving Your Child

Seeing your adolescent child wrestle with questions of identity, values and life goals can be difficult and threatening, if you yourself haven't come to terms with these issues.

"What do you mean, 'you have to find out who you are'?" a father demands of his son. "You know who you are. You're Jimmy, and you're fifteen, and you're a sophomore in high school. In a couple of years you're going to college, and then you'll go out and make a living." The man stares across the dining table at the boy.

"But suppose I don't want to just make a living. Maybe I want to do something different. Don't you ever stop and wonder what you're getting for everything you're putting into the company? What's all that work and pressure really for?"

"What kind of jackass questions are those?" the father explodes. "It's for your private school, your tape deck, our two cars and all of this!" The father gestures furiously around the room.

"Come on, hon, take it easy. Jimmy didn't mean anything." His wife tries to make peace. "Can we please have a pleasant dinner together for once?"

"You stay out of this!" The father can't tolerate his wife's "siding" with the boy. "I work my tail off for you and that kid, trying to give him things I never had when I was young, and what do I get? Well, don't expect me to sit here listening to this . . . ."

It is important for a father to realize that his son's critical attitude is his unsubtle way of separating from his parents and establishing his own identity. By belittling all the luxuries, he may well be denying his desire for them. He may adopt his father's values later on in life, but as an adolescent he has a need to question them.

If a father isn't secure in his own identity, if he doesn't feel sufficiently fulfilled or satisfied with his own life choices, then how can he tolerate his son's questioning of the values he himself doubts? He gets angry as a defense against his own anxiety. A father can also be sure of his values, but can't understand why his son is criticizing him. His lack of understanding of adolescent dynamics may make him impatient and angry.

Besides the negative effect this reaction may have on the youngster, this conflict is also apt to spill over into the relationship between husband and wife. **Typically, conflicts that start out between one parent and child quickly broaden to involve both spouses.** They can get caught up in an argument that's one step removed from the real problem . . . for instance, whether Jimmy should be allowed to express his own ideas, whether that's disrespectful, whether criticizing one's parent is permissible. But they won't deal with the primary problem of what the father is feeling about his own life that makes him react so emotionally to Jimmy's criticism. Perhaps the father, having worked hard all his life and reached the age of forty, is suddenly not sure it's been worthwhile, not sure that his efforts are appreciated or valued by his family, and not sure whether he might want to change his life. Feelings like these need to be confronted and shared between two people in order to continue an intimate relationship.

Enid and Pat

As parents feel their control over the children being drained away from them, they typically try to compensate by becoming even more rigid. "You can't go out looking like that . . . clean up your room this minute . . . I don't want you to waste your money on that . . . you're to finish your homework *before* you . . . ."

In a sense it's understandable to fight the slipping of your authority, especially if that authority is necessary and important to you. But beyond a certain point, attempts to actually control an adolescent are futile, and may be detrimental to the child. By overprotecting and not allowing the youngster to make his own decisions, you may infantalize him. Your attempts may also provoke the teenager into doing exactly the opposite. The power struggle that ensues usually pits the parents against each other.

I worked with a couple whose regular source of conflict was the daughter's diet and figure.

"You really are putting on weight," Enid would tell her child. "I know it's not so terrible for a girl of fourteen to be a little heavy, but you're getting fat. You have a pretty face, but how do you expect to keep a nice complexion and figure when you eat all that junk? It's not good for you. Do you like having pimples? Don't you want to be popular?"

"I'm popular enough," Pat would mutter, reaching for something in the refrigerator.

"What are you taking now?"

"Food. I'm hungry."

"How can you be hungry? We just finished dinner. If you have to have something, eat a carrot instead . . ."

"Dammit, I don't want a carrot. *You* eat a carrot . . ."

"Don't you dare talk to me like that!" Enid would turn to her husband. "Are you going to let her . . ."

"Why don't you just lay off? You're at her all the time. She sits down at the dinner table and it's, 'Listen, Pat, if you're going to eat like that, you're going to get as fat as a house.' Give the kid a break. Don't you have anything else to think about? So what if she's got a little baby fat?"

"Are you serious? The difference can be her whole social life, her health and her future. What's the matter with you? Don't you care what happens to your own daughter?"

And so things would go at almost every meal.

After some time in therapy, however, Enid began to develop in ways that enabled her to deal with her daughter in a remarkably different manner. She recognized that she needed more of a life of her own and that she was capable of doing things for and by herself rather than through her child. At the same time, she came to understand that her special distress over Pat's weight was related to echoes she was getting from her own past. Enid had been a pudgy, often-teased teenager who wasn't asked out and feared she'd never have a boyfriend. Naturally she hoped to protect her daughter from the same experience. Moreover, she felt *driven* to control Pat because she herself couldn't bear her revived feelings of her dreadful "fat phase." Enid gradually began to separate her own anxiety from her daughter's situation. She began to fill her own life, put her memories into perspective, and finally view her daughter as a young adult who by now should be given the responsibility for her own eating habits and appearance.

One of the hardest things for parents to do is to step back and ask, "What is my child trying to show or prove? What is he testing or developing within himself? What does his behavior mean to me? What will be the realistic, long-term effect of his actions on himself? If I share *my* thoughts, concerns, and values with him and he still insists on doing what he wants, is it something that could result in serious harm or permanent damage to him? Does his behavior suggest inner problems he may need help with? Is this, instead, a relatively safe situation through which he can *learn* what it means to be responsible for his own decisions? Is it to this child's long-term benefit that he now start facing the consequences of his actions?"

By emphasizing the importance of understanding your own motives and involvement in trying to control your child's behavior, I don't mean to suggest raising children without any kinds of restrictions. Parents have the right to set rules and limitations. Particularly if the child is doing something that could result in serious harm to him, parents have an obligation to use all their *power* to deter him and all their *understanding* to find out why the child is acting in a self-destructive way. If a girl is so fat that it's actually a threat to her health and a sign of emotional disturbance, or if she has a physiological condition that makes it dangerous for her to be overweight, then one has to discover what her behavior means when she over-eats, what kind of help or attention she may be seeking, and what kind of anger or rebellion she may be displaying.

Reaching Your Adolescent

Most parents are genuinely concerned with how to reach a youngster who is searching, rebelling and forming values. It's often only by understanding yourself and being able to share your own feelings that you can communicate with your child *and with your partner* in a meaningful way. Here's an illustration.

I was working with a woman named Peggy, whose husband Mel finally joined us in a therapy session for the first time after he'd become very upset over their son.

"How could you let the kid apply for a summer job looking like a slob?" Mel shouted at his wife. "Shep wants to work as a counselor at a nice respectable camp, and you let him turn up at the interview looking like a bum who never even had parents."

"*I let him?*" Peggy challenged with unaccustomed indignation. "Where were *you*? I told him I thought he ought to change his clothes and do something about his hair, but he refused. What did you want me to do? Dress him and carry him into a barber shop?"

"Listen, you've spoiled and babied that boy from the time he was an infant. He never had to shape up. Well, now you see the results." Mel turned to me. "I'll tell you plain and simply what it comes down to. I'm ashamed of my own son." He stared belligerently from me to Peggy, then asked harshly, "Do you think that's easy to say? Do you think that's a good feeling to have?"

"I don't think it's easy at all," I answered. "I think it's a very difficult thing for you to say, and I think it's very hard for you to feel that. But let's see if we can understand it a little bit. Shame comes from the discrepancy between how you wish to be viewed and how you actually are viewed. It has many implications, including that you're making other people your judges. When you say you're ashamed, whom are you ashamed in front of?"

"Anybody. I mean friends come over to the house and . . ." Mel shook his head. "It's not just the way he looks, which is bad enough. I mean, the kid is dirty, and he wears torn filthy jeans—he looks like he just crawled out of a ditch. But the real issue is the way he *is*. He doesn't *do* anything except shoot off his mouth. I don't need him sounding off in front of my friends about how stupid school is—instead of doing his homework and getting some decent grades for a change. I don't need him hanging around making cracks about how they're going to legalize marijuana or invent booze that doesn't give you a hangover, or God knows what."

"So you're really ashamed of everything about him," I said. "You're ashamed of the way he is, how he looks, talks and everything . . ."

"No, hell, I'm not ashamed of everything. Don't put words into my mouth."

"Oh. What aren't you ashamed of?"

"Well, deep down—if you can scrape through the crud—there's a good decent kid in there."

"Do you really feel that?"

There was a pause. "Yeah, some of the time. The rest of the time I just don't know. I mean, sometimes he just disgusts me and I feel like I've had him up to here." He made a slicing gesture over his head.

"You know, a lot of fifteen-year-olds are sloppy, dirty and rebellious. But I wonder what that evokes in you. What makes that so important to you? What makes your *friends'* judgment so important? It seems to me that there are those two different areas to explore. When you were growing up, were you made to feel less significant or that you had to conform in a certain way?"

"*Conform?* Are you crazy, lady? *I had to go out and earn a living.* I had to put myself through college. I didn't have time to know conform from uncomform."

"So in a sense you never had a chance to get away with the kinds of things that your son is getting away with now. Is it possible you would have wanted to?"

"What's that got to do with anything? I'm trying to tell you I've got a kid who doesn't care what he does and who's screwing up his life. Can you understand that? Between you and me, he never wanted that camp job in the first place. All he wants to do is 'hang out'—you should pardon the expression, it's his, not mine—"

"I just can't help wondering," I said softly, "is it possible that when you were growing up, you would have wanted to be able to be sloppy and *not* have to work as hard as you did, be able to go off and do whatever you felt like?"

Mel hesitated and finally said, "Sure!" Then more quietly, "Of course I would."

"That doesn't mean a fifteen-year-old can't act like that and Shep take the consequences of whatever he does. If he's going to be rejected on the basis of his appearance, and he knows that, it's one thing. And he may *not* want to work. But then what else is he going to do? How is he going to cope with the rest of the summer? Have you thought about that?"

"Maybe that's part of what's bugging me. I'm worried about him being on the loose all summer because I think he's hanging around with a bad crowd. So far he's stayed out of real trouble, but I think he's heading for it."

"What kinds of trouble?"

"Hanging around with the wrong people."

"What do you think is going to happen to him?"

"I think he's going to pick up their habits, start getting stoned on dope."

"Yes? What does it mean to you that he might get stoned on dope?"

"It means he can get hurt. He can get arrested or flunk out of school."

"Pretty dire consequences, aren't they?"

"I think so."

"Do you think that's really liable to happen to him?"

"I don't *know.* I don't know where you draw the line. I don't know when you start to really get worried and say, '*This is enough*, this kid has got to do these things *now* before he turns into some kind of juvenile delinquent . . .'"

"He's got to do what? What are the things he's got to do?"

Mel paused. "He's got to see that there's danger in the

world," he said finally. "He's got to see that things won't always be easy and he can get hurt. He's got to see that I won't always be there to protect him."

"Do you think you *can* prevent him from facing any kind of danger?"

"Some kinds, I hope."

"What kinds?"

"I don't know. I can't talk to him." Mel spoke slowly now. "If he won't listen, how do I teach him values? Where do I set some disciplinary limits? How do I tell him that some things are important? How do I make him see what can happen if he starts fooling around with dope? Suppose he starts dealing? Look, I even know the vocabulary because that's what I hear on TV all the time. Kids in high school are dealing dope."

"Is that what you think is going to happen to him?"

Mel shrugged. "I can't answer you. I don't know any more. Dope, alcohol, something else—he's just like a stranger to me."

"I wonder why all of this is making you so frightened."

"Because I'm not going to be able to help him any more." Mel's voice was low.

"Ah. And you've been able to help him in the past? He has listened to you, and now suddenly he's not listening to you any more?"

"Yes."

"And when he doesn't listen to you, then what happens to you?"

"I guess I get frightened for him. It's just not an easy world."

"Have you ever talked to him like that? Have you ever shared some of these feelings with him?"

"I've told him what I thought he ought to do."

Peggy said apologetically, "It comes out like orders or a lecture."

I said, "You didn't sound as though you were lecturing now. I didn't feel you were lecturing. I felt you were really sharing something that was very deep, real and meaningful. I really *felt* it. Are you in touch with that?"

Mel nodded.

I turned to Peggy. "How did you feel about it?"

"I never heard him talk that way."

"You know, this is a way for both of you to talk to each other. You can learn a lot about each other even from this. How did you feel when Mel spoke like that, Peggy? How'd that make you feel about him?"

"Close to him."

"Sure. Closer than when he lectures?"

"He doesn't lecture me so much, he just tells me what to do and then drops it."

"How does that make you feel? Being told what to do?"

Peggy thought for a minute. "Like I wish he really knew what would be good for me because I'm mixed up myself."

"Perhaps you'd like to be a little girl and have him tell you what to do?"

"Sometimes."

I smiled. "Sometimes all of us would. But you pay a price for that, too. The price is that you remain the child and he becomes the parent. Then you have this kind of inequality in terms of who has the power and who makes the decisions. Are you sure you want to do that?" It was something we'd touched on before.

Peggy gave me a small smile. "I know, it's something we have to explore and examine," she teased gently.

Mel looked at us thoughtfully.

Some Parents Emulate Their Children

Today some parents do not seek greater control over their adolescents but want to imitate them instead. Perhaps it's a result of the increased emphasis on the youth culture, or the simple fact that the young seem to have fun in a much more permissive society than their parents knew. The parents feel the excitement the kids bring into the home and naturally want to get involved. As a result, they may identify with the child, choose not to set any limits at all, and in fact, try to eradicate the generation gap ("Don't call me 'Mom,' call me 'Maggie' "). By denying the parental role, they may also be avoiding the sense of aging that comes with being the parents of an adolescent. Thus you'll find mothers and fathers who dress and talk like the kids, become disco dancers and generally try to reexperience their own adolescence through the children. It can be a helpful release and a lot of fun for the couple if they're both on the same youth trip. But if only one is participating, the other may feel deserted and will probably ridicule the partner. "Adult adolescence" can also make parents seem absurd to their children. On the one hand, this may aid the children in separating. Yet it's always better to separate from stronger parents—adults who know themselves and are not going to be devastated when you leave them. For the parents, keeping up with the kids can turn out to be quite a strain! It's usually more rewarding to face reality and choose your own ways of having fun.

Using the Child

When parents of adolescents come to see me professionally, it's almost always because they're having serious trouble about the children. Time and again a husband or wife will say, "If it weren't for the children, things between us would be fine, but how can we enjoy ourselves when Johnny's always doing something to upset us? How can we ever go away on vacation, or have a decent sex life, or feel happy doing things together when we spend all our time and energy worrying and fighting about the child?"

By the time things have reached this stage, the youngster may also need some professional help. But the couple should recognize that their own relationship needs examining, too. Usually this kind of focus on the child is a diversionary tactic, a way of avoiding some problem between husband and wife.

I saw one couple whose fifteen-year-old daughter, Nancy, had been in therapy with a child psychiatrist for several months. Finally, the doctor sent the parents to me because he felt that the child's problems stemmed largely from the couple's marital difficulties.

"I guess you know about the terrible time we're having with our daughter," Jack, said. "We can't even talk to her any more."

Madge lowered her voice. "There's this guy who's almost ten years older than Nancy, and she's been spending nights with him. . ."

I said, "It sounds as though it was a wise decision for you to have arranged for Nancy to talk to someone professionally."

Jack scowled. "There wasn't much choice. Madge and Nancy are at each other's throats every other minute. I walk into the house and I don't know what to expect—except that there'll be some kind of situation where I have to make the peace."

"Some peace." Madge's tone was contemptuous. She eyed me. "*He* walks in from the office anytime between eight and eleven at night, then spends a big five minutes playing family court judge. Well, you can see all the good it does."

"Nancy might be a little different today if you'd have put some limits on her when she was younger," Jack said. "But no, you always encouraged her to grow up too fast and be popular, to flirt and date . . ."

"What do you know about it? You've never been involved. You're never even around. A girl needs a father, but you were always too interested in the business. So now she's out looking for love from a father-figure . . ."

"Oh, God, what crap have you been reading now?"

I said, "I think what we're really here to talk about is the relationship between the two of you. You sound very angry with each other. Has this always been your way of relating?"

"Well, we're just so damn upset over the girl."

"Okay, but your daughter is with a psychiatrist. He can handle her problems, and they'll work things out together. What's important here and now is the two of you."

"Who the hell knows whether that doctor's any good or not," Jack muttered.

I avoided his attempt to keep the conversation focused on the daughter. "Let's try to see what this concern for Nancy is doing to both of you. It seems to be taking you away from each other and forcing your attention upon something else. What do you think that means?"

"It means we're good parents who put our child first," Madge stated flatly.

"That's right, it does. But what happens when your child leaves in a couple of years? What happens to the two of you?"

"Are you trying to say we shouldn't be concerned about our own daughter?"

"Of course, you should. Children are important, and it's necessary to pay attention to them. But so much of your attention seems to be diverted away from yourselves; so much of your energy seems to be dissipated or converted to anger. I wonder what could be causing that."

"It's what Jack said. We're upset. There's never a minute's peace. Things would be different if Nancy were all right."

"Is that true?" I looked at each of them. "Is it true that you had a good relationship when your daughter was younger?"

There was a moment of silence.

Finally Jack said, "Possibly our marriage isn't perfect, but we're making out one way or another."

"Why are you here?"

"To find out what we can do to help our child."

"I thought that's why you took her to the child psychiatrist."

"Are you saying there's nothing we can do to help her?"

"That's a whole different ball game, and maybe something we can talk over with the psychiatrist and your daughter. Perhaps have a family conference. But let's see what really belongs to the child and what belongs to the two of you."

"Are you saying the psychiatrist told us to come see you because he really thinks there's something wrong with *us*?" Jack was shocked and disbelieving.

"With the *relationship* between the two of you."

"I'd like to know why the hell he thinks that."

"Well, are things so ideal? Is there anything you'd like to improve? Do you enjoy being together, doing things with each other? Right now, when you look at each other, what do you see?"

Very quietly Madge started to cry. "We don't make love very often." Her voice was small. "I'm not exciting to Jack the way I used to be."

"*Nobody* stays exciting or excited for twenty years," Jack said.

"But we don't do much together."

"What are you talking about? We spend every weekend together."

"No, not just the two of us doing things together. We're either alone by ourselves, or keeping an eye on Nancy, or with other people. And then, most of the time, we're drinking a lot." Madge paused. "It's not the way I thought it would be. It's not the way I think it could be, if we could just . . . try something . . ."

I looked from Madge to Jack. "Do you think there are ways in which your sexual life can be improved? Would you like to find new ways?"

Jack's voice was dull. "It seems a little late at this stage in the game."

"You sound resigned, as though you've given up. Is that so?"

"I don't know." He was avoiding Madge's eyes. "I'm just not sure."

"Well, what counts here is a commitment to wanting to improve the relationship, sexual and otherwise. And without such a commitment very little can be accomplished." They were silent. "Why don't you give it some thought, and then let me know how you feel about continuing to explore the aspects of your relationship that might be altered. If you decide that's something you want to do, I'd like to spend a little time with each of you individually so I can get to know you on a one-to-one basis. Then we can talk together again."

In thinking about what might be going on with this couple, many questions and possibilities came to mind. Had their sexual relationship ever been satisfying? If not, what had kept them together, and why was that bond now weakening? Possibly the presence of an adolescent daughter had heightened their sexual awareness and aroused a sense that time was passing. Were they now regretting or resenting the absence of better sex between them? Seeking it elsewhere?

If this couple *had* a good sex life at one time, when had that changed, and why? What might their daughter's burgeoning sexuality have brought to the surface? Possibly the father felt aroused, then became so concerned and anxious about his feelings that he withdrew from the family completely, causing repercussions with his child as well as his wife. Had he become involved with someone else? Had the wife's competitive feelings with their daughter unconsciously caused her to collude, in the child's rebellion?

If I worked with this husband and wife, we'd have to trace the development of their marriage and family interaction from the beginning. Possibly the pressures of this period had worn away the veneer covering many of the weaker aspects of the couple's relationship. We'd have to see what had made the daughter such a central concern, and whether they shared enough other things to provide the basis for a viable relationship. As things were now, Jack and Madge were clearly arranging their lives with little opportunity for real intimacy or confrontation with each other. The focus on Nancy, the constant company of other people and the drinking were all mitigating against intimacy.

By stressing the importance of a couple dealing with their own relationship, I'm not suggesting that it isn't natural for parents to feel a deep and abiding concern for their children. Of course, we love and worry about our children, and try to protect, guide and help them. And sometimes your child *is* in a crisis that requires all your energy.

But normally, the fundamental interaction within the family is first between husband and wife. Only if parents can see themselves as individuals and as a couple separate and apart from the adolescent can they act in the child's best interest—or their own.

Children in Trouble

I sometimes work with couples whose adolescent child is in serious trouble involving drugs, alcoholism, theft, homosexuality and so forth. It's almost impossible for any parent in these circumstances not to feel some guilt, shame, embarrassment and failure. You look for somebody to blame because it's very hard to accept responsibility for the negative development of your child. The usual scapegoat is your partner, and the effect on the marriage can be disastrous.

Assigning of fault is absurd and useless. It's never a case of one parent being the villain while the other is the hero or so-called "neutral observer." **It always takes two to create a situation and permit it to develop.** Any time partners find themselves accusing

("If only you had . . . , I told you we'd better . . . ."), they should be reminded that the responsibility must be shared. There may have been some way in which one might have been collusive, or a time when one neglected to take action, or reinforced either the partner's behavior or the child's.

Sometimes parents unintentionally and unconsciously encourage or maintain a child's destructive behavior because it serves their own purposes or needs. For example, if a couple can't confront each other directly, it's sometimes useful to maintain a child's acting out so that it can be used as an indirect form of communication or a club: "See! If you weren't so cold and authoritarian, the boy wouldn't have been afraid to ask you for money instead of stealing it." The child's actions can also serve as an excuse for the parent's behavior. For instance, a wife may justify not going to work: "I have to stay home and watch out for this kid." A husband may excuse his inability to advance in his career: "Who can come home and work when that child is always raising hell and driving me to distraction?"

Until parents are ready to deal with their individual anxieties or the marital problems that may exist, they won't be able to understand their interaction with the child or the real meaning of the child's behavior.

(I don't mean to imply that parents are solely responsible for their child's development. Besides genetic factors and interaction with siblings, the minute the youngster leaves the household, he interacts with others who become significant in shaping his life. There's also the impact of educational institutions, the larger social scene, and perhaps especially the media.)

An adolescent's extreme actions convey more than "just a rebellion." One must ask, "Why drugs and not alcohol? Why promiscuity and not dropping out of school?" Reasons have to be uncovered as to how and why a particular behavior developed at a particular time.

There are also warning signs that can be recognized as cries for help before the behavior gets out of hand. If a youngster is constantly yelling, screaming and flailing against his parents; or if a depressed, sullen and withdrawn child retreats to his room and shuts the door on conversation; if there's extreme chaos or ominous silence in the household; if there are signs of self-destructive behavior or evidence that the child doesn't want to be at all honest with his parents; if there is no way of making real contact with the child, then these are absolute danger signals and it's time to seek outside help.

When a youngster gets into serious trouble, the parents have to face the immediate reaction within themselves: "My God, how could she be so stupid as to get pregnant with all that's known about birth control today?" Or, "Why didn't I tell her about contraceptives? What have I done wrong? I didn't even know she was sleeping with somebody."

Some of the most devastating self-doubts are awakened in parents who discover that their adolescent is homosexual. "What have we done to cause this? What's going to happen when our friends and relatives find out? We're never going to be grandparents!" Individual feelings about homosexuality come to the fore. A father whose son declares himself a homosexual may fear that some of his own secret wishes have been picked up by the boy. "Was there something in me that came out in him? Is it because I experimented when I was seventeen? Did he get ideas because I go out with the guys for a weekend of hunting?" The mother of a homosexual son may wonder, "Was I so harsh that now he can't stand women? I don't remember being that bad, but I must have been a terrible mother for him to hate all women now."

Similarly, when a daughter is a lesbian, the father says, "My God, what's wrong with me? My daughter hates men? What did I do to make her feel like that?" The mother may agonize over what's hidden within herself that she hasn't recognized. "Am I so tough-looking that I'm like a 'dyke'? Is it because I haven't taught her to care about being feminine?"

Whatever difficulty the child is in, each parent will respond with a personal reaction or identification that he or she must confront. Just as people must develop beyond blaming each other, they must also work through their self-accusations and guilt. They need to find compassion and forgive each other for mistakes they may have made. Only then can the child's behavior be examined and understood, the relationship between spouses explored and strengthened, and perhaps the interaction between parents and child restructured.

PART 4:
Common Crises
Between
Husband and Wife

One of the themes we've been discussing is the way in which change tend to trigger various feelings and fears. A baby enters the household, your child starts school, your adolescents test you. Each significant change causes you to respond according to your own personality, and it also necessitates a corresponding adjustment of the marital interaction.

Whether it's a change for the better (inheriting a million dollars or making an outstanding personal achievement) or for the worse (losing a job or going into debt), the very fact of the change creates stress. The results can be either positive or negative for the couple. Adversity sometimes draws people closer together, while good fortune may divide them. Again it all depends on your needs, your partner's needs, the resources you have for dealing with the stress and the stage in your life and marriage when it occurs.

For instance, if a woman begins to win great acclaim at a time when her husband feels he has already reached the peak of his career, he may not be able to tolerate his wife's success. The jealousy and rival feelings may be overwhelming because they have occurred at a point when he's too vulnerable. Had his wife's success come during an earlier period when this man felt he was still developing and had his whole life ahead of him, it might not have been such a threat.

In the following chapters, we're going to explore the dynamics of a number of events, some of which are apt to play a significant part in almost all our lives.

15. Sexual Problems

Bette had reddish hair and alert brown eyes. She moved gracefully and had a pleasant voice. "Dr. Singer, I came to you because I was told you're a sex therapist and a marriage counselor, too."

"Yes, that's true."

"I think my husband and I need help." Her voice dropped a little. "We've been married less than a year and we're not . . . we don't have a good sex life. The real trouble is that it's starting to affect our whole relationship, and I'm frightened."

"What frightens you about it?"

Her eyes met mine. "There's a lot of tension between us. There are times when I'm sure we're both thinking things, but we're not saying them. On weekends or when we're coming home from a party, I can feel the tension even though we're not talking about whether we're going to . . . to make love. I thought that before it got worse—I mean, before we were in real trouble . . ." she paused. "Greg doesn't know I'm here. I was afraid to ask him to come with me because if he said no, I thought it would make things even worse. I thought maybe there were some things I could do alone that you could tell me about."

"Well, let's find out a little bit more about what's going on between the two of you. You say you've been married about a year?"

"Yes. We knew each other first for about four months. And we slept together before we got married."

"Sleeping together—you mean you had intercourse with him?"

Bette flushed and nodded. "I don't feel very comfortable talking about this to a stranger."

"Sure, I can understand that."

She smiled faintly. "Well, we did have . . . intercourse."

"Under what kinds of circumstances? In a hotel room? In the back of a car . . ."

"Oh no. In his apartment. I wasn't living with him, but I spent a lot of time there because I had a roommate and Greg lived alone."

"And how was sex between the two of you then?"

Bette relaxed slightly. "It was exciting. Greg was very aggressive, and he had a lot more experience than I did. I just let him take charge. I think I liked the idea that he knew what he was doing. I think I felt very reassured—and excited just to be in bed with him."

"And now? Is he still in charge?"

Bette spoke softly. "No, not in the same way." I had the feeling that she'd thought about this before. "You see, I never used to ask Greg to do anything special. Before we were married I let him do everything his way and never commented about it. It was just that whatever he did seemed okay to me." Bette looked at the legs of my chair. "I knew I wasn't completely satisfied, but I thought everything would get better when we spent more time together, or when we were married." She paused, then said with an effort, "I thought I would start to have orgasms." Her glance met mine and dropped again. "I always acted as though I did. I mean, I faked it. But I never had them with him. After we got married, things didn't get any better. Greg seemed satisfied. At least he always got his satisfaction, but I didn't, and at some point I started feeling disappointed and angry—as though there should be more."

"Have you told Greg about this? Did you raise this at all with him?"

"You mean faking? *No.*"

"You've never shared that with him."

"Absolutely not."

"What do you think would happen if you did?"

"I think it would devastate him. I'd rather correct it and stop faking, but if I told him, he'd never trust me. It would wipe him out and I'd never do that. I love him."

"Maybe you're sensing Greg's feelings of vulnerability. One of the things that can happen with sex is that you become much more intimate and much more vulnerable as a result. People sometimes do feel as though their very essence is being challenged or their selfhood brought into question. A man can feel very threatened. But it can also be ruinous to a marriage if you're not being satisfied. And if you feel you must continue to fake it, that builds up distrust and resentment that is lethal to any marriage."

"That's why I don't want to keep faking it. I want to know how to get him to do some things—like not rush so much, or touch me more." Bette was shaking her head and frowning. "I'm sorry. I'm not being very clear about what's happening. Maybe . . . maybe I can be more specific. I've tried to tell Greg how to do something, or I'll put his hand where I want it, but he says I spoil things by always correcting him. And since I've been doing it, he's been much less . . . aggressive. Sometimes he has trouble getting hard." Bette took a deep breath. "Two weeks ago we had an incident. We were together and he hurt me, and I said, 'That *hurts.* You always do it too hard.' "

"Stop right here," I said quickly. "Let's see if we can understand just this. When you say to him, 'You always hurt me,' how do you suppose that makes him feel?"

"*Terrible.* Believe me, I knew the minute I said it that I shouldn't have."

"How could you have said it differently?"

Bette spoke quickly, impatiently, defensively. "It would feel better if you didn't do it so hard—I understand I did something the wrong way. I was just so upset because it did hurt, and I was angry because I've asked him to be more gentle. But it was still a stupid thing to say—and now I don't know what to do. We haven't had sex since then. I don't know how it will be when we do try again. I only know I'm not supposed to correct him, but I don't see how *else* you can show someone what you want."

"What do you think would happen if you could share with him the fact that your needs are a little different than he seems to realize?"

"But then he says I'm criticizing."

"Have you tried to talk to him like that when you're *not* having sex?"

Bette flushed. "No, not really. It seems so awkward. I mean, when? Over coffee?"

I smiled. "Or in front of a fire, or any time you select. I think timing is terribly important because when you start something and then you stop it precipitously, you can easily feel turned off or put down. But if you can talk at a time when you're just feeling close and enjoy being together, when you're *not* having intercourse, not trying for an orgasm but just stroking or touching, then that's one way of really showing one another what you like and discovering what pleases you."

Bette was silent.

"How do you feel when you think about being with Greg in that way?"

She shrugged.

"You seem uncertain about something."

"I don't know how to set things up like that."

"Couldn't you share some of the things you've been saying here? Suppose you said, 'I feel bad that we're having sex and I'm not enjoying it as much as I'd like to. I don't have orgasms as often as I'd like, but I think I could if we could talk and experiment a little, maybe learn a bit more about each other's bodies . . . .' "

Bette shrugged again.

"What are you feeling?"

She looked at me. "I couldn't say those things."

"I wonder why not. I wonder what's standing in the way."

"For one thing, I think Greg would be terribly upset. He'd say, 'When did you start feeling like this?' and I'd have to say I've felt this way for a long time. I just couldn't bring it up. I thought maybe you could tell me some things to do without having to talk to him about it."

"It doesn't work that way, unfortunately. I wish there was some magical formula, but that's not the way it is between two people."

"But how can you tell someone you haven't been enjoying sex with him?"

"Maybe you can say it in another way. Maybe you can say something to the effect that you'd hoped things would improve in terms of *your own reactions* after you'd been married for a while, but now you realize you haven't really shared some of your feelings with him. And you think it's a good idea to share feelings in an area where there could be resentment building."

Bette was agitated. "But the whole point is that I'm afraid my *saying* these things would create worse resentment."

"Why should it, really?"

"Because I'm telling him that I'm not satisfied."

"Well, nobody says that anybody else *has* to understand about satisfying you, nor is that his job. It's really your job to please yourself, to learn how to get the greatest amount of pleasure, and to share with your partner what you have discovered about yourself. Nobody else can know what's going on in your body or mind."

"I know you're right," Bette said faintly, "but I just couldn't get the words out. I'm sorry. I think Greg would be so angry at me."

"And what's so terrible about anger?"

Bette hesitated. "It's frightening to me. I'm afraid he would . . . he would push me away. He would be less aroused by me. He would stop wanting me."

"He would stop wanting you," I repeated gently. "Why

don't you say that to him? Say, 'You know, I've been scared to death to talk to you because I'm afraid that if I do, you'd get so angry you wouldn't even want me.' What happens if you take that kind of risk? What do you suppose would happen?"

Bette stared at me, clearly wishful and wistful, but still not convinced she could act on her feelings. I wondered if it was, in fact, a simple problem in communication, or if there were deeper reasons preventing her from becoming truly intimate, vulnerable, trusting, or demanding with her husband.

Of all our natural characteristics, sexuality is the one we probably feel least comfortable with and least free to explore and express. The majority of us have been conditioned to think of sex as something one shouldn't be open about, something that's not quite nice, bad or maybe even dirty. Perhaps we think of it as frivolous or unimportant. The Puritan ethic that you're not supposed to enjoy yourself too much still pervades our society.

Our evaluation of whether sex is "good" partly depends on what we've been led to believe it "should be" like. Paradoxically, our Puritanism persists with a society that emphasizes superficial sexuality and considers orgasm the ultimate experience. The earth should shake, and if it doesn't shake and keep on shaking, then a man or woman may think, "Is this all there is to it? Is something the matter with me?" The sense of having had a loving and/or pleasurable experience dims in view of the Fourth of July expectations of what should have been. All the "musts" and "shoulds" tend to turn sexuality into an effort, a risk and a problem instead of a relaxed, spontaneous experience that can be fun, furious, loving, relieving, replenishing, soothing, enjoyable, ecstatic and also casual.

Perhaps the greatest misconception of all is that sex means intercourse. Sex is much more than just intercourse. We're being sexual in the broadest sense when we're holding, touching, kissing and loving—even when we're speaking certain words or using an intimate tone. Our sexuality, including intercourse, can be filled with variations, and they're all good. If both partners are giving, receiving and being fulfilled, then nobody outside the relationship can say what's right, wrong, preferable or best.

Gradually we are becoming enlightened, but there's always a gap between the time an idea is discussed and the point at which it becomes fully accepted and incorporated into our thinking. I believe it's a hopeful sign that more and more of the people I see professionally are coming in with sex as a "presenting problem." People are more open about sex, and it's become a more acceptable presenting problem than ever before. There's a greater awareness that many couples have these difficulties, and that it's a positive step to do something in order to enjoy a rich and fulfilling sexual life together.

Usually what frightens people enough to create an immediate crisis in a marriage is either the onset of impotence in the man or the woman's unresponsiveness and disinterest in sex. Then one of the partners wonders, "What's happened? You were responsive six months ago. What's changed? What's wrong?" The problem can't be hidden or denied.

Sometimes sexual difficulties begin as some sort of dissatisfaction and escalate until they assume crisis proportions. Perhaps there's an acceptance of a situation for a while. There may be enough good in the marriage and/or enough insecurity in the partners to delay acknowledging and exposing troubles that can be kept buried. In the past, many sexual dissatisfactions were acted out indirectly. A husband would make snide remarks about his wife in front of company. "If I hear about one more headache, I think I'll go up the wall." A wife might say, "I think I'm going to trade you in for the young one over there." Those little quips mask a tremendous amount of hostility, anger and aggression, although the cause may never be discussed. Today, more people seem to be saying, "I've put up with this for as long as I can, and now I won't tolerate it any more." They decide to try to help themselves or get outside help.

In most cases, sexual problems tend to indicate that something else is wrong underneath. These problems are easier to pinpoint than, say, fear of closeness. How is a person to identify *that* anxiety and understand the part it may be playing within the marital relationship? But you do know when something is bothering you concerning sexual rapport and satisfaction; so the problem is identified as sexual.

For a long time, professional sex therapy was highly categorized and very specific in terms of the mechanical paces that patients underwent. But in the last few years, sex and marital therapists have come to recognize that sexuality is a much more complex phenomenon, and that, with some exceptions, sexual problems are rooted in our most fundamental male-female relationships.

The body isn't a physically autonomous entity with its own patterns of behavior. Rather it's an extension of our whole being, expressing our deepest feelings. Seldom do sexual difficulties stem from something as simple, for example, as ignorance. If they did, partners would quickly remedy the deficiency through mutual exploration. They'd have the confidence and freedom to ask for and do whatever felt good. But the fact is that all kinds of emotions and teachings influence our physical sensations, and as a result often block or distort our communication with a partner. It's our underlying feelings we most often need to explore in order to understand what's really happening within our sexual relationship.

Impotence

Impotence is usually defined as a man's inability to achieve and/or maintain an erection sufficient to enable coital penetration. Primary impotence refers to a condition in which sexual penetration has never been achieved. Secondary impotence, which is what we're talking about here, refers to the condition of having once been potent but becoming impotent either for a single encounter or over an extended period of time.

The first and most important fact to understand is that *nobody* can be potent at all times and under all circumstances. It just doesn't happen. There are too many physical and psychological variables that can cause occasional, temporary episodes of impotence. Practically every man learns this through experience, although many are unnecessarily terrified about what might be wrong with them when it does happen.

It's estimated that approximately ten percent of impotence has some physiological basis. If it persists over a period of time— and this measurement must be subjective—then a logical step would be to have a medical examination to rule out physical causes.

However, the vast majority of potency problems have a psychological basis. Usually, they're rooted in various anxieties, conflicts or unresolved problems. Often the difficulty is temporary, and it can come from stresses that may or may not be related to the marriage. It's important for women as well as men to recognize this and thus relieve a great many feelings of guilt and inadequacy.

Impotence is usually a man's way of expressing something with his penis that he hasn't been able to put into words or deal with in some other manner.

A man who loses his job and feels like a failure or "less of a man" because his self-esteem is based on his earning power may become impotent. Until he can feel that his value as a human being and his importance to his family are separate from his ability to make money, he may be unable to function sexually in a complete way.

A man who is terribly overworked and under tremendous job pressures may unconsciously feel that orgasm is going to further deplete him and therefore may become impotent.

A man who is depressed or consumed by worries may have difficulty achieving the sense of fullness and outgoingness needed for an erection.

One of the most helpful things a couple can do at times like this is immediately take the emphasis off intercourse. That, in and of itself, seems to relieve the man—sometimes enough for him to have an erection. In effect, he's being shown that he doesn't have to perform. There's no pressure or possible failure to make him anxious.

Men have a tremendous concern about performance because of the overemphasis in our culture upon the macho male who's always ready and eager, who has total sexual adequacy and perfect technique. Sex becomes a real production, and men then have performance anxiety, which is a major cause of impotence. Ironically, with women today declaring their own right to be sexual, assertive and open, many men are feeling even more threatened. Although the male fantasy of a passionate, sex-hungry woman may be exciting, the actuality can place rather threatening demands on the man. Women are complaining that now it's the men who have the headaches; and men have indicated that it's because of the demands they feel stemming from women's "excessive" sexuality, their great needs, their explicit desire to have many orgasms, etc. Men seem to withdraw or withhold from play and sexuality more often these days. And there are indications of increasing male impotence.

Perhaps the greatest danger with impotence is that if the episodes recur, the fear of failure leads to a greater likelihood of failure the next time. Thus, a reinforcing pattern is established. By recognizing our broader sexuality, this pattern can be broken. Pleasure doesn't depend solely on the man's ability to have an erection. By being able to say, "Okay, let's be with each other without having intercourse, let's hold and kiss each other, find out what feels good on different parts of our bodies, and what ways we can satisfy each other," partners can become sexual in the more complete sense. They can find out a great deal about themselves, one another and the many variations of sex and love-making that are pleasurable and satisfying.

Impotence can signal or stem from many different emotions within a man or a relationship. While initially the most helpful move is to eliminate any pressure on the man to perform, eventually he may have to confront the deeper issues that are being expressed sexually in order to regain his potency.

Feelings of guilt may have to be overcome. It's remarkable how many adults have had poor or distorted sex educations and still believe that all kinds of things are wrong or bad. Reassurance, support and education can go a long way toward alleviating guilt, and gradually, if we are open to new experiences, we may be able to modify our earlier learning.

Unexpressed anger is one of the most common underlying causes of impotence. A man's pent-up rage may result in his bottling up his sexual feelings. Sometimes, if one can pinpoint the cause of the anger and encourage the man to express his feelings about some specific incident or person, he may become much more potent in the sexual act.

Frequently, anger and resentment arise from within the marital relationship. If a husband feels that his wife has been excessively harsh, has neglected him, isn't doing what he wants her to, or is looking at other men, then he may become impotent as a way of showing his rage. He can punish her for what he experiences as an affront to his self-esteem. Thus, the power struggle is played out sexually. (The same thing sometimes happens in reverse when sex is used as an aggressive, hostile acting out. Anger and resentment can be expressed through rough, hard love-play. People can get rid of a great deal of annoyance and anger sexually, and if it's a release for both of them, this may be very helpful.)

When considering the underlying causes of impotence, you should place it within the context of the life and development of the man and the marriage. For instance, if a husband gets impotent shortly after he's been married, I have to question the part played by the marriage itself and the interaction with the partner. Sometimes the very act of marriage makes a woman less of a sex object in the man's eyes. She's his wife, and a wife is in a different category than a girlfriend or lover. The man may become impotent or simply less interested in sex. It's also true that availability can reduce desirability. In fact, there seems to be evidence in parts of our society that we've been so satiated and bombarded by sex that we may be entering a period of diminished excitement and interest in it.

Newlyweds sometimes discover that they're "out of sync" in terms of timing. Perhaps the husband is a day person and the wife is a night person. Their body rhythms are different. She wants to have intercourse when he wants to go to sleep. He wakes her in the morning to make love, but she's not feeling sexy. However, if people have real desire and there's no other underlying problem, it's usually possible to compromise.

If the timing of love-making becomes a real problem, you have to look for other causes. For instance, there may be a power struggle that's being acted out. If each person has a need for control and one gives in and has intercourse at a time that the other prefers, the other has won. However, if the man gives in and then is impotent, the woman has not won—and the man (in a self-defeating sense) has triumphed.

There can be all kinds of reasons for a change in a man's sexuality after marriage. It can reflect a feeling that the partner is too demanding or a fear that she wants to swallow him up with more closeness than he can tolerate. If a man hasn't worked out his competitive feelings with his father, he may fear that winning this woman will bring some sort of terrible retaliation. Once he has his prize, it becomes dangerous. He feels safer if he doesn't enjoy it; then he can pretend that it doesn't exist, deny its reality and diminish the parental threat.

Sometimes a man can unconsciously project onto his wife the aspect of the angry, punitive mother. Possibly he could tell an angry, punitive wife to go to hell. But if he's unconsciously a little boy to a mother-figure/wife, he can't tell her to go to hell, so to protect himself, he withdraws his penis.

If impotence occurs later on in the marriage in a man's middle thirties, it can reflect the tensions of business, where the man may be striving to achieve and make his mark. It can also be the beginning of that self-doubt which often takes place between the ages of thirty-five and forty-five. It might reflect a need to explore and confront his identity as a male and a husband.

Impotence that occurs around a man's fifties deserves careful consideration of what's happening between the couple and within the home. Have the children left? Is there a conflict taking place between the partners? Has the wife entered menopause? Is she unable to be responsive or available? Sometimes the husband takes this as evidence that he's no longer desirable. He may see her menopausal symptoms as an indication that she's getting old, and he may become frightened and turned off. This, combined with his own sense of aging, can militate against his being able to have an erection.

The dynamic between husband and wife is highly individual, and therefore generalizations are useful only as a starting point to encourage further exploration.

A husband once said to me very angrily, "Can you picture screwing a woman who never shows any emotion? I mean, she's warm and loving as long as it's not connected to sex, but the minute she senses I'm getting interested, she turns to cardboard. So I'm not interested anymore."

Taken by itself, this statement might suggest that the wife's needs were for the kind of cuddling and warmth that a young child receives. She was afraid to be responsive on a mature sexual level because she hadn't developed to a point where she was ready to have "genital" love.

But when the wife entered the dialogue, her perception of this same sexual relationship was, "My husband can be gentle and warm, like when we're in bed watching TV together. But whenever he wants to have sex, he just jumps on me and expects me to somehow be ready. I'm not. I need to be held and kissed first."

It now becomes clear that these two people have defined sex in different terms. The husband feels that there's a sharp division between warmth and loving sexuality in the broader sense and the kind of sex that happens during intercourse. To him, genital sex has to be aggressive, an act of conquering. He has to leap on his wife and take her, but he's resentful when she just lies there and doesn't respond. He doesn't want a dead object because who can conquer a dead thing?

His wife, on the other hand, cannot tolerate this division between aspects of sexuality. She needs to feel totally loved, wanted, secure and desirable, not just wanted genitally. She needs to feel that she's accepted as a loving human being. Possibly she's having some difficulty defining herself as lovable or she wouldn't need so much reassurance.

A couple's success in dealing with problems of potency depends to a great degree upon their understanding and the quality of communication they can establish with each other. If the impotence continues and fear, resentment or guilt are great, it's wise to seek help from a qualified marital or sex therapist.

Premature Ejaculation

A man has the ability to learn when he's going to have an orgasm, and he can learn how to control it consciously for a long time if he really wants to. What may be preventing control is his lack of awareness of what's happening to him, his inability to postpone gratification or some underlying anger or anxiety. Premature ejaculation can be symptomatic of a conflict in the marriage, in which case the man is determined (perhaps without being aware of it) to hurt and frustrate his wife by getting things over in a hurry. It's his way of saying, "Piss on you," and in a sense, it is almost like urination.

Premature ejaculation usually requires ongoing therapy under professional care. For it to be successful, both spouses must be unambivalent about wanting to help each other and make the marriage work because they both have to participate in the two techniques commonly used. One is the *squeeze technique* developed by Masters and Johnson, in which finger pressure is applied to the underside of the penis near the head just prior to orgasm. The other is the *stop and start technique*, invented by James Seamens, in which the woman is moving on top of the man; when he reaches the point of ejaculation, she then gets off. Both techniques are effective when used under the guidance of a sex and/or marital therapist.

Female Unresponsiveness

When a woman is aroused, one of the physical changes that takes place is a moistening of the vagina. Conversely, if she's feeling sexually unresponsive, her vagina doesn't become wet; and for a woman, this is approximately the equivalent of a man's not having an erection.

In a small percentage of cases, a woman's lack of arousal has physiological causes. For instance, some women experience dryness in the vagina after menopause due to a lack of estrogen. Effective treatment under a gynecologist's supervision may include the use of a local estrogenic cream or hormone pills.

For the great majority of women, psychological factors are the underlying causes of sexual nonresponsiveness or "frigidity," a word I dislike. Beneath the woman's cool exterior are some of the most powerful feelings anyone can experience.

Low self-esteem and/or a poor body image seem to be the factors that most frequently contribute to making a woman unresponsive. Until a woman has worked through her view of herself as a worthwhile person and a sexually attractive being, she can't experience the freedom and trust that are so crucial to her ability to respond sexually and feel aroused or erotic.

After all, moments of intimacy expose us both physically and emotionally. When you feel a need to hide or withhold parts of yourself from another—usually because you fear being rejected if you reveal everything—then you can't be open, relaxed and spontaneous. If you feel inadequate, unattractive, unlovable, unworthy, then you can't believe this other person really loves and accepts you. How can you respond to him? How can you trust him to be caring? You may have tremendous difficulty asking for something, or giving, or accepting what's offered. In a sense, we all unconsciously protect ourselves from an expected rejection by rejecting first.

Body image, the way a woman sees herself, is a subjective phenomenon, not related to physical appearance. A woman who might objectively be described as ordinary looking or even unattractive may have a positive view of herself, whereas a stunning model may be anguished because she feels she's too fat or thin, her breasts are the wrong shape, her body is too hairy. Such views usually go back to impressions we formed during childhood and adolescence.

I had a patient who was an extraordinarily beautiful woman. She was a talented designer who married one of New York's most eligible bachelors. They looked like a couple created by Hollywood. They were also both intelligent and articulate. But this woman had grown up in a home with rigid standards. Her father was a super-achiever and a distanced person; her mother, a highly critical, demanding person with an underlying sense of her own inferiority. This beautiful, gifted woman thought of herself as "shit." If there was an extra ounce of fat on her body, she felt hideous. She dieted regularly and rigorously. She considered herself too tall, something she couldn't change, which made her feel hopelessly and permanently awkward.

She couldn't believe this marvelous man had married *her*, and she constantly feared she'd lose him to another woman. She frequently provoked him into attacks against her because she actually found it less confusing when his opinion of her appeared to coincide with her own terrible view of herself. Gradually he became confused. Here he thought he'd married a princess, but she kept broadcasting messages that she was worthless. Their sexual activity became a reenactment of their emotional life, filled with her provocations, his attacks and her self-disparaging comments. Finally she withdrew from both the sexual and marital relationship.

Another woman came to me because she didn't feel sexually attracted to her husband. She couldn't discuss sex with him because she felt guilty about her lack of responsive arousal. She'd feel herself physically tighten up as soon as there was any attempt to have sex. Still, she'd grit her teeth and try to perform the way a "good wife" should.

Although a very complex psychological picture was eventually revealed, I think it's worth simplifying and summarizing the basic elements.

This patient had been brought up by well-educated parents in a household filled with fine music, literature, and so forth. There were vigorous demands made for her to perform on the highest level. At the same time, there was a hidden message from her parents that sex was dirty and one should focus on the "better things in life."

This woman had married her husband even though his physical appearance didn't fit her ideal, and she wasn't strongly attracted to him at the time. She said, "I didn't think the physical aspect was that important."

Marrying a man who wasn't especially attractive or sexually appealing enabled her to keep sex in its "proper place." Consciously, she thought that her selection showed what a profound person she was because she wasn't taken in by looks or superficial concerns. Subconsciously, because her self-esteem was very low, she needed somebody who could make her feel desirable without making threatening demands upon her. And part of the soundness of her selection was that her husband was a steady, stable person who provided a nurturing environment and helped her reach the point where she could accept and express her own sexuality.

Unfortunately as she became more secure and her self-esteem developed, she began to say, "What am I doing with this guy? Why am I here? What's in it for me? I could do better than this." At that point she came to see me. She had become extremely critical of her husband. While she still loved him, she was convinced he could never be the man she wanted and now had begun to feel she deserved.

I thought she needed help to grow further in terms of her feelings of self-worth. Then she could at least see that her mate didn't have to be an extension of herself. A woman may try to win a particularly handsome man as a way of showing that she's desirable, but she doesn't have to do that if she already knows she's desirable. Furthermore, while this patient believed herself ready for a more passionate, fulfilling sexual relationship, she still wasn't secure enough to be able to talk to her own loving husband about what she wanted within their sexual life. Essentially, she was hoping that a different, more attractive man would sweep her away, bring out her sensual nature and take over the responsibility for her sexual fulfillment. However, this kind of dependency would probably maintain her immaturity and vulnerability. I felt that if she continued in therapy, alone at first, then jointly with her husband, there was a good chance for a solid relationship to develop between these two people.

There are many possible reasons besides low self-esteem and a poor body image that can cause a woman to be sexually unresponsive. She may be reacting to a fear of closeness or an anxiety about her performance. There may be an underlying conflict about allowing herself to have pleasure with a man. She may unconsciously feel she doesn't deserve and shouldn't have this enjoyment. There may be childhood feelings of guilt attached to it or unconscious fears of punishment from her mother if she competes by winning a man. In rarer cases, there is a fear of penetration, a fear of something foreign entering her body. This is related to very early childhood and can result in vaginismus, or a severe contraction of the vagina.

Occasionally a woman expresses anger at her husband, or hostility toward men in general, by non-responsiveness. A woman may feel that a man isn't acting like a man in other areas of their lives, and rather than express this directly, she won't permit him to feel like a man in bed. Sometimes she denies his masculinity by taking over the dominant role and becoming more aggressive than is tolerable for him.

Sometimes it's possible for a woman to do a lot of self-exploration and also get support from her partner so that she can begin to work through some of the deeper feelings that may be determining her attitude toward sex. In other cases, it's best for her to get professional help.

Female Orgasm

One of the most common problems I hear from women is that they begin to be responsive, but then something happens before they reach orgasm. There's a halt and they turn off even as they sense the possibility of a climax.

Orgasm is a separate physiological phenomenon from arousal. While most men progress quite naturally from one to the other, women frequently experience more complications. Often they feel there's something wrong with them. Yet orgastic dysfunction and sexual unresponsiveness are the two most common complaints of women seeking sexual counseling. I think our cultural conditioning plays a major role in this difficulty women have.

Although the emphasis today is on a woman's right to express her sexuality openly and fully, most women have absorbed a different message in childhood. "Ladies don't do that. It's not nice. Take your hand away from there. Don't get messy, you won't look pretty. Don't you want to be our pretty little girl? Now, you get control of yourself and act like a civilized young lady, not a savage." But how do you reconcile the need to do what's "nice," to look pretty, to keep control and to "be a lady" with the excesses of letting go and reaching orgasm? Should it really be surprising when a woman unconsciously fears that if she allows herself to let go (becoming sweaty, noisy, messy or violent) and reach the point of orgasm, her partner will see her as ugly or undesirable and think of her as an animal? The idea of a sexually free, unrestrained, aggressive woman is still a new concept. Someone who's been taught to be passive and obedient will understandably fear that her sexual requests and demands will bring rejection from the male.

Furthermore, lack of restraint may be a threat to the woman's own sense of boundaries. "Where do I stop? Can I contain myself? What's going to happen to me if I'm not in control?"

A woman may unconsciously go through all kinds of maneuvers to avoid losing control. She may adjust the lighting, the temperature or the bed, or require certain things of her husband before she's ready to have intercourse. This "program" is her way of controling her environment. This mastery is her way of dealing with her anxieties about sex. Usually the woman explains her behavior logically: "I don't like the room too bright . . . it's more romantic to have music . . . I need time to get relaxed first . . . ." But the clue to the pattern lies in the rigidity of the steps she insists on taking one by one and in the proper order.

"I tell him what I want and he doesn't do it," Ginny said unhappily. "How am I supposed to feel good and want to make love when he ignores all the things that might put me in the mood?"

Her husband, Artie, said, "My God, before she's ready we have to go through a whole script that starts with fixing the lights, taking the phone off the hook, then I should hold her and kiss her and undress her slowly . . . ."

"Well, what's wrong with any of that?" Ginny demanded.

Artie ignored the question. "It's as though the minute we get in the bedroom, every move is choreographed like a ballet. But by the time her program gets around to intercourse, I don't want it. I'm not ready anymore."

I asked, "What do you think is going on between the two of you? What do you suppose you're really doing to each other?"

Ginny said, "He just wants everything his way."

Artie slammed his hand against the side of his chair. "That's ridiculous. You're the one who won't give an inch. Everything has to be according to your outline."

"That's *right*," I said. "*Both* of you feel that the other one needs to have everything his way."

"Well, shouldn't he want to please me if I tell him what makes me feel good and if I'm ready to please him? Why won't he do some of the things that make me feel ready to have sex with him?"

"What Artie has just said to you is that this preparation is so lengthy and prolonged that it turns him off."

"But I can't help that." Ginny sounded frightened. "I need to be kissed and held and stroked. Maybe there can be some aggressiveness, but I can't enjoy anything if he's suddenly grabbing me and it's bang, bang, bang."

I looked at Artie. "Is that what you want to do? Grab her and bang, bang, bang?"

He smiled uncertainly. "Sure, I think that would be terrific some of the time. I mean, it would really be super if just once when I had a hard-on she'd say, 'Great, let's screw.' "

"You know," I said, "you are both describing things that are fine and acceptable. And some people can really run the gamut, trying and enjoying many different ways of being together. But let's try to find out what it is that's turning you off and making certain things totally unacceptable. Because the greatest source of our sexual excitement and response stems from within each of us. After that it can be enhanced· by our partner." I turned toward Ginny. "Suppose, for example, *most* of the time Artie held you, kissed you and made love to you the way you prefer. Do you feel that you might be able to react more spontaneously at other times when he might prefer to do things more quickly and aggressively?"

Ginny hesitated. "I don't know. I guess maybe—if I really felt he was ready to do things my way, then sometimes I'd . . . ." She stopped, startled. "I didn't mean to make it sound like my way against his," she apologized.

"But is it possible that that's part of what's happening here?" I asked. "Do the two of you think there may be other phases of your lives where you're each trying to dominate or maintain equal control with the other? Do you suppose that each of you feels threatened when the other takes over?"

In order to be able to give up some control some of the time, people may have to explore general feelings toward power in the marital relationship, as well as the more specific question of control in sexuality.

One of the things professional therapists suggest to non-orgastic women is learning how to masturbate first. If you discover how to excite yourself and allow yourself to be out of control, then you may learn to be more comfortable with this new sensation of abandonment. We also suggest that the man masturbate the woman to the point of orgasm, then introduce the penis while he is masturbating her, and then ultimately explore full vaginal intercourse together.

Trust is essential. If a woman gets to the point of orgasm and lets go, she has to have complete trust that her lover will not hurt or reject her.

Communication is essential, even about "details." No one is

a mind reader. A graduate student of mine told me after a seminar on sexuality that she always felt a little uncomfortable and self-conscious because her husband would stare at her when she became sexually excited. Finally she asked him if he'd rather close his eyes and he said, "Are you crazy? That's one of the sexiest things about it—watching your face!" And my student said, "Suddenly I thought, why not? After all, it turned *me* on to see him when *he* was excited. For the first time I really started relaxing and going with my feelings. But the ridiculous part is that we'd been married two years before we talked about this."

In the past, it was relatively common for women to lie about having had an orgasm. I don't believe that pretending helps anybody. Coming isn't the be-all and end-all of everything, and by understanding this, you can work toward a better sexual experience. Perhaps the woman wants to say, "No, I didn't come, but I enjoyed it and I feel great," or "No, I didn't come and it's not okay. Maybe if you manipulated me now . . . ." or "If we went on a little longer, I could have come. Maybe next time we can do . . . ." There are so many different ways of having an orgasm that it seems totally unnecessary for a woman to say she's had one when she hasn't. Why lie unless there's a tremendous fear of inadequacy on the woman's part or a feeling that the man is too fragile to take it?

As people begin to demystify the orgasm, women lie less and less about it. It certainly doesn't represent a man's success in "giving the woman an orgasm" as it's usually described and thought of. Sexual satisfaction really depends on the woman's ability to take responsibility for her own sexuality, to respond and request, and to feel comfortable with the special kind of self-involvement that's part of the sexual climax.

There are two issues that in and of themselves seldom cause couples to seek counseling, yet they come up time and again when people are in therapy.

The first is sexual boredom.

You're bound to get used to another person after a certain amount of time, but what are you doing to alleviate that? There's a prototypical conversation that I have with couples on this subject:

"Have you been trying to do things to reduce the boredom? We know all kinds of fun and games. Have you tried anything different?" I'll ask.

"Well, that's not really our style, trying anything freaky or kinky," they'll say.

"I'm not talking about freaky, just stimulating. The opposite of boring. When do you usually have sex?"

"At night. You know, when things are quiet in the house."

"How is sex when you go away for a weekend on your own?"

"Well, come to think of it, it does get more exciting then. Sometimes we make love in the morning. And it's kind of fun to be in different beds . . ."

"Sure. That's right. And what does that tell you?"

"That a change of surroundings . . ."

"Sure, and also changing the way you do things. Usually after a period of time couples fall into certain ways of making love. A few kisses, a few touches, a few this, a few that, then intercourse and that's it. Try something else. Try massage. Try entry from different positions. Try delaying. There are many variations and they're all good. There are good sex manuals available, which you can look at together and see what turns you on. Go to a porno film as an adventure or do something else that's offbeat, to make life more interesting and exciting."

The second issue that couples may want to consider is what it means when they let other activities take precedence over making love. If they never have time or are always too tired from doing other things, is it a sign that love-making causes them anxiety so they try unconsciously to avoid it? Or are they perhaps just ignoring the fact that in this busy society of ours, if we really want something, we have to plan for it, reserve time for ourselves, and feel we have the absolute right to shut the rest of the world out.

When my husband and I went to Norway, we noticed that in some of the small hamlets, the houses had flags. Some of them would be up, others would be down. We asked someone what that meant and he said, "When the flag is up, it means the people in the house are ready to accept visitors. When the flag is down, it means the people do not wish to be disturbed. Everybody knows these signals and accepts them."

I think that's a perfectly marvelous way of saying, "It's not that we don't like you, but we are otherwise engaged and unavailable to you right now!"

16. Extramarital Sexuality

"Thank you for seeing me," Mrs. Griffin said.

"I'm glad I . . . ."

My patient cut off the conventionalities in a dull voice. "That was in our mailbox this morning." She gave me an envelope. "It's my husband's handwriting and that's our return address. I don't know who Cynthia Webster is."

The letter was addressed to Cynthia Webster in Los Angeles, but the envelope had no postage. Stamped across the front was a bold, red message: "Returned for Postage." I took out a single sheet of paper.

Dear Cinny,

Arriving the 19th for a week! Where have you been? I've been trying to phone you for three days. Will be famished when I get there.

Love,
R.

The informality added to the note's intimacy. I folded the letter, reinserted it and put the envelope on the table between us. Linda Griffin watched, expressionless. She wasn't wearing makeup, and her face looked puffy.

"I feel like such a fool." Her voice was low. "I still can't believe this is happening. I don't even know what I'm doing here because I don't want to cope with any of it or even try to solve anything. I just can't stand the pain." Her voice broke and she started crying. "I don't want this. It hurts too much." She bent forward in the chair and wept.

It was evening. Mrs. Griffin had called me that morning while I was in session. The message service told me she was crying and sounded terribly distraught. I didn't know her, but she'd left the name of a former patient who was a friend of hers. I called her back, listened briefly and told her to come over after my last scheduled appointment.

She stopped crying. "We've been married for fifteen years." She took a deep breath. "We had our problems, but we worked them out. By ourselves." There was a hint of a challenge. I nodded and waited. "I thought we were getting along better than we had in years. Do you understand, I loved and trusted this man. We've been through a lot together. And I *believed* he loved me. This morning before he left for the airport, he kissed me on the mouth and told me he loved me." Her voice started to break and then grew harsh. "He told me not to work too hard and that he'd call me tonight. I hope he enjoys not getting any answer. I hope the bastard's worried sick." She gave an anguished laugh. "Worried. He's probably phoning while he's with his little chickie. All this time that son of a bitch was living with me and lying to me while I'm getting his laundry and packing his fucking valise—there's an appropriate use for that word. How long? Six months? Six years? Oh God, he's been going to California since his company bought a factory out there nearly six years ago." Her voice rose, and the pain spilled out. "And I'm worrying about his flying so much. How could I have been such a stupid, blind fool? Poor Richy, coming home exhausted, needing to be taken care of almost like a little boy. The cheating bastard. I never thought I could hate someone this much. Now I know why he was so exhausted. He used to come back on the red-eye special, Sunday nights. He'd make the evening plane out of LA and get in around six in the morning. And I'd be up, asking if he'd like some scrambled eggs. I'd put him to bed for a couple of hours and he'd practically fall asleep while I was holding him, telling him it was so good to have him home. I was holding him probably just hours after she had. And he let me. The bastard *let* me after he'd been with her, doing things with her. When I picture the two of them together—oh, no." She buried her face in her hands. "No."

After a moment she looked up. "You want to hear something funny?" A dry, mirthless laugh escaped. "A couple of years ago I almost had an affair with a guy at work. I said no, I couldn't because if my husband ever found out it would break up our marriage. Don't you think that's amusing?" The sarcasm left her voice abruptly. "I don't know why I'm here." She stared at the envelope. "Our marriage is over. I guess I just didn't know what to say to him." The words were soft and questioning.

I said, "I wonder if your marriage is really over." Her eyes sought mine. "It doesn't sound to me as though it's over." I was speaking gently, watching her shake her head. "I know you're terribly hurt now. You have great pain. I can feel it. But let's see whether your marriage really is over or not. Let's see what the marriage is all about. Obviously if you almost had an affair a few years ago, something must have been going on in your marriage for quite some time. What made you want to do that?" She looked away. "Can you tell me a little about the kind of marriage you had, why you married him, how old you were? Tell me something about yourself. I really need to get to know you.

Discovering that your spouse has been having an affair is almost always a devastating experience. Even for the strongest, most autonomous kind of person, there are usually deep feelings of pain, rage, anxiety, inadequacy, rejection and distrust. "I've failed . . . been betrayed . . . I'm not loved. He (or she) has been unfaithful. Our marriage is destroyed."

Yet the implications of extramarital sex are far from obvious. It isn't necessarily a sign that love has ended or that the "betrayed" partner has somehow failed. **Sometimes there are reasons that have nothing to do with the parnter that cause the spouse to turn elsewhere, and act out his or her needs with someone else.** There's so much that must be considered. My initial interview with Linda Griffin barely touched the real issues. But even her first brief description of what had occurred raised many questions we would have to come back to. What *was* her marriage with Richard all about? What problems did she feel they'd worked out? She feels she takes care of him "almost like a little boy." Is that a dynamic in the relationship? How does it affect Richard? Is he acting out something with Cynthia that may have very little to do with his wife?

He kissed his wife and told her he loved her. No one had a gun at his head. He has apparently known this other woman for some time, yet has always returned to his wife. What makes him stay with Linda? What are the strengths in this marital relationship? And why did the letter to Cynthia come back in the first place? Had a postage stamp simply fallen off, or had Richard mailed it without postage, subconsciously wanting to be discovered? What made Linda immediately open the envelope? Was she aware of the situation on some level? She seems to have recognized there was an unusual element about her husband's travel schedule. Was it something she wasn't ready to face until now? And finally, can this marriage and these two people withstand the impact of what has happened?

Today we almost all live with a major conflict and contradiction about our sexuality. On the one hand, contemporary society has adopted an increasingly open and permissive attitude toward sex. Many people who believe in their right and need to be responsive human beings want to feel free to experiment sexually and have relationships outside marriage. But the fact is that a lot of feelings we think of as old-fashioned and discarded *still exist.* Our deepest attitudes, ingrained since early childhood, may well prohibit extramarital sexuality. So the partner who indulges in it feels guilty or may actually be inhibited and unable to respond. The spouse who discovers it experiences all the emotions we've described. And almost inevitably, when "infidelity" comes to light, the marriage is thrown into a crisis.

I don't like to use the words "infidelity" and "unfaithfulness." They're too negative and can make it more difficult to deal with an already distressing situation. However, for those people who feel that extramarital sexuality is morally wrong and involves the breaking of sacred vows, there *is* a sense of having been totally betrayed. If these vows can be broken, then there's nothing. The one who did this is wicked, unfaithful, morally corrupt.

To make a marriage like that function again takes an enormous amount of patience and effort and also requires a basically good, solid relationship. And I don't think it's ever the same. There always remains some doubt and uncertainty, some feeling of betrayal. However, it may still be possible for such a couple to cope with what has happened, and for the first time face the fact that they haven't had a good sex life together or haven't been communicating closely with each other. Even if they can't restore the marriage to its former condition, perhaps they can establish a different relationship that in some ways may be more rewarding.

Generally, when two people have a deep moral or religious commitment, it seems ill-advised for one of them to take the chance of having an affair. What could you gain that would be worth all that you could lose? Yet even a morally committed individual can do something that seems totally out of character. Everybody has all kinds of feelings. An observer might be astounded. "But he was a church-going man, and he had such high moral values. How could he . . ."

As a psychologist, I raise many questions about why some people become utterly rigid in their values, why they have to hold themselves in such tight check and why they are so punitive about things a spouse might do.

Speaking as a layperson, I suggest that even people with the strictest moral and religious code might do well to remember that forgiveness is a biblical injunction. When we set ourselves up to be moral judges, we really have to question *our* motives, too. "Let he who is without sin cast the first stone."

Perhaps a man says, "I never had an affair. I knew it was wrong. And if she had a decent character, believed in our marriage vows, and loved me the way I love her, she would have controlled herself." In this case, one must ask, "What goes into your view of what constitutes love? What kind of love has no room in it for mistakes? Is your feeling loving or possessing? Can you value the other person for who *she* is? While your experience is terribly painful and requires a lot of healing, is it possible for you to feel some element of understanding and forgiveness in order to suspend absolute judgment?"

I honestly believe the concept behind an open marriage, in which partners have mutual freedom to form outside alliances, is theoretically ideal. Wouldn't it be marvelous if people were mature enough so that they wouldn't be the least bit hurt or threatened when a spouse entered into a relationship with another person? But it just doesn't work that way. Open marriage is only an ideal. Most of us can't tolerate the feelings that arise when we share an intimate part of our spouse with somebody else.

"I'm having—or want to have—an affair."

A man in therapy once called me from Madrid, where he was attending an international conference for his company. He was forty-five years old, a successful top executive. He'd been married for twenty-two years, and had a college-age daughter. For some time, he'd been thinking about having intercourse with other women, and we'd been discussing some of his reasons. He felt that he'd given his best years to his family, and he was feeling increasingly restless and dissatisfied. He wanted a passionate relationship. Now he was phoning to tell me that he'd met a marvelous, attractive executive at his conference. He'd slept with her three times, and suddenly this sophisticated, intelligent fellow believed he was head over heels in love. He was talking seriously about leaving his wife for this new love which had only existed for three or four days.

I said, "I certainly can appreciate the experience you're having. Sometimes people do fall in love at first sight, and sometimes it can last. But in light of the fact that you've had an ongoing marriage for so many years, and that a lot of what you've been saying about the marriage has been positive and good, it seems to me that we need to take time out to think and talk about this exhilarating, new experience and what it might mean."

Many people feel that the only thing that justifies having sex outside of marriage is love. Therefore, if they do become sexually involved with someone, *it must be love* with all the consequences that implies. While there's a liberated, largely urban segment of our society that doesn't believe this any more, the idea still exists widely. And people sometimes do get divorced for absurd reasons. A man suddenly gets turned on by somebody, says, "My God, I haven't felt this way in fifteen years," and walks out on his marriage. Sometimes, of course, people can bring that arousal into the marriage and become very responsive again. You see this kind of activity quite often at cocktail parties, where people have stimulating flirtations—then they go home and have exciting sex with their own mates.

There are all kinds of reasons that may cause a person to engage in extramarital sex. Perhaps there's a need for variety or for reassurance that one is still sexually desirable. It may be a way of feeling more valued, more exciting and excited, stimulating and stimulated. It can be an acting out of rebelliousness, a feeling that your spouse is like your father or mother, and you're going to break the rules. It can be a way of saying, "I'm my own person; I'm going to assert my independence." Sometimes it's the result of a fear of closeness; an affair is one means of establishing distance from the spouse.

Extramarital sex doesn't necessarily reflect a lack of love for the spouse and certainly doesn't have to mean the end of the marriage. A person can have one or two experiences with somebody else and see it for what it is—a temporary but exciting fling. Perhaps it was a good experience: "It put a fillip into my life and I feel better about myself. I'm even able to be more responsive to my husband." Maybe it was a mistake: "I don't know what I was thinking. She seemed so attractive, and my wife was off visiting her family. But I found out she's not half the woman my wife is. I feel like an absolute jackass and very ashamed."

Under some circumstances, extramarital sex can be constructive to the marriage. It's possible for two people who have a rich and rewarding relationship in almost every way not to be on the same sexual wavelength. An outside liaison may enable a spouse to release some sexual tension and take a lot of pressure off the marriage.

One of the most destructive aspects of even a "trivial" affair is the way in which one's feelings toward the spouse are acted out. Frequently, the person who's having an affair leaves a trail. Unconsciously, he or she wants to be found out. The wanting usually is rooted in either hostility or guilt.

In addition, there's often an impulse or need to confess. "I was so curious to know what another man was like because I never had anyone except my husband. In a way, I'm glad I did it. Now I know there's not such a big difference! And I wouldn't give up my husband for anything in the world. But I'm worried. Should I tell my husband about it? *Is it fair not to tell him?*"

I'm all for honesty in most situations, but I think a person really has to question his or her motives for telling a spouse about having had intercourse with someone else. Are you using the confession as a way of showing hostility and dissatisfaction, as a means of getting back at your mate? Do you feel so guilty that you can't stand it and want to share the guilt? If so, was it mature to have entered into an experience when you weren't able to bear the consequences? Rather than risk devastating your spouse, perhaps an outside counselor might help you to deal with the guilt in a less hurtful way.

Sometimes there's a wish to verbally explore what's been happening within the marital relationship. But is a confession the appropriate or constructive method? In most cases, I'd have to doubt that.

When an affair is extremely intense, continues and remains important, one must question its meaning closely. "Is it because this is forbidden? How would I feel after I was married to this new man or woman for three years? What is *not* going on in my marriage?" After all, having an affair is very complicated. It takes a lot of time and energy. You have to arrange for it and do a lot of lying. Sometimes it's bound to be frustrating. Therefore, if it does endure, the chances are that something in addition to sexual passion is involved.

When a person feels there's something missing in the marriage, it's vital to ask whether it legitimately belongs within a marital relationship. Can it be gratified within marriage? If you need a variety of sexual partners, your spouse can't satisfy this. You then have to acknowledge the need and say, "What am I willing to do for it? What risks am I willing to take?" In the long run, it may be helpful to consider whether the need should be gratified, or explored and possibly modified.

For instance, some men and women continually become involved in one affair after another. Maybe they say, "I need variety," yet it's likely that something else is going on here. The three-way relationship of an affair evokes all kinds of earlier feelings about Oedipal and pre-Oedipal triangles. Adults who engage in repeated affairs are often acting out a competition with one parent. There has to be a forbidden element to it, as well as a lot of guilt and anxiety, which maintain the high pitch of the fantasy. It's like a man capturing his mother away from his father, then feeling guilty about it. It only works as long as he can keep it sub rosa. Once he has her, she's no longer forbidden, so she becomes trivial—like his wife—and he goes after another woman. Women, as well as men, go on like this. The capture is the element that's exciting. Capturing the male, knowing you're winning out over another female—over mother—proving your desirability as a woman. But if this is not a life pattern one wishes to maintain, then professional help is needed.

Pre-Oedipal feelings have to do with the insatiable wish to be loved and satisfied in the way you wish you had been when you were a baby. To be "one" with mother is a universal need of every human being regardless of sex. If the baby is not helped by the mother to separate gradually and become an autonomous person, he or she may continue to seek that idyllic relationship all through life. A man or woman may constantly seek this kind of loving from others than the spouse, taking primary pleasure not so much in adult sexuality, but in haunting childhood memories of being one with mother.

I think that part of today's extramarital sexuality stems from a desire for a passionate, exciting relationship—the kind of consuming attraction that is perpetuated by the media, but cannot be sustained in a long-term marriage, no matter how creative the two people are. You have to make a choice. You have to ask yourself, "Do I want to and can I contain a very exciting, emotionally stimulating affair and still go on with my marriage? If not, is there enough of value within the marriage so that I want to maintain it even though I'll have less passion than I'd really like? Or do I feel that my marriage is insufficient in so many ways that I have to terminate it for a different kind of relationship?"

Many people question and even refuse to tolerate the dwindling of passion, and finally they question the whole marital relationship. There are very few marriages so solid that they can withstand the lack of passion, especially when alternatives are offered. So people say, "Why should I stay in this? I want something more." It's a dilemma that has no completely satisfactory solution.

"I think my spouse is having an affair. What should I do?"

Some decisions have to be made. Do you want to know? Do you want to confront your partner? Perhaps you're looking for a denial, but you must be prepared to hear your spouse say, "Yes, you're right, I've been seeing someone else."

Suppose you do want to raise the issue. The least constructive approach is to make accusations or vent your feelings in a name-calling attack. Your partner will probably withdraw or strike back. Nothing useful will be accomplished, and great damage can be done.

It's most helpful to try to bring up the subject at a time when you're relatively in control of your feelings. Perhaps you can simply say, "I may be crazy, but I have a feeling that you're having an affair with somebody." In this way, you leave the options open for the partner to say yes or no. If the partner says, "No, that's not so," you have to be prepared to accept the fact that this may or may not be true. You can try to examine it and say, "The reason I feel like this is because of the way you've been acting. You don't come home at the usual time. When you do, you seem distant. We used to be close and have a drink together before dinner, but now you want to go off by yourself." If you can document the things that are causing your unease, then frequently it gives the partner an opportunity to explain. "I had no idea that's what you were thinking. I'm sorry. It's just that there's been a major change at the company and it looks as though my job . . . ." I knew of a wife who was absolutely positive her husband was being unfaithful. They had a tremendous fight, and she nearly walked out of the marriage. It turned out that he was going for medical treatments for a problem he didn't want to frighten her with.

If your partner acknowledges that there is an affair or has confessed spontaneously, can you then establish the kind of communication that lets the two of you discuss what's been going on and why? When the confession is a shock, people react in a variety of ways. Sometimes they freeze, say nothing and walk away. They may feel it's the end of the world and, emotionally at least, collapse. There's almost always pain and distress, yet some people pretend to be casual and say, "So what else is new?" Sometimes the person who asked to know if there was an affair is nonetheless shocked upon hearing an affirmative answer. If you're too hurt or angry, discussion at this time may be impossible, and you can say so. But what can be done when the conscious, rational mind takes over? Once you have some self-control, how do you choose to handle the situation? In order to deal with the reality, you eventually have to find out why the affair was necessary. What has your partner been feeling? What does your partner need from a new relationship that wasn't or perhaps couldn't be forthcoming from the marriage?

"Are you having an affair?"

If you're asked this question and you're not, then your answer is easy. It probably should be followed by, "What made you think such a thing?"

If you are having an affair, you have to decide whether or not to admit it. Certainly there are times when that response will be inappropriate. For example, if your spouse has been sick, unavailable or in tremendous personal difficulties, and you know that your outside relationship is trivial, then admitting it might be destructive all around. It can obviously devastate someone who is having problems about the way he feels about himself. You really have to evaluate all the circumstances, including your motives and the probable impact on the other person, before giving an answer.

It does seem to me that if we're honest with ourselves, we'll consider questions like these before we are confronted with them. I don't think that's being cold-blooded. Rather it's appropriate and mature to recognize the possible consequences of our actions and to take the responsibility for coping with those consequences with a minimum of damage to another.

17. Financial Changes

In our society, the significance of money is enormous and highly complex. Not only does it sometimes represent love and power but also hostility when it's withheld. Money is a kind of bartering device that gives us control over other people and situations. Money represents our entry into the adult world, where we get to earn and use it. Money is closely related to status, to our sense of self-esteem. Lack of it makes people feel inadequate. Money can be economic security, but it can also be a form of emotional security for many. We confuse what we have with who we are.

When finances are stable and there is X amount of money available, couples tend to establish patterns and methods of handling whatever quantity there is. But if there's a sudden financial shift, a stressful situation is initiated. The previous equilibrium is disturbed. Whether it's a question of shifting from having no money to having a great deal or from having a lot of money to much less, the change almost invariably exacerbates earlier fears and upsets primary ways of relating.

For example, a sudden increase in fortune may cause a man or woman to think, "I'm a big shot now. You knew me when I was nothing, but I don't want anybody to view me that way any more. I want to be seen as someone important, successful, powerful. You make me feel little. I look at you and I think of my poor origins. I want to have somebody who looks at me with adoration and makes me feel I'm totally wonderful." This person may go out and buy a new house, a new wardrobe, a new car, a new mate and a new self-image. (Something similar often happens when women help men get through law school or medical school. The wife works hard for the man, but as soon as he gets to be a lawyer or a doctor, instead of adoring her for helping him, he leaves her.) What's revealed is a person whose own values and sense of self are uncertain and dependent on outside factors and opinions.

Some people react to a significant increase in money by suddenly going on wild sprees. They acquire without an end in sight. What comes to the fore is an inability to postpone gratification, a need to fulfill immediately all one's materialistic wishes like a hungry child. The spouse, who for the first time sees this need in his or her partner, is often shaken and very uncomfortable about it. "Will the control return? What does this stem from? Who *is* this person I married?"

The opposite of the person who goes on wild sprees is the individual who receives some money and develops a kind of tension about it, a feeling that "Now that I have it, I'm going to hold on to it. It says I'm great, I'm powerful, I'm successful. I'm not going to let anything happen to take this away from me."

The spouse of such an individual may be frustrated, angered or even frightened by the partner's need to retain every cent and his apparent satisfaction at just knowing it's there. "What's the matter with him? Aren't we going to spend a penny on anything that will give us some pleasure or make our lives more enjoyable? How can he get more reward out of having the money in the bank than from the things it could buy? Is he selfish? Sick? What's going on?"

In long-term therapy we help people to realize and deal with the underlying causes for their actions: why it's necessary for one person to cling to money while another has to go crazy with it, and what the symbolic meanings are for each. These are questions you and your partner may wish to explore together to whatever extent is comfortable or possible.

However, you can sometimes regain a sense of balance if you realize that what's happening now is really not unrelated to what has gone on before hand. You can usually trace earlier indications of this behavior if you look at a person's previous patterns. Rarely does somebody who was always very penurious inherit a fortune and suddenly become a mad spendthrift. People *usually* stay in character—although they may go to an extreme that wasn't possible previously. The "new" behavior may be a little less threatening if it doesn't create the impression that your partner has become a totally different person. (Obviously if somebody is out of control and you see money vanishing on luxuries when it's needed for essentials, you may want to seek professional help in exploring whether this person may have a self-destructive wish.)

I think the first thing to do is *question your own response* to your mate's behavior. In other words, we start with ourselves and try to see why we're reacting as we are. Then perhaps we'll be able to grant the other person more leeway to do what's necessary or satisfying for him. The questions you might ask are, "How does his behavior make me feel? Why does it make me feel that way? What meaning does it have for me? How much of this can I accept? Why does it pose a threat to me?"

"If suddenly my husband decides that he's going to go out and buy twenty-five suits with his bonus, why does that bother me? Do I think it means he wants to go out and seduce every woman he meets? Do I suddenly see him as a narcissist who's only involved in his own body? Am I afraid that *I'm* going to be bereft? That he's taking something away from me? If that's my fear, how realistic is it?"

For some people money represents the original source of supply. It can become like a mother's breast, the infant's source of milk, comfort, well-being and security. Anything that threatens to diminish it produces tremendous anxiety. "Something's being taken away from me; I'm being robbed." When money has this significance for someone, he can't tolerate a reduction in the bank account, since with the symbol gone, he feels in danger of starving to death. He visualizes himself as being destitute. Of course, the sense of destitution has nothing to do with reality. Yet this obsessive need can outweigh an actual need—for medical care, for example. This person is so desperately tied to the symbol that he'd prefer his spouse to borrow or obtain the needed money elsewhere.

Often such a person justifies wanting a nest egg with rational explanations that having money in the bank gives you a certain amount of choice and freedom of action. This is perfectly true, but the clue that something else is going on comes from the degree of anxiety exhibited when there's a necessity to disturb that center of security. For example, if you're talking about a couple who are relatively young, in good health and both capable of earning more money, then you have to question the desperate need for the security of an untouched nest egg. When money represents this kind of emotional as well as economic security, it generally requires professional help and a great deal of understanding before a person can recognize its symbolic significance for him. He needs to develop to the point where he can feel that he is, in fact, an adult, a competent human being who doesn't really need this symbolic source anymore because he's not going to starve to death without the breast in his mouth all the time.

Money is sometimes completely tied up with a person's sense of identity and self-esteem. An individual who feels hollow, incomplete and worthless as a human being may use money as a means of completing himself and acquiring a sense of worth. There may be nothing a partner can offer to compete with this person's need to earn, work and accumulate more. If anything happens to the financial "support," the person sees the loss as personally jeopardizing. People commit suicide because of lost fortunes. Marriages are shattered. Observers may say, "It just shows she loved him only for his money." But in fact, women who view the riches they receive as reflecting how valued and desirable they are may have great difficulty in dealing with the *self-doubts* that are raised by the spouse's financial loss.

In relationships where the partners have a certain amount of autonomy and inner security, a sudden increase or decrease in fortune is much less apt to become destructive to the individuals or the marriage. The stress of financial reversal can make a husband and wife rally and decide that they can work together as they did when they were younger. They may feel it gives them the chance to restructure and rebuild, the freedom to consider new career choices and different life-styles. It can be an exciting and rejuvenating experience.

Money and Power

A financial change can be especially disruptive when it also involves a shift in the power structure between husband and wife. In a typical relationship, the person who is generally more assertive and makes more of the decisions is the one who's bringing in the money. If this person suddenly loses a job or has a significant drop in income, or if his partner gets a tremendous raise or inherits a large sum, there is a shift in power. A relationship that's been comfortably balanced can be thrown out of kilter unless the partners are aware of what's happening and able to deal openly with the money-power question.

One of the first issues they must face is how the money is to be reallocated. There are many possibilities. I've known wives who began to earn more and took over the distribution of the money. I've also known women who've asked their husbands to handle their money, as well as those who gave their husbands an allowance. In every one of these cases, one or both partners resented the arrangement. The resentment arose out of the very concept of one person getting to hold the goodies and make all the decisions. Even when the allowance is generous, the very element of control that one spouse has over the other can lead to bitterness.

Women who have traditionally been in the position of receiving an allowance may remain quite satisfied as long as the generous dole continues. But if the money is taken away, or if the husband can no longer supply it at the same rate, she begins to resent the loss and feel that she's no longer loved and indulged as she deserves to be. As her feelings are manifested, the elements that money has masked are revealed.

For instance, when a husband's income is cut, the wife, who formerly might have been quite open about her spending, may become secretive and conceal her purchases from him. Rather than confront the situation and say, "This is what's happened, what can we do about it?" she takes on the role of the frightened, sneaky child, hiding things from her husband. But since the bills eventually arrive, she has in a sense arranged for her own punishment because her husband does discover what she's been doing.

To the degree that people can recognize and discuss the ways in which money is apt to give one of them a controlling factor over the other and to the degree that they can feel comfortable mutually deciding on its disposition, they're apt to avoid a great deal of the stress and resentments that arise whenever one partner is in control of the assets.

It's very difficult for people to share equally in money that has been acquired unequally. I've heard many wives say to their husbands, "Getting an allowance makes me feel like a child. It reduces me in my own eyes."

The husband will reply, "Oh, come on, that's not the way I think of it."

And the wife has to say, "You may not feel that way when you're giving me the money. This feeling may all be on my part. But I'm sharing my feelings with you. And as long as this situation does exist, I think I'm bound to have some resentment toward you. Could we try to work out a different way of handling this whole thing?"

Perhaps they can put a certain amount of money into a joint checking account on which they both can draw. On the other hand, one partner may *need* to hold on to the assets and the various kinds of control which that represents.

It takes a tremendous amount of maturity for people to be able to say, "The money really belongs to both of us. We each contribute to our marriage in different ways, and money is just one form of contribution."

18. Job Changes

"I don't think you're being realistic," my patient, Martin, said. I had seen him some years before with his wife. "I was fired. I've been out of work for three months. I'm depressed as hell, and things are a mess at home. I can't make love with my wife. I can't stand hanging around feeling like a failure—and a fool for not having seen the budget cut coming in my department. And my wife can't stand having me under foot all the time. I still don't see anything turning up in my field, so I'm thinking of settling for a job that's not going to use most of my qualifications. It will downgrade me professionally. *That's* what I came to discuss. Why bother going into why I feel like I've failed? Obviously, I *am* less of a success than I was three months ago."

"By whose standards?"

"By *my* standards."

"Okay, but can you see that your standards are a part of our culture that you've internalized? Since we're raised on the work ethic, it's natural that you feel the way you do. What I'm asking you to do is reexamine the basis of this feeling. Your experience with your job doesn't mean a damn thing about you as a human being. What has it got to do with who you are, or your ability to function in a relationship? What has it got to do with whether you're a loving, supportive *person*? Where does this holiness for work and success originate? If you can accept the fact that some of the shibboleths we've all been conditioned to accept are really just sacred cows, you might find you've reached a turning point in your feelings about yourself, and I think it would give you a tremendous sense of freedom."

"I can't afford freedom."

"What does that mean?"

"Well, if I really had a sense of freedom, I'd probably take a job that pays even less than the one I came to talk to you about."

"Why don't you tell me a little about it."

Martin started describing a position he'd been offered and was about to reject. As he talked, he leaned forward and his voice came alive. Suddenly I thought, "This is what he really wanted to discuss when he called me. This man, who's depressed because currently there are no jobs in his field at his salary level, is really facing an opportunity to do something that will give him a great deal of fulfillment and gratification. And he knows it! But he's constrained by a lifetime of conditioning and can't free himself."

We spent the rest of the hour exploring what this more appealing job might actually mean to Martin—and his wife. He was deeply concerned about her reaction. We talked about how involvement and enjoyment from your work can enhance your whole being, and as a result, your relationships with others. If you've had a day that's productive and fulfilling, you don't come home to flop in front of the TV or go off by yourself, depressed and withdrawn. You come home wanting to share your excitement, and therefore your partner benefits from your involvement.

In recent years, we've begun to question a lot of beliefs about what women can and can't do. Women's consciousness is being raised. I think we have to do the same thing with men. We have to take a closer look at the values that equate work with masculinity, money and sexual potency. These things have become one big equation so anything that goes wrong may well be a body blow to the masculine ego. A woman may also feel that her work and earning ability are closely related to her sense of self-esteem and identity, but the loss of a job is seldom felt as a negation of her essential femininity.

Changing our values is terribly hard, yet it can enable family members to rally and support each other in the most positive ways. If a wife can feel that a man's ability to earn money, while important and significant, is not a function of who he is, then it matters less who goes to work. Maybe she has some skill for which there's a ready market. If the husband can accept her earning power without his masculinity being threatened, the couple have the kind of role flexibility that can help them enormously. The man can stay home and take care of the children or go back to school for additional training. Maybe he can try a job in a completely different field. Happily, we are starting to revise our attitudes in ways that offer people more and more of this new kind of freedom to find out what's best for them individually and together.

When Wives Want Outside Jobs

One issue which still causes stress between spouses is that of the wife's taking a job.

"I don't want you to go to work," a husband will say. "We don't need the money. I make enough. If you want to do something, take a volunteer job."

"But I want to get paid. It's a different feeling. I've done volunteer work."

The husband shakes his head. "There are plenty of things that you can do around the house or on one of the committees over at the hospital. I don't want to come home at night to an exhausted wife—or to an empty house because you're working late. I love you and I want you here. I need you here."

In the face of these and other arguments, a woman is often baffled as to what she can possibly say or do.

What's needed is a lot of tact, determination, empathy and, most of all, an understanding that in some important way, her taking a job is a threat to her husband. The more she can find out about the threat and the more they can discuss it, the greater the chances for reassurance and a new sensitivity to the needs of each partner.

Perhaps a man wants his wife at home, in a stable spot where he can always get hold of her, where she's not meeting other men and where she'll be available to meet his needs. In a way he's feeling like the child who wants Mommy to be home when he comes in from school so he can touch base with her and know she's there if he needs her. But there are other ways in which a husband and wife can make contact and still retain their freedom of action.

Often a man sees his wife as the "little woman" who is absolutely dependent upon him for support. With a job comes the threat that "she'll be so self-sufficient, she'll be able to walk out of the marriage." Until recently, that hasn't been a threat to men in our society. In fact, it's been the opposite: women worried and men left home. Working women can say for the first time, "I'm staying in this marriage because I want to, not because I have to." When both spouses have this attitude, it's a potential source of even greater strength and value in the partnership. However, it does change their relationship. Suddenly, the man's traditional feeling of being secure is in question. He may need reassurance that he's loved in many ways that have nothing to do with money.

This kind of questioning is a very good thing because it helps people acquire a different understanding of what's involved in marriage. They're less apt to fall into the rut of accepting the status quo and taking each other for granted. It encourages respect for the other spouse. A woman's salary well may represent a significant contribution to the family. It may expand the opportunities open to the children and enhance the whole family's way of living. And a woman who works because she wants to generally becomes more interesting, more certain that she has something enriching to contribute to the marriage, and much more alive to herself and within the entire family relationship.

Sometimes a husband objects to his wife's working because he needs to uphold his own self-image. Among his associates, a working wife may signify that the husband can't support his family. As one corporate executive told his wife, "It just isn't appropriate for you to work. It wouldn't be accepted in view of the position I have in the company!" Her life and career choices are viewed in terms of how they will affect his career, the problems she might raise with his image at the corporation. Many companies seem to support the concept that a wife shouldn't work because it makes for a more stable home life. I think that's a myth worth dispelling. A marriage in which both partners are fulfilled and accomplished is much richer and more viable than a token marriage, in which the woman feels stifled and may turn to alcohol or other men as an escape from the vacuum surrounding her.

The success of a wife's taking a job depends not only on easing a possible threat to her husband but also on the way the resulting changes are incorporated into the family's routine. Sudden, unilateral pronouncements—"From now on, you can cook your own dinners"—are anxiety-provoking at best, and may correctly be seen as thoughtlessness or hostile demonstrations of power. On the other hand, unless a woman is able to accept and express the fact that she can't hold down a job and still be responsible for most of the work in the household, she's apt to find herself trying to fulfill the impossible role of working super-mom.

When a woman takes a job, her husband and children are bound to resent losing certain comforts and "services" they're used to. These losses need to be recognized and discussed. At the same time, it's crucial for everyone to understand what the job means to the woman and to the whole family. If husband and children can empathize with a woman's hunger to do something satisfying, or if they recognize the importance of her financial contribution, they'll probably be better able to accept the changes her job will cause in their lives. Ideally they'll offer as much help and support as possible —even though they may still have moments of resentment.

Some wives react to their new role of wage-earner by suddenly seizing power over financial matters. "*You* always got to choose where we went on vacations and I never said a word. But dammit, I never liked those camping trips. Now that I'm working, I intend to decide how we spend our time off." All the resentment and frustration that might have been building up for years may explode. Yet one must realize that a momentarily satisfying power play may well cost the relationship in the long-run. The constructive approach is through discussions about the feelings and needs of each person.

19. Moving Your Home

Sometimes moving is like leaving one's mother. This may actually or symbolically be true. For instance, if you leave the place in which you have grown up and made a lot of friends, it's like leaving the breast. The separation and sense of being uprooted can be deep and powerful.

The move needn't involve a great geographical change in order to cause anxiety. I knew a Manhattan couple who only moved across town from a brownstone-lined block off Central Park West to a cooperative apartment on Park Avenue. The husband wanted to move because he felt the new, wealthier neighborhood was more suitable to his position. It was also more convenient to the high school their oldest child was about to enter. But his wife had spent her whole life in the old neighborhood. Residents and storekeepers knew her. She'd walk down the street and people would say "hello." She'd been active in a block association and was recognized and valued. Her attachment to her home transcended the usual sense of comfort and convenience one gets from familiarity with a place. This woman was working through some of her own needs, which were terribly important in terms of her identity and self-esteem. She had her own network in this neighborhood. Her identity there was something special, and the community was like her extended family. For her, the move was devastating and triggered a serious depression.

Moving to a new home creates a certain amount of stress for almost everyone. Even an exciting move means giving up old friends and taking on new ones, building a different network within the new community. It's a whole different territory. The quality of the space itself is different, and one has to adjust to that. You can say, "Oh, look how large. It's just splendid. But what am I going to put here and how am I going to deal with this?" You wake up in the morning and nothing is the same. Adjusting takes a certain amount of doing, and it becomes increasingly difficult as one grows older and longs for familiarity.

Depending on who's responsible for what within the household, each spouse may face different kinds of stresses. For instance, in a family where the husband works and the wife stays home, the move may have been occasioned by the husband's transfer to a new job. In a sense, he's going to a prearranged place at work, where he's wanted and he can count on certain things. At the same time, he's under pressure to live up to certain expectations and make himself effective in a new career situation. He may naturally feel compelled to devote most of his energies to his job. The result can be a lack of support for his wife when she particularly needs it.

For a woman whose life is focused largely around her family and home, the move may raise anxieties about how she's going to be received, where she's going to fit in to the existing network. She has neither the distraction nor the support of an outside job. She doesn't walk into an office Monday morning and automatically start making contacts to establish a place for herself. She may turn to her husband for reassurance and the security of his presence. "I wish you'd come home early tonight."

"How can I come home early? I'm starting a new job and I'm up to my ears in work."

"They waited two months to get you here. Don't tell me another two hours are going to make such a difference. You can't expect me to unpack and do everything here all by myself." Her uncertainty and loneliness are translated into a plea for help with tasks that he may regard as minor, just as his concern over his job is translated into a statement about being busy.

If the spouses don't recognize the real, underlying needs, they can't communicate, set priorities or offer each other support, and the situation may start to deteriorate. Sometimes the wife reacts to the stress of moving by withdrawing and becoming very childish, isolating herself like the new kid on the block. Her husband may react with annoyance to her "sulking" and her lack of enthusiasm. Yet in its own way, her withdrawal is also an implicit demand that needs understanding and response.

The more completely the spouses can anticipate the kinds of problems they're apt to encounter—and if possible, allot enough time to ease into the new situation—the more they'll be able to support each other and make a relatively comfortable adjustment within the new community.

20. Vacations

I don't know how many couples have sat in my office and said, "We're coming to vacation time again, and we're both in a panic. Last year was a fiasco—we spent so much money and had a terrible time. This year we just don't know what to do or which way to turn."

There are many, many factors that go into determining the kind of vacation experience you have. Who made the decision about where to go? Did the two of you arrive at your choice mutually, or did the husband just say, "Listen, honey, we're going on that marvelous trip you've always wanted to take! We're going to France, Switzerland, Germany and Italy on a special company tour for seventeen days with a great group of people and you're going to love every minute of it." And the wife hates the very thought of it, but it's already done and she feels, "How can I possibly object? Look how happy he is. He's trying to be thoughtful . . . ." Sometimes the feeling is, "What can I say, it's his money." But it is far better to raise all sorts of questions beforehand.

The fantasies and expectations people have about what's going to happen during those few weeks of vacation need to be shared. What do we hope it will be like? How can we make this a special time for reengaging with each other and delighting in the change? Maybe the wife thinks, "We're going to this beautiful resort with beaches and time to be together, dancing in the evening, sleeping late in the morning—it'll be like another honeymoon." They get there and the husband is up at eight o'clock every day taking tennis lessons. After eating breakfast, he heads for the golf course because this is his chance to indulge in all the sports he missed during the year. The husband and wife may be in the same place, but they're not on the same vacation.

Some people find that taking separate vacations is a helpful and rejuvenating experience. They go off by themselves or with friends to a place of their choice, and they're delighted that they can spend as much time as they want doing whatever they enjoy without making their partner suffer through a miserable time. They find that the experience makes them happier and more loving at home.

Frequently, when people look forward for an entire year to one important holiday, they want to do everything. They want to have a rest and excitement, too. They try to crowd everything in, then they get home too fatigued to even know if they've enjoyed themselves. Everything is just one big blur that's supposed to last until next year.

Some people have difficulty enjoying their vacations because on a deeper level they don't feel that they really deserve this pleasure. Have they actually "earned the right" to this luxury and enjoyment—not in a financial sense, but in terms of deserving to be gratified or just plain happy? Anxiety of this type may stem from early childhood and our sense of not being valued as human beings who have the right to pleasure and enjoyment from life. When this sense of self-worth is lacking, professional counseling is often important and effective.

People on vacation are together much more than when they're at home, particularly if they're traveling and are then thrown together in a hotel room. They have very little time for privacy or any kind of emotional withdrawal, and this can create a strain. I think it's important for many couples to arrange things so that each spouse has some time to be alone. If plans like this are made in advance, the private time becomes one of the comfortable elements in each day. Otherwise, there can be a sudden urgent need to "go off by myself," and the withdrawal is interpreted by the spouse as an exclusion or rejection.

Vacations frequently bring physical irritants or discomforts. There may be noise, no air conditioning, mosquitos, too little drawer space or whatever. If one spouse has made the vacation decision unilaterally, the irritations are often blamed on him. "Didn't you ask for a double bed? Don't you know by now I can't sleep in a bed with you? Just look at this dinky room. Do you mean to tell me we're paying . . . ." When vacation quarters are much less spacious or luxurious than those that people are accustomed to at home, it may be worthwhile to consider shortening the stay slightly and using the extra money to upgrade the accommodations.

The relationship between couples on vacation often reflects

resentments that have been building up, perhaps for years. Some people can get rid of a lot of hostility and aggression in front of strangers they know they're not going to see again. Perhaps one partner may snipe at the other, feeling, "I can get away with it now because in front of these strangers my spouse isn't going to say anything back to me. I'm safe." Sometimes one spouse criticizes the other as a way of declaring to everyone else around, "I'm not the same kind of person this creature is. I know better. I'm socially aware. Don't put me in the same category." The critic's own self-esteem is threatened by the partner's "inadequacy."

The balance of power between two people often changes in response to the new surroundings. A man may derive a great deal of strength from his success and position in his home community. But at a resort, his wife may outshine him as the better athlete, dancer or raconteur. She may also be a strikingly attractive person. She then becomes the star, and the husband, whose background and success aren't known, loses in terms of power. He may respond by seeking out his wife more than usual or trying to demonstrate possession and control of her. Many variations may occur depending on the relative strengths of the individuals in the new setting. For some couples, these changes in pattern can be refreshing and exciting.

When vacations regularly cause difficulties between spouses, there's usually a need to examine not just the holiday arrangements but the individual people, their values and the fundamental interaction between them.

21. Live-in Parents/In-Laws

"I can't believe this is happening now." Carolyn pressed her fingertips against her forehead. "Phil and I have just straightened out our problems and now he wants his mother to come live with us. It's either that or put her in a home, which he can't face. But if I have her with me, I'll be miserable. And if I refuse, I'll be guilty the rest of my life. How can I win?"

I said, "That concept of guilt is horrendous. What's behind it? Haven't we talked about your primary responsibility being toward yourself? And toward Phil?"

"Phil is the one I'd feel guilty about, not his mother," Carolyn exclaimed. "If I were just a nicer person, I wouldn't make this into such a big deal because I'd know it means so much to Phil. But I'm *not* like that. And as happy as it would make Phil, it would drive me absolutely crazy. I don't *want* somebody else in my home. I've just started my own little catering business. I don't want to have to take time away from it to care for a dependent old lady. It's easy for Phil to say he wants his mother with us because he won't be there all day taking care of her. *I will.* I know it isn't nice, but that's the way I feel."

"What has 'nice' got to do with any of this? Aren't you saying that you're unhappy about having to do something you don't want to do? You're probably unhappy that your husband expects you to undertake a task you feel unable to cope with."

"That's exactly right. And I'm saying I'm too selfish to cope with this. I'd be standing on a window ledge every morning not wanting to face another day."

" 'Selfishness' is a badly misused word," I said. "To be concerned about yourself is not selfish. It's realistic and honest to be able to say, 'Look, this is who I am. This is where I am at this time

192

in my life, this is what I can do and what I cannot do. I need my privacy and space, and I cannot cope with having somebody else here.' Recognizing what you're able to do and what is beyond your capacity is vital. When you say you'd be on the window ledge every morning if you had Phil's mother with you, what good would that do for anybody? *That* would be selfish: that would be trying to play a game, assume a role, be somebody you're not, and do it at a tremendous cost to yourself and everybody around you. How do you think it would make everybody else feel if they saw you at the end of your rope? If they saw you dangling from a ledge?"

"Let me try to answer that. Right now Phil figures his mother hasn't got a lot of time left. If you said to him, 'Make a choice. Would you rather have your mother in an institution or your wife dangling out the window?' I think he'd say, 'If Carolyn could just manage to dangle for a year or two, it would make me feel great!' "

"Undoubtedly!" I had to laugh despite the seriousness of the matter. "I'm sure that's probably so! And it may be the result of a lot of guilt on his part as well. Who knows what's going on between him and his mother? He might very well feel the way you said. But this isn't limited by time, is it?" Carolyn shook her head. "You see, people can usually cope with something they know is just for a brief period. But there are no limitations here, except fairly long-term ones. And I think you have to question to what degree you're able to discount your own self and well-being. What price would you be paying by doing that? Is that a price you want to pay —feeling depressed and resentful most of the time?"

"If I say no, Phil is going to feel resentful and hold this against me for the rest of my life."

"He probably *will* feel resentful. But the two of you have achieved a pretty good relationship. What makes you think Phil is going to hold this against you forever? Is that realistic or absurd?"

"I don't know. Right now, it's the most important thing to him."

"Sure. Right now it would be the best thing in the world from his point of view if his mother were a little less dependent and you were able to cope with it. That would make life easier for everyone, but that's not the way it is. The reality is something else."

"Phil asked me last night if I was ready to have *our* kids say, 'Hey, you didn't take care of your parents, why should we take care of you? We're going to put you in a home.' "

"What did you say?"

"I told him I'd rather be in an old age home than be a pain in the ass to my kids. And he said, 'You don't know how you'll feel until you're that age.' "

I nodded. "There's no doubt that when we get older we have very strong dependency needs and wishes. Everybody feels more vulnerable. And it's also true that whatever you do now is setting an example for your children. I think you do have to keep that in mind, but I don't think it can be the deciding factor. You can talk about future possibilities involving your children, but you don't know what's going to happen. You could drop dead before it ever came to that. And what they do or don't do will finally depend on the kind of relationship you have with them, and what their own needs are. But you're living today, and I think you have to consider what's going on at this point in your life and face that."

Extending the Family

There are no easy answers when partners disagree about bringing parent(s) into the home. Husband and wife may have strong, opposing feelings on the subject, and this may be a time when both of them can *not* have their needs or wishes met. Then a choice becomes necessary, and that's very hard for anybody.

On the other hand, it's sometimes possible for two people who disagree to share their concerns and come to some kind of an arrangement that will be equitable for both. This means, among other things, negotiating how much responsibility each one would take in caring for the older parent *if* this person came into the household. While not all situations involve an infirm or incapacitated relative, most often there are limitations and needs that will have to be met. How? By whom?

The husband may say, "This means enough to me so that I'll take the major responsibility for caring for my mother on weekends. I'll do whatever chores have to be done for her, and on weekday evenings I'll take over after I come home from work." Depending on the health of the parent, this care may entail taking her shopping, to visit friends, to a show, or to the doctor. It may even require helping her to eat, bathe, wash her hair and so forth. Once the partners become realistic and specific in planning the details, they may feel they can *try out* having this parent in the household.

Under the best of circumstances, taking a parent or in-law into your home is difficult. Most of us have not learned to accommodate an extended family. Most of us don't have that kind of later intimate contact with our parents. We're not all members of one household, as was the case many years ago. Of course, the situation may be different for some people. For years everybody in my family gathered for the summer in an enormous house at the shore. We learned how to get along with several generations living together. But many people have grown away from their parents. Members of the older generation coming into the household may be relative strangers. They may be people we scarcely know. The mother who comes in at this time is not the mother you knew in your youth. Both of you have changed through years of living totally different lives, developing different customs and different ways of being. Many of the things you did in your parent's home you no longer do, nor want to do. There are sociological irritants as well as early feelings and conflicts that reemerge when parents and children are suddenly forced into living together.

Typically, the strongest tensions in this interaction arise between the two women. What happens to the younger woman is that all the old competitive feelings and fears of being sucked back into an infantile role of being criticized and prevented from assuming the primary female position within the home or with her husband become exacerbated. For the older woman who is entering the household after giving up her familiar bailiwick, finding a place within this new setting is extremely difficult. Any time she tries to assert herself, it seems an intrusion.

Usually there's added anxiety because of the impact of role reversal. You have to come to grips with the fact that your parents have become the "children" and they're now looking to you as "parents." That's often unsettling or scary.

In order to give this new family grouping the best possibility of succeeding, everybody has to participate to some extent in the decisions. Husband, wife, children and the person who's coming into the situation need to get together and discuss some of the changes that will be taking place. The husband and wife must then talk as honestly as possible about what they think might be the dangers, what they particularly need to be aware of, and what might be positive aspects of the situation. Questions of privacy, dependency and responsibility are particularly important.

When parents or in-laws are brought into a household that may not be spacious enough to easily accommodate additional people, there is an immediate lack of privacy for everyone. The intrusion alone can be enough to upset the apple cart. The older people may feel they have to withdraw and become isolated so as not to intrude or become too demanding. As a result, a lot of anxiety and guilt may be aroused in the younger couple. "What am I doing to my mother? How can I treat her this way? Why are they distancing? Have we offended them? Are they unhappy? Don't they like us?"

Yet at the same time, the younger people want their privacy; they want the right to continue certain customs and activities which are part of *their* lives and don't include parents or in-laws. The ambivalence and tension grow.

One of the most helpful preparations is to structure the household in a way that provides the maximum privacy for everybody concerned. This might mean not putting your mother-in-law in the bedroom next to yours, nor adjacent to the children's where she'll be hearing their rock music and complaining about the noise. If you can provide the older couple with their own kitchen, or even just a hotplate and refrigerator, I'd say that would be a big step forward.

You cannot expect an elderly person—or anybody else, for that matter—left alone in a household not to be curious. Everybody wants to know how someone else lives. If there are things you absolutely don't want seen, you have to lock them up or put them away. You have the right to your way of life, your private possessions and areas. But if you take somebody else into your home, you also have an obligation to respect their ways as much as you can and try to make some accommodations that are important for them. It doesn't always work, but there's a chance if you make an honest effort.

Privacy includes providing opportunities for husband and wife to be alone with each other, perhaps absent from the home altogether. The spouses might discuss their needs in order to decide which ones they may have to modify and which can be maintained. Explain these needs openly to the in-laws. Help them realize, for example, that privacy doesn't mean exclusion. Since these relatives may come from a home in which the habits were very different, they don't know what to expect. Being told can set their minds at ease. "We always have a family dinner on Friday night," or "The two of us generally spend Wednesday evening in town together." Unless the older relatives are completely helpless, it's fine to suggest that occasionally they're going to be eating or staying alone. Often it's a relief to them. In effect, they're being shown that you respect their ability to be on their own and do certain things for themselves.

Sometimes older people bring specific, serious problems into the home. A senile grandfather who is incontinent or acting out sexually can be difficult for everyone in the household. A parent who is severely incapacitated is bound to be an enormous burden. If the children are away at school, it may be easier to cope with these pressures. However, both the dependent person and the one who is depended upon resent the situation. Sometimes the best solution may be to place the older person in a suitable home or to hire professional help if that's feasible.

Wherever possible, it's important to promote the older

individual's activity and independence. Trips outside the home and invitations to guests are supportive. If chores around the home are delegated to the relatives, it can make the elderly parent feel useful and less of a burden. It also benefits those freed from these tasks.

As usual, a change in life-style is apt to cause a shift in the power structure between spouses. The alignment of husband or wife with one or both of the in-laws can become a touchy and potentially devastating issue. Who gets supported by whom? What does that do to the other partner's sense of importance and power? When this kind of alignment is recognized, it helps if the partners discuss it and decide how to check it before it worsens. One effective solution may be to state the problem clearly to the parent or in-law.

There are some circumstances when living with an older person can be a rewarding experience . . . especially if his health allows him to be active. He may establish a cherished relationship with the grandchildren. Furthermore, there's always a lot of unfinished business between grown children and parents. Often it remains unsettled when the parent dies, and then it's too late. A person may then need a lot of hours on the analyst's couch. If it's still possible to resolve things with the parent, there are more opportunities if you're both under the same roof. I'm not suggesting a rehashing of old issues or arguments, but coming to grips with the relationship and trying to understand the other person and what was going on in his or her life when you were being raised. You probably have no idea what your mother was going through when she was carrying you, the struggles your father might have been engaged in when you were young, or what your parents' relationship was.

There are many areas that can be explored in order to see these people in a different perspective, more completely and with greater empathy and understanding. This kind of exploration can help you to understand who you are and what was happening in your own early years. It's your last chance to grasp firsthand knowledge of your own history and "roots."

PART 5: Remarriage

22. Starting Over

When you remarry, you are influenced from the very beginning by the experience of your first marriage. You enter with a certain predisposition and certain fears, expectations or resolutions. If you've been divorced (rather than widowed), you are usually somewhat negative because the first marriage was a failure. At the same time you're hopeful and determined to make this new relationship work: to see that this time everything turns out better. Immediately there's a built-in tension with remarriage, and like any other stress it has its negative as well as its positive aspects.

For the most part we've talked about the emotional and practical adjustments that have to be made by people marrying for the first time and raising children together. If you consider the complexities inherent in that situation, then add previous marital experience *and* the complications of relationships with ex-husbands and ex-wives, ex-in-laws, children from one or both former marriages who may or may not be living full-time with the new couple, children from the current marriage, alimony, child-support and visitation rights, you may *begin* to understand some of the ways in which remarriage is different from first marriage.

It's not possible to treat the subject of remarriage in depth here. However, we *can* indicate the most common problem areas and help people to understand the major stresses in order to avoid many unrealistic expectations. **Remarriage is essentially an opportunity to create the nucleus for a new family unit that can be affirming and can provide many of those things which may have been lacking in the first union.**

Remarriage after a Partner's Death

Frequently the surviving partner who remarries remembers

all the wonderful things about his or her spouse and none of the real difficulties of their everyday life together. This is sometimes called the "halo effect."

The ghost of the dead partner can threaten the new marriage unless you've had a sufficient period of mourning to come to grips with that first relationship, work through the feelings of loss, and develop a balanced view that enables you to see both the good and the bad in your dead partner and your marriage. I don't think you can ever have a successful remarriage when strong, unsettled emotions are still tugging and stabbing within you. You need to settle this part of your life so you can let go and move on to something else.

This applies to cases of divorce, too. No matter how angry, negative and horrendous the parting may have been, you need to be able to develop a balanced view of your former partner and remember that things weren't all bad and that there were reasons you married this person in the first place. Prior to remarriage, it is necessary to lay ghosts to rest.

Problems can arise when the surviving partner continues to have close emotional ties or other connections to the dead spouse's family. (Occasionally this happens after divorces, too.) In some instances there may be a business relationship or an independent friendship with the in-laws. Most often, however, the connection is maintained for and through the children. If there are children from the first marriage, the surviving parent still wants the youngsters to have grandparents, aunts and uncles on that side of the family. A living divorced spouse is usually the channel for the kids to these relatives, but the widow or widower must maintain the relationship, and sometimes the new husband or wife finds the connection difficult to accept.

A woman I had counseled after the death of her husband came to see me some years later after remarrying. She had two children from her first marriage.

"I'm in trouble and I don't know what to do," she said. She reminded me that she and her first husband Bill had been been married for nine years before he died. "It was a good marriage and my in-laws were always great to me. I used to tell you how specially loving and supportive they were after Bill's death—even though they'd lost their son.

"Well, my new husband, Andy, resents them terribly. I just can't figure it out. He doesn't want me to spend a minute with them. I mean that literally. If the children are going there for a visit, he wants me to drop them off and come right back home without even seeing Mom and Dad Selby at all. And these are people I love, who have been wonderful to me and the kids. How can Andy be jealous of them? What can I say? We fight about this all the time."

"The chances are that Andy feels excluded, as though he doesn't have a part in all of this." Lynn nodded. "But from what you say about your in-laws, it sounds as though they'd welcome the addition of somebody else into your life. And into the family. Of course, it will take some doing, but I really think you can engage Andy and help him to join in."

"I asked Andy to come and meet the Selbys when we were first planning to be married and he gave me a flat 'no.' "

"Well, that was a while ago, and now you *are* married. Maybe you could tell him you were part of this family for a long time, and they did lose a son. Maybe you could tell Andy that because you love him and because these people love you, he'll be welcomed as a part of their family. He might be ready now to accept the idea that you and your in-laws want him to participate. Be very clear in what you say: 'Andy, this way you're left out of the whole thing and I feel very bad. It makes me feel terrible when you're left out. I would love to have you sharing with us, and so would the Selbys. So can we try it? See what happens?' "

Lynn nodded again. "That's exactly how we all feel." She hesitated. "But if Andy won't try it?"

"Then I think you have to wait for a while. His feelings come ahead of the in-laws'. Sometimes these things do happen in time. Meanwhile, it might be wise if you saw your in-laws when it didn't impinge on Andy's time with you, if he can't tolerate that right now. Perhaps in the future when he sees that they really don't want to take you away, or that you're not threatening to remove any of your love or time from him, he may be more inclined to go along with you."

Often when the "new" spouse senses a partner's commitment to the new marriage and becomes more secure, he or she no longer feels threatened by figures intimately associated with the former spouse. In cases where the threat continues, one must look for deeper reasons. There may be a struggle in progress between husband and wife over who's going to set the rules of the new marriage. Feelings about their own parents may be reactivated. In any event, one must explore why one spouse is unable to accept the relationship *and also* why the other partner needs to maintain it despite the spouse's distress.

"One divorce is enough. I won't make that mistake again."

Because of a determination to avoid problems that caused

difficulty in the former marriage, issues that normally should and would be discussed by a husband and wife may not be confronted. A woman is apt to say, "I just can't talk to Jim about money. It was such a sore subject in my former marriage—all I'd have to do was mention it and Bob would blow his top. I just can't bring the issue up with Jim." In all likelihood, the ostensible subject—money—wasn't the real problem; rather it reflected other underlying difficulties between the partners, perhaps unresolved dependency needs or low self-esteem. Avoiding the subject in this marriage can only lead to trouble.

Another area remarried people are often reluctant to talk about is sex, even though sex tends to be very important in remarriage and much more open than it was in the first marriage. But if something goes wrong with the sex in that second marriage where it's supposed to be so great, there can be hesitation in confronting the issue. Especially if sex was fought over in the first marriage and became a sensitive, painful subject, people won't want to bring it up. Men and women will tell me, "It's better to be a little disappointed in our sex life than to start something." Of course, this attitude tends to leave things tense and unresolved and leads to growing disappointment, resentment and blaming.

In order to make this new marriage solid and realistic, it's imperative that the partners don't avoid opening up areas for discussion. Issues, especially important or sensitive ones, *need* to be discussed. Above all, it is important to deal with this marriage as it exists and not try to pattern it after the other nor use the other as a guide for what *not* to do in this one.

I don't mean you can't try to change some of the underlying attitudes that may have caused problems in the first marriage. But now we're talking about changing, not covering up or denying. Usually, without professional help, it's hard to identify what went wrong. However, if you're tuned in to who you are, open about what you did and able to accept responsibility for your role in the marriage, you can sometimes say, "I was a real fool. I tended to shove him away. I tended to keep him out of my own interests, to guard zealously my own little sphere, and I can see why he felt rejected by me. So maybe I'm aware enough now to try not to do that in this marriage." You may realize, "I was such a baby. I went into that marriage expecting to be cared for and served, and as long as I brought home the check, I thought all my decisions should be accepted. I never took her feelings into account. I was so anxious about my own position, I never considered her needs. But now I think I'm ready to have a different kind of relationship." *One way to reinforce a real desire to change is to share it with your partner.*

Money is almost always a problem
in remarriage after divorce.

If you've been through a divorce and had to deal with settlements, alimony and child-support under adversary conditions with your ex-spouse, chances are you have bitter feelings attached to money. When you enter the new marriage, as much as you commit yourself to it on one level, on some other deeper level you're just not quite able to trust the commitment.

After all, the first marriage was 'till death us do part,' and it ended. It's only natural for you to have some reservations about trusting a new mate utterly and completely. There's an "iffy" feeling that's especially apt to emerge over financial considerations. The tendency is for the man, if he's the breadwinner, to try to conceal how much he has or feel diffident about revealing how much money he earns, perhaps because he's afraid he's going to be taken again. He's frequently reluctant to change his will, alter the insurance policy or make other monetary decisions that indicate acceptance of the new situation. He's got a "let's wait and see" attitude.

The woman tends to feel that she absolutely must put aside some money for who knows what's going to happen some day. If she earns a salary or has any private income, she may be secretive about it. She may try to squirrel away part of the household money as a kind of security against the future.

There's a general discomfort, fear and/or suspicion about money—how much there is, whose is being spent on what, who's going to handle it and how. If you can acknowledge the problem and say that there *is* this apprehension, then you've taken the first step toward dealing with it.

I worked with a husband who had kept secret a substantial Christmas bonus and raise. His wife found out about it and there was a huge explosion. The couple came in, and after we'd talked for a while, Ray finally acknowledged his need for secrecy.

"You know, I'm still too sore from the alimony fight not to feel like this," he said. "I got burned by Sheila and I'm afraid it's going to take me some time before I get over it. I *want* my finances to be private. I know it's my craziness, but right now, part of me feels like all women are out to get everything they can from any man."

"And that includes me?" His wife, Erica, was thunderstruck.

"I . . . I'm afraid so."

Erica turned to me. "I've been telling you he hasn't accepted me. Well, now you've got it in his own words. We all know he doesn't trust me as long as he goes on filing his precious separate tax return."

I said, "Maybe that's *so*. Maybe that's a reality for both of you to understand and accept. It takes time to get over certain experiences and develop a complete trust in a new person and relationship."

"But that makes me feel like I'm on *trial*," Erica protested.

"Well, in a sense all new relationships are a kind of trial, aren't they? There's nothing wrong with that. We all test each other out. We try each other to see how the other one is going to be. Developing real trust takes a long time. Some people never reach it. And when there has been a lot of pain and heartache, it takes that much longer. Sometimes we may have to accept the fact that for the time being, a relationship is not the ideal that we'd like it to be, but we can work and grow toward it." I paused, and then said to Erica, "You feel as though you're on trial. But in a sense, aren't *you* saying that unless Ray accepts you totally, he doesn't love you? So the trial is going *both* ways. You're testing his love. You're saying that he should be able to accept you without reservations, otherwise he doesn't love you. That's an unrealistic expectation at this time."

It's natural and positive to strive toward an ideal, but unless you recognize that it is an *ideal* and base your expectations on reality, you end up denying your true feelings. This can only lead to problems, and work against the development of trust.

When children are part of a remarriage, finances become more complex and anxieties about money expand in scope. Often a man is paying alimony to his ex-wife and support for his children from that marriage. He, and usually his new wife, feel the financial drain and also the stress of this tangible obligation to the past. This man may be the sole provider for his current wife, who may have children of her own that he's helping to support. He goes from one family group to the other, and in one he hears, "Daddy, I have to have money for school," while in the other it's, "Walter, the kids need shoes and clothing," someone has medical bills, and this child needs braces.

Even in cases where there's no shortage of cash, the person who's constantly doling it out is bound to experience some resentment. Money isn't just a simple commodity; in our society, it's a symbol for many things. Through money a man may sense the emotional as well as fiscal demands being made on him, and he can come to feel depleted or used, which is where his resentment is usually rooted. He may start to wonder who's taking care of him, who's giving something to him in return. And unless he and his wife realize what's happening, he may start letting out his resentment on her.

Chances are his wife and ex-wife have their own feelings of hostility and guilt. Typically a woman with children from a previous marriage feels guilty about whatever the children are costing the second husband. Yet, when he decided to marry her, he knew he was marrying the total family. She didn't spring the kids on him. He was aware of their existence and apparently willing to accept a certain amount of responsibility. If she can share her doubts and guilt, he may be able to reassure her. If her guilt is excessive or persistent, she may have to explore the real reasons for it. Is there some area in which she's not carrying her weight and he's carrying the burden for two? Does she have old, deeper feelings of unworthiness that are now being exacerbated by the current situation?

Sometimes the answers are complex and difficult to uncover. Yet always, it's better to raise the questions and see what can be learned together.

Establishing the New Household

"We had Rick's two boys with us for three weeks." Vera looked down at the handkerchief she was twisting in her fingers. "They're nine and six. And Debby, my daughter, is seven." Her voice was low and tense. "It was a disaster."

"You saw to that," Rick said.

"I didn't have to. You and the boys did a fine job on your own. I told you it wouldn't work out with them sleeping in the living room—not for three weeks. They were only supposed to come between Christmas and New Year's." Vera was straining to keep herself under control.

"I know that. But it's not my fault that Mona extended her damn ski trip. All I got was a cable from Switzerland saying she wouldn't be back. What was I supposed to do, send two kids home to an empty apartment because their mother's an irresponsible bitch?"

"I think it's very strange that your ex-wife manages to do everything she wants to at her convenience and we end up being built-in sitters."

"You don't mind having me as a built-in babysitter for Debby, do you? Well, why can't you be more flexible about the boys?"

"Flexible? What they need is a little discipline. Maybe they could even learn a little thoughtfulness." Vera's voice was getting unsteady. "It was bad enough when they practically ruined the living room, but how could you act as though their behavior with

Debby didn't matter? She's a little girl and she's not used to boys in the first place. She's certainly never seen a naked one in her life. And your two roughnecks go tearing around in their underwear . . ."

"Jesus Christ, Vera, their mother didn't *pack* any pajamas or robes. What did you want them to do? You were going to go buy them that stuff. What happened to that idea?"

"I gave up the idea after they sneaked into Debby's room and woke her up with their Indian massacre." Vera flushed and her voice shook with suppressed fury. "They were stark naked except for my lipstick and make-up smeared all over them from head to toe. They scared Debby half to death."

"Come on, they were just fooling around. You're over-protective of Debby. It didn't hurt her one bit."

"Don't you dare tell me what does or doesn't hurt my daughter. You just get your own children under control because I'm not going to have this going on every other weekend, at Easter and all summer long."

"Is that some kind of a threat?" Rick asked coldly.

"I'm sorry." Vera turned away suddenly.

"I don't want you to be sorry. I want to know what you meant by what you said."

"I didn't mean anything."

"Bullshit, you were threatening me about the boys."

Vera started crying.

"Will you stop crying and talk to me?" Rick sounded angry and upset as he leaned toward Vera. She shrank back in her chair. "*Stop that*," Rick shouted. "Stop acting as if you're afraid of me. Have I ever touched you except with love?" His voice resounded in the office, and Vera cupped her head between her hands.

I waited a moment and then said quietly to the two of them, "What upset you so much?"

Vera's answer was almost a wail. "I'm afraid he'll get fed up and leave. I'm afraid I'll end up with a second divorce."

"Why don't you talk to me?" Rick demanded. "I don't want another divorce, either."

I said, "Perhaps you're both threatened by something else. I wonder how you see your ex-wife, Rick. It sounds to me as though she's exploiting both of you. Are you aware of that?"

"Well, what am I supposed to do when she cables from Switzerland that she's not coming back?"

"Obviously there's nothing that can be done at that time. But it sounds to me as though there's a lot of exploring you have to do with her, and you've got to be prepared to be very definite in terms of what you will do and what you will not let her do. She's really controlling both of your lives and it's a willful act."

Rick spoke vehemently. "You don't begin to understand my ex-wife if you think there's anything to explore with her. She'll go along with whatever I say, then she'll do the same rotten things all over again. She'll send the kids to us without the right clothing, or phone and say that she's not picking them up Sunday night after all . . ."

"Truly I don't buy that," I said.

"What?"

"I don't buy that."

"What does that mean?"

"It means that we've discovered that when people are really very firm, they get their points across. There is something that's coming through to you from your ex-wife that's causing you to allow certain things to happen. You're seeing her as someone stronger, more definite, more controlling than she really is. I think we have to find out what this means. I think we have to explore why you're willing to go along with what she does."

"Well, dammit, I don't know *how* to be firmer with her. One time last month when I was going to drop the kids off at the end of a weekend, she called from Long Island to say she wasn't at home. The kids would have to stay with us Sunday night and go to school from our place on Monday. What could I do?"

"What do you think you could do? You could say to her, 'Long Island isn't the other end of the earth. You come back home now; I'm driving the kids to the apartment.' "

"She'd say, 'I won't be there. If you want to leave your children alone in the apartment, that's on you.' "

" 'That's not part of our contract. Our contract says that you're supposed to be home at a certain time. I'm bringing the kids there.' "

Rick shook his head and sighed. "I think Mona just wouldn't give a damn. She'd probably just let me bring the kids."

"What's coming across to me is uncertainty. And your uncertainty is what gets across to her. She knows she has a patsy on her hands. I think that if she felt you really meant it, she'd give in. But she knows you don't." Rick rubbed his hand across his brow. "It seems to me you have a complicated relationship with your ex-wife, and it's carrying over into your current marriage. Look what's happening between you and Vera. I think we have a great deal to explore. I also wonder how you and Vera feel about your boys, about setting some limits for them."

"She doesn't love them." Rick looked at Vera. She averted

her eyes. He said more strongly, "She doesn't love them. None of this would be happening if she did. The kids know it. You can't fool kids. And *I* know it, too." He stared at Vera as though waiting for a contradiction.

She sat silently twisting her handkerchief.

I said, "Okay, okay, you may be right! But why do you think Vera can really love your boys at this point?" They both looked up at me, startled. "Loving is something that grows in a relationship. It's really expecting a hell of a lot from someone to jump right in and start loving."

"But I love Debby."

"And that's great. When it happens, it's just glorious. From what I understand, she loves you, too. She wants to cuddle up with you and have you be her 'Daddy.' She hardly ever sees her real father. She accepts you, and you've said you enjoy having a little girl around the house and getting to know what that's like. But sometimes it doesn't happen that way. In reality it's often difficult to become accustomed to new children, especially if you're not used to having children of the opposite sex around." I looked at Vera. "You said you were an only child?"

She nodded.

"I wonder how it makes you feel when you see little boys running around naked in your apartment?"

"I don't think it's right."

"Let's stay with how it makes you feel in terms of your personal reaction."

Vera looked uneasy. "I don't . . . know how to handle them."

"But do you think you can tell us how you feel?"

She hesitated. "I feel uncomfortable. They're such complete strangers. I mean, so different from Debby and me." She shook her head. "I don't feel as though I'll ever understand them or make the same kind of contact with them that I have with Debby."

"Are you ready to try gradually to get to know them? How does it make you feel to picture that?"

"I'm not sure. They really are like mysterious, wild, little Indians." She shot an apprehensive look at Rick, then lowered her eyes. "It sounds crazy but they're very intimidating to me."

"Intimidating!" Rick was surprised. "But they're just a couple of little kids. They just need an occasional firm hand and a lot of hugging the rest of the time."

"Maybe." Vera smiled tentatively. "Maybe I just need a little time to find out that that's true."

Vera and Rick's experiences are common to many couples

who are adjusting to remarriage. People often breathe into an ex-spouse something that really doesn't exist. "She's a demon," or "He's impossible to deal with and will never agree to anything." You begin to see that part of the interaction is one person's inability to be resolute. The very things that led to the destruction of the previous marriage can continue to plague the couple after the divorce and can also threaten the second marriage. Rick couldn't confront his first wife within the marriage so he divorced her and married Vera, a softer, gentler woman. But he still had the same old difficulty with Mona. He ended up feeling helpless and unable to do anything about her manipulations. Moreover, his new wife was also telling him he wasn't doing the right thing. He just felt helpless, hopeless and bewildered. Not knowing which way to turn, he exploded. His own feelings of inadequacy were displaced onto Vera.

Vera, meanwhile, had to come to terms with the feelings she had when confronted with two naked boys in the presence of her "baby" girl, who is actually between the two boys' ages and not all that little! Vera was raised in a relatively quiet household and boys were still something of an enigma to her, strange and intriguing like her husband. Her first husband, who walked out of the marriage, scared the hell out of her because he was distant and unavailable. In Rick she had somebody responsive and warm, as well as exciting and masculine, but she hadn't counted on having two other males to contend with.

I helped Rick and Vera become more assertive with each other, less frightened, able to negotiate how they felt about the children and what was behind their feelings. Once they were able to get these issues into the open, they had the groundwork for a good second marriage.

Young children are involved in approximately sixty percent of remarriages. In my experience, the chances of making the new family unit work are infinitely greater when you discuss ahead of time your plans to incorporate the children into your lives. Although the marriage may start out with an initial period of euphoria with everyone bending over backward to be nice and keep things happy, suddenly buried emotions come to the surface and often what seems like an overwhelming problem develops.

The following points may be helpful in anticipating potential stresses and maintaining a realistic perspective after remarriage.

1. *Your "ex" or your partner's will be a factor in your lives.*

The biological parent, even though married to a new partner, continues to be a co-parent with the first spouse. There are joint decisions that still have to be made concerning the children's health, schooling, vacations, and so forth. The new partner is apt to resent the time, energy and money that's being funneled toward these ends.

The relationship to the ex-spouse is always a complicated one. Occasionally divorced people will truly want the former spouse to be happy and to achieve a good remarriage. This hope may reflect not only a concern for the other's welfare but also a recognition that it will be better for the children if the "ex" remarries a warm, loving mate.

Often, however, there's a great deal of hostility between former partners, and the newly married couple can be drawn into their own arguments over what the "ex" has or hasn't done, should or shouldn't do. Because the ex-spouse is and will continue to be a factor within the new household, all the questions of role relationships must be discussed and settled. Sometimes it's necessary to renegotiate agreements between divorced partners or to clarify details of those agreements. Occasionally I even have an ex-spouse come in with the new family for a therapy session to make everyone realize how complicated this situation is and to open up more direct channels of communication.

2. *Adjusting to new living patterns takes time, patience and a lot of open communication.*

A tremendous amount of adjusting, both emotional and practical, has to take place for two different families to be absorbed within one household. People must adapt as they gradually experience this new home, the various activities that go on within it, and the whole new way of being.

"Ice-skating!" a husband exclaims to his wife. "Hon, I haven't ice-skated since I was twelve. Besides, I need Saturday mornings to get myself together after the week. Couldn't the kids do something with you or on their own?"

"But they love ice-skating. And I've had them all week. I always used to count on some time for myself on Saturdays."

A new living pattern is being formed.

"But Mommy, *before* we always went out together on Sunday for Chinese food. Why aren't we going out now?"

The children are bound to ask questions and make comparisons between the old and the new ways. Parents have to decide which traditions they're ready to continue and explain why other activities will no longer be part of the new life.

3. *During the first year of remarriage, new family relationships are developed, and people need time to acquire the feeling that they belong.*

Suppose a woman gets divorced and remains in her home with her children. She then remarries and the new husband moves in with or without his own children. He comes into someone else's home, and feels somewhat like an invader entering somebody else's territory. On the other hand, the children are apt to feel, "What's he doing here? How can he be sitting in Daddy's chair or sleeping in Daddy's bed?"

The adoptive parent needs a chance to relate to his partner's children privately on a one-to-one basis. It requires patient effort and hard work for this parent to establish his or her position with the child. Realizing this in advance can diminish your sense of frustration and rejection. It takes a long time to build trust, and it's natural for the child to feel hesitant, awkward and guilty. For instance, if a youngster is nice to his adoptive mother, does that mean he's being disloyal to his real mother? But if he's antagonistic toward this new woman, isn't he jeopardizing his position with his father and within the new family? The child doesn't even know what to call the new parent. "Am I supposed to call you Jane or Mama or what? How do I introduce you to my friends?"

The more relaxed the adoptive parent can be during this time of adjustment, the more naturally and easily the new relationship can develop. It's difficult for a step-parent who's trying hard to meet with rejection. Nevertheless, he's got to be able to overcome his own needs and say, "This child is under pressure and needs a lot of time. I'm ready to spend that time and keep making the effort." The partner's encouragement and support are important, too.

4. *Husbands and wives should avoid comparisons with the past.*

In remarriage, criticism often comes in the form of comparisons with the former marriage. A wife may comment, "One thing I'll say about Jack, *he'd* never question my buying a new outfit. He always liked me to look my best. Sometimes I wonder why the hell I ever left him. Oh, I know you're paying alimony and it's not easy, but aren't we supposed to live, too? How long is this going to go on? When is she going to remarry? Hell, she's such a bitch nobody will ever marry her." The husband may react angrily, "Listen, my first wife wasn't all *that* bad . . . ."

Comparisons with the past are usually odious to start with and can be very destructive. It's far better to be open and direct with the present than to bring in the ghosts of the past and use them as means of letting out hostility.

5. *Realistically, the adoptive and biological parent are not equal when it comes to their relationship with the child.*

We've all been raised to believe that love makes everything easy and can even work miracles. "I love my fiancé so much, I can't help loving his kids. It'll take a little adjusting, but everything's going to be great." But this attitude doesn't take into account the feelings of resentment and hostility you have even toward your *own* children. How can you then expect things to work out easily with somebody else's child, where there's greater distance, less involvement, and more resentment and competitiveness?

The first shock may be in realizing that you don't necessarily love or even like the offspring of your beloved mate. Then, regardless of the affection you feel, you're surely not going to like everything about the child.

"I really think Jeffrey's acting selfish."

"What do you mean, Jeffrey's selfish? How can you say such a thing about a sensitive child? Look at your precious Debby. She saves all her tricks until bedtime so she can stall around for hours. Why don't you do something about *that*?"

It's perfectly natural for either partner to become uptight about a critical evaluation of his or her children by the new non-biological parent. The underlying feeling is, "*It's not your child.* If I or my former spouse want to criticize him, that's one thing. We're the child's real parents. We can say he's a slob, but we know we still love him. You're the adoptive parent. I don't know how involved and loving you are with this child. You have to earn the right to be critical."

I don't think there's anything to be gained by pretending there are no differences between the biological and adoptive parent. Of course there are differences, especially at first. There should be no sense of blame or failure if one parent says, "You know, it's really hard for me to take your criticism about Jeff because I can't be certain you really love him. I think it may be too soon for that to have happened. Anyway, I feel awfully protective of Jeff partly because I've seen what he's been through with the divorce and everything . . . ."

I've seen a great deal of anxiety dissipate or be replaced by relief and understanding after a couple are able to be open and discuss feelings like these.

6. *Discipline is one of the most common problems couples have, and in remarriage, it's an issue that should receive careful consideration.*

How are you going to handle the situation when a youngster

objects to a step-mother, "I don't have to eat things I don't like when I'm with my own Mommy, and I won't do it here." What happens when an adolescent says to a step-father, "What do you mean, I shouldn't use the basement to rehearse my rock group? You're not my father. You can't tell me what to do. It's not your house, it's *our* house."

How appropriate is it for the newly adoptive parent to take an active part in disciplining the child? Based on my experience, it's apt to create more problems than it solves. On the one hand, discipline can be a part of loving and concern for a youngster. But this new parent is just getting to know the child. The exercise of discipline has to begin very slowly, and the parents have to take into account the child's own stressful reactions to all that's happening. If the spouses discuss the various sides to the question, it may be wise for the biological parent to say, "Look, let's see if we can try to live as naturally as possible and keep the need for rules to a minimum right now, at least until we've really built up some trust and love. I'll try to take over whatever discipline is necessary because I find that I get very uptight when I hear you yelling at Cathy. You don't know much about four-year-olds, and she's just getting used to the new household and all the changes. She doesn't really know you, and she has to learn how to trust you. And she doesn't understand what's happening to Mommy. She's had me all to herself for the past couple of years, and now she has to share me with you."

7. *One of the most common feelings in remarriage is that there's not enough of you to go around.*

Sometimes, rather than take anything away from the children, parents shortchange themselves. They don't turn to each other because they don't want the kids to feel neglected. However, in order for this marriage to be solidified, they absolutely must have privacy and time to themselves.

The opportunity for time alone is one of the biggest differences between first marriages and remarriages where there are children. In a first marriage, there's the chance to learn how to be together. There's a great deal of freedom to make love when you want, to joke around, to do anything you want whenever you want. In remarriage with children, the need for some of this kind of privacy still has to be respected. The partners must carve out time for themselves and guard it scrupulously. It's best to make the children aware of this need, and perhaps allow them to take part in some of the decisions. "Your step-mother and I need to have time together. We don't know each other as well as we want to, and we have to learn more about each other, the same way you have to learn more about her and she about you. It'll be better for everybody in the family. So we're going to take this weekend off and go away together, and we wondered if you'd rather go to your Grandmother's or have Aunt Susie come stay with you here."

8. *The need for open, realistic communication can include children.*

Children can be brought into discussions of almost all the critical areas we've mentioned with beneficial results. Even a three-year-old can be told, "This is how we're going to be doing things at dinner time because your new Daddy doesn't get home from work until late."

I think it's especially wise for parents to say, "We all have to get to know each other to find out what we like about each other and what we don't like. And if we're hurt, let's always talk about it and see if we can make it feel a little better." That way you're giving them permission to feel angry or resentful and to get those feelings out, rather than hiding them and feeling guilty for having them.

If you and your partner can give each other the same kind of understanding, take the necessary risks, and share whatever is bothering—or delighting—you, then gradually, as your trust and empathy increase, the risks become easier to take and your relationship grows stronger and deeper.

PART 6: Mid-Life and the Later Years

23. Now That the Children Are Grown

For many years I saw couples who were devastated because their children had left home and they were now abandoned in the so-called "empty nest." Women in particular were apt to feel depressed, forsaken and lost. There's no question that this can be an uncertain time for people, especially if they have not resolved their own inner problems.

Recently, however, there's been a significant change of attitude. For the first time a lot of people are acknowledging that it's okay for the nest to be empty. Often they're relieved at having the kids out of the house. One woman summed up this attitude when she said, "We love it when the children come home from college— and we're so happy when they go back!"

The byword of many parents during the years of child-rearing is "wait 'til the kids are grown." When that moment comes, some people seize the opportunity to do more things on their own and also share more with their partners. They try new activities together, travel, move, take second honeymoons. Some even have their first *real* honeymoon, if theirs was a remarriage in which children lived with them from the very beginning.

However, I've also known husbands and wives who've awaited "freedom" with very different anticipations. "I can't break up the family as long as the children are still at home," one told me, "but once the kids are out, I'm going right behind them. I've been taking care of others and putting them first for long enough. Now it's my turn. My husband hardly sees me any more when he looks at me. But *I* see something else for myself. I've got a job and my own income, and I'm ready to grow. What do I have to hang around here for, when there's a big, beautiful, sexy world out there?"

214

In fact, this is a time when a great many divorces take place as people react to fundamental changes in their lives and their feelings about both themselves and each other.

Whether you've planned for it or not, the departure of your last child from home produces a dramatic change that's bound to affect you and your partner profoundly. There's a totally different feel to the household now that there are no adolescents always coming and going. There's a loss of the youthful energy, company and excitement that was pouring in and a loss of your identification with the young. You no longer have your teenager to bring music into the home and to tell you about the latest songs, styles and the "in" things to say. You're apt to become more aware of the distance between you and your child and also between you and your own childhood.

Suddenly you're not called upon to do things for your youngster. You're relieved of whatever everyday responsibilities or "services" you were handling as parent. There's one less mouth to feed, one less person to be sustained. You have less to do, and you have more time and energy available for reflection.

On a deeper level, the fact that your children are no longer living with you changes something about who you are. You have to separate from a role that has been a crucial one for you.

I don't mean to suggest that your children are completely out of your life. You probably continue providing an economic and emotional support system for them. (Some couples continue to focus on the children in absentia.) But on the whole, you and your partner have gained a substantial amount of freedom, privacy and time. You confront each other alone for the first time since the early days of your marriage. Now, face to face, you see what's left to keep the two of you together.

Some couples heave a sigh of relief and feel, "Thank God! We could never get a word in edgewise before. Now, at least we have a chance to talk and share." Other couples find communication difficult, even paralyzed, if they've customarily used the children as their main "connection."

Yet if the only problem were two people sitting opposite each other and feeling they had nothing to say to one another, they still might recognize what was happening and overcome it without critical stress. They could realize that it was only logical to need some time for readjustment and rediscovery. They could accept it as natural that with the children no longer bringing excitement into the home, they'd need to develop other interests and releases for their energy.

But the fact is that most couples at this time not only face

an identity crisis in their marriage, but also face their own great individual identity or "mid-life" crisis.

With the children gone and a crucial phase of your life completed, the question arises, *What am I going to do with the rest of my life?*

Childless couples also face this question, usually between the ages of thirty-nine and fifty. Parents, however, experience a much more dramatic confrontation because of the sudden absence of their children.

Depending on your personality, your past experiences, goals, dreams, drives, emotional development and physical health, you may experience the mid-life transition not as a painful crisis, but rather as a splendid opportunity. Yet this opportunity may or may not be—or seem to be—compatible with your marriage.

As the term "mid-life crisis" connotes, this is the time when you recognize that you've entered the last half of your life. The realization that death is approaching begins to filter in—not imminently, of course, but less remotely.

No longer do you feel that you can do anything. Suddenly time is running out. Certain options are no longer available or won't be for long. "If I really want to study law, or go on an archaeological dig, or change my life drastically, I have to make my move now or else it will be too late." A man may think, "I always expected to have a large family, now I wouldn't ask my wife to have another child, but I'd really love to have a baby at this point in my life." Fantasies come to mind. A woman may feel, "This is my last chance for a wonderful, glamorous affair. Soon I won't be able to compete with the younger women." Her fantasies blossom with the realization that a last chance *can be taken*.

At the same time, all too many people feel that almost all opportunities are over. They sense that life is winding down. Instead of saying, "This is a grand chance to write the novel, produce the play, start the business, go back to school," the attitude frequently is, "If I haven't done it up to now, I'm never going to do it."

With the children at home, you were always looking forward to something new happening. Now you may be in a sort of holding pattern. The kind of optimistic planning of the ascendant period is apt to turn into a questioning, restrictive curtailment of activities. Suddenly you begin to wonder whether you should bother to redecorate the house or whether it's sensible to buy land. There may be feelings of depression, frustration and futility that are compounded by other circumstances which may have become part of your life.

For instance, this is frequently a time of diminished energy and less than perfect physical functioning. There may be illness, which further dims your optimism. Even if your own health is good, the knowledge that your partner is sick can raise fears about what will happen if you outlive him or her. "What am I going to do when I'm alone? The children will be off on their own and I'll be left with no one." Fears about the future can darken the present.

Many people start having doubts about their looks, attractiveness and sexuality. For women, the sense of crisis is often compounded by the menopause. While a great majority of women—perhaps seven or eight out of ten—have no distressing physical symptoms from the hormonal changes they're undergoing, the emotional aspects of menopause are always significant. The woman is now at the end of her ability to fulfill what our society has regarded as her primary function: motherhood. If she's had no other purpose in life than identifying herself totally with her mothering capacity and her ability to become pregnant, then the loss she now feels is devastating. Even if she decided long ago not to have any more children, the option was open until now. Now the choice is gone, and she may feel a sense of despair, humiliation and worthlessness.

Women who are creative or productive in other areas may be much less troubled by the menopause. Many welcome the freedom from contraceptive concerns and devices, and menstrual inconvenience or discomfort. Furthermore, there can also be a heightened sexuality in some women because of hormonal changes. And yet there is still a finality, a tangible signal of aging.

Men may also be going through hormonal changes, although it's not yet clear just what the cause and effect relationship is between the emotional and physiological male climacteric. It *is* known that depression and chronic stress cause a sharp drop in the production of testosterone, possibly leading to sporadic impotence. Certainly men at mid-life are likely to enter a period of unconscious despair, humiliation at the loss of powers and disintegration because of the whole aging process. But one of the questions still being researched is whether there may sometimes be a spontaneous, age-related drop in testosterone levels, which can then cause emotional symptoms such as anxiety, irritability, moodiness, depression, insomnia, impotence.

Another factor which may enter your life at about this time involves a "role reversal" with your parents. If your parents are elderly or infirm, or if one has died and the other is left alone, they now need attention. No longer are they a source of support and practical help for you; they now depend on you to give them these things. This change heightens your sense of the passing of time. It can be frightening because it makes you confront your own vulnerability and aging through identification with your parents. Further-more, whether the parents' need is economic, social or emotional, it creates a burden for you and your spouse. Here you've just "lost" your children, and now you "lose" your parents because they're no longer strong enough to give to you. You have to take over the parenting, and it's natural to respond with anger, dismay and re-sentment. "Dammit, I don't want this at all," or perhaps, "I'm frightened, I'm not ready, I'm not strong enough." The sense of fear and loss can be sharp. "Just when the children were finally gone and I thought I'd finally get some loving care for myself, there are new people dependent on me. When do my obligations to oth-ers end? Who's going to give me what *I* want and need?"

Each person experiences the mid-life crisis uniquely and not necessarily painfully. However, the self-questioning and self-doubts that are its essence frequently lead to recriminations against your partner. It's *difficult* to say, "I've made a lot of mistakes in my life. I've made poor decisions, avoided taking responsibility for my life, and I've failed to become the person I might have been. Now I must face who I am and what I still can do."

It's easier to forget that as adults, we each have the power to lead and shape our own lives. It's less threatening to blame a part-ner for our disappointments: "I just opened my eyes and I see where I've been the last twenty years. What a *fool* I've been. I could have done all kinds of things, but you kept me down. You kept telling me I didn't know how to do this, that and the other thing. It's you who held me back all this time. If it weren't for you I could have . . ."

When someone feels he has wasted his life, there's a tenden-cy to try to do something about it—and one of the easier things to do may be to dissolve the marriage. It can be much more difficult to acquire new strengths, attitudes, values, habits or skills than to get a divorce and acquire a new mate and life-style. Of course, without the internal changes, the mistakes and disappointments of the past are apt to repeat themselves.

Sometimes doubts about one's own self-worth are displaced onto a partner: "All this time I've settled for someone who didn't really love and value me. I've just been a convenience. Well, now the kids are gone and I've got my chance to find real love and pas-sion." Seeking outside love and reassurance may be an attempt to get from someone else what you can't give yourself.

Very often people feel that what's missing in their lives can only be found outside the existing marital relationship. And some-times this is true. One can't have the consuming passion of a new love with a partner of twenty years. Of course, the new passion also will eventually be domesticated by the passing of time. One must carefully consider what's being forfeited for a temporary state of exaltation. Sometimes an affair can satisfy the needs of people at various stages in their marriage without forcing the marriage to dissolve. Whatever the decision, one must evaluate the possible consequences before acting on desires.

There's always potential in any basically good relationship for the partners to grow and change and help each other to develop new aspects of themselves. However, making these changes within the context of the marriage can be more difficult than starting fresh with someone else because you have been a certain way, thought of yourself in that way, and your partner has also formed a certain image of you. If you want to change, you may find it easier—or necessary—to seek out a new partner who sees you differently and who evokes different kinds of feelings within you.

Ellen and Bennett were about to become divorced when I talked to them. I asked if they were sure about this divorce. They said yes. I knew that Ellen had a younger lover, and that there wasn't much chance for reconciliation here. I asked if they knew what had been the most difficult problem between them. Bennett said, "Well, Ellen is not a very sexual woman. She's just not tuned in to that whole area." Ellen said, "Oh, that was before I met Larry. It's true, I thought I wasn't sexual, and you somehow perpetuated that myth. But now I find that I'm very sexual and responsive with Larry." For whatever reasons, her lover, Larry, was able to evoke feelings in Ellen that her husband didn't even think were there.

Partners may feel they *know* each other, yet individuals are different with different people. You've probably heard or even said things like, "I don't know why it is, but when I'm with Joe, I always feel terrific. He brings out the best in me." We each have many aspects, but sometimes there is such rigidity in terms of our responsive behavior that it seems as though we can't alter the reactions a particular person evokes in us, nor can we change our fundamental way of relating to that individual.

Marital therapy tries to help two people recognize on a deeper level the causes of a particular interaction between them, so they can, if they wish, find ways of changing the pattern. I worked with one couple, Audrey and Tom, who fought (among other things) over her wit and his lack of appreciation of it. There can be a variety of reasons why a man can't "hear" his wife's humorous side or doesn't respond in ways that encourage it to emerge. Perhaps in the original relationship, the man was the raconteur and the woman was the appreciative audience. He may feel he has lost ground with the change, or he may feel very competitive with his wife: she's getting the goodies, the response, and he's not. Because he's unconsciously competitive with her, he turns her off.

The wife Audrey complained to her husband, "You never laugh at anything I say."

"I laugh, if it strikes me as funny," Tom answered.

"Well, maybe your sense of humor needs first aid. It does seem curious that other people seem to find me damned amusing. Like when I'm with Richy, I make a lot of funny comments and tell stories well. If you ask me, it's because he really listens to what I'm saying, and he laughs when it's funny. You just sit there like a bored lump, and it gives me a pain."

"Oh, come on, Audrey. I know you're clever," Tom finally answered. "What do you want from me? Sometimes I'm just tired or preoccupied so I'm not a very good audience."

"Maybe not for me. But you've always got enough energy to laugh at others. Why should I bother making an effort with you? In fact, why shouldn't I spend my time with someone who appreciates me?"

I asked Tom, "How do you feel when Audrey is being humorous or when others are laughing at what she's saying?"

He shrugged. "It's fine."

"But I wonder whether you might not be experiencing something that you'd like to share with us."

He looked at Audrey and said mildly, "I think it's very nice that she has a flair for being funny."

"And yet Audrey has explained that she's not getting the response from you that she would really like to have. I wonder why that could be. Is it possible that *you're* not getting something you need?"

"What do I need?"

"There could be many things. What do you think?"

Tom looked at Audrey for a long moment. Then he said to me, "It might be nice if she were more interested in things I want to talk about. She's very good at turning me off and taking the conversation where she wants it to go. I may not laugh at her jokes, but a lot of the time *she doesn't even listen to me.*"

"Were you aware of that?" I asked Audrey.

She flushed.

"Well, is it possible we could do something about all of this?" I looked at each of them in turn.

In order to change the views that a husband and wife have formed of each other over years of marriage, it's necessary first to acknowledge that these attitudes *exist.* "He/she isn't interested in

. . . wouldn't like . . . would never try . . . doesn't think I am . . . doesn't want me to be . . . ." If you can see the premise you're operating under, then perhaps it can be questioned, reevaluated and changed, if it is no longer useful to you.

There is nothing more important at this stage in a marriage than to consciously open yourself to new possibilities, fresh ways of seeing yourself and your partner, and new ways for each of you to be.

In practical terms, this means:

1. Focus on the moment. A preoccupation with the past is apt to get you into trouble. Try to be aware of what's happening today, of what you're feeling, seeing and experiencing. Share these things with your partner.

2. Make something happen now, instead of allowing old routines to keep trundling you along. Take some risks and try out new ways of relaxing, communicating, entertaining, making love, being.

3. Realize that we all keep growing and changing every day; that there's always something new to be uncovered and shared. Look for the new aspect in yourself and your partner.

One of my primary purposes here is to help you unlock the potential that's inside you and understand that this doesn't have to be a frightening or threatening experience. Patients I'm working with frequently fear that the analysis will somehow alter the essence of their being. They say, "I'm so afraid you're going to change me into somebody I won't know." Nobody really changes a person. A person won't give up anything until he or she is ready. A great deal of what we all *can* do involves changing behaviors, modifying ways of thinking and granting ourselves more freedom to emerge as multifaceted human beings.

24. Becoming Grandparents

Becoming a grandparent affects individuals and marriages in a vast variety of ways. "It's the next best thing to having your own children all over again," one person will rejoice. "Oh, *no*, I'm not ready to be a grandmother," another will wail. And still another will feel relative indifference.

The way you respond to being a grandparent depends largely on your personality, your needs at this time in your life, and your relationship with your partner as well as with the grandchild's parents. Also important are practical considerations such as what is being asked or expected of you.

Let's explore some aspects of grandparenthood that most commonly raise questions or difficulties between partners.

A New Concept of Yourself

1. *Aging*

"I really don't want to be called grandmother. It makes me feel old. I'd rather just be Dottie." My patient was slender, lightly tanned and in her mid-forties. She and her husband, Charles, had first come to me several years earlier about some marital problems that emerged when their only daughter went away to college. Now their daughter was married and had just had a baby girl. Dottie continued, "Anyway, I told Charles how I felt and he said, 'That's ridiculous. You *are* a grandmother and that's what you should be called.' So I said, 'Well, I trust you're not going to call me that,' and he said of course he wasn't, but then . . .'' Dottie paused. "I suppose all this sounds a little silly to you, but it's been building into a real problem between the two of us."

"I don't think it sounds silly to be concerned."

"We went to this party last Saturday and Charles walked into a room full of people and said, 'Well, I never thought I'd be sleeping with a grandmother!' Now, I don't need that kind of crack. It made me furious."

I asked, "why do you think it disturbed you so much? What made it so hard to take?"

Dottie sat up straight. "It was like I was being labeled with something that was the opposite of pretty or sexy—that was a completely negative sign of age."

"What's so terrible about aging?"

"Almost everything!"

"Like what?"

"Like the fact that I can't play tennis singles the way I used to. A seventeen-year-old girl just beat me in the finals at the club, and last year I beat her easily. Sometimes I think this is the beginning of losing everything I have that's strong and good, and anything I'm getting in return in no way makes up for what's going. Sure it may be fun to have a little baby around again, but it doesn't compensate for the fact that I'm changing and losing my strength and speed and physical ability. This is the beginning of a downward direction for the rest of my life."

I said quietly, "That's a reality, and the only way to circumvent it is to die early."

Dottie stared at me for a moment. "But just because I'm getting older, why should I have to rush it? I don't wear old-looking clothes. What's so odd if I don't want the label of 'grandmother' pinned on me right now?"

"What comes to mind when you think in terms of 'grandmother'?"

"My own grandmother."

"And she was . . ."

"As I remember her, she was kind of heavy and wrinkled and she looked very old by the time she was sixty, when she died."

"And if you look around you today, is that what's really happening to the women you know?"

"To some of them. Of course a lot of others are getting face lifts and they look much better, or they're going to exercise class and it's not happening to them in the same way."

"So what you're saying is that you want to be one of the ones who remains as vital and young and affirmative as you can. And you're afraid that labeling you as grandmother will call to mind the old, stereotypical image." Dottie nodded. "It's interesting, because we have more grandmothers now and they're younger and living longer, so we really have to revise our thinking about what being a grandmother *means*. You're now forty-six years old, and part of being forty-six in this day and age and in your situation is being strong and attractive and actively engaged—and also being a grandmother.

"You've got a good thirty or forty years ahead of you if your health continues. You and Charles have to talk about how you want to live those years. To live them as fully as possible means living them in the present. It means trying to come to grips with who you are right now."

Dottie sighed. "You're saying the bottom line is that Charles is right and I should stop telling him I don't want to be called grandmother."

"No, I don't think that's what I'm saying. You can tell Charles and anyone else that you're not ready to be called grandmother yet. You have a right to be called anything that you want, but I think the important thing here is the acceptance of self at any given stage of one's development. And that includes accepting your own aging process. There's no question that seeing your body deteriorate feels like a betrayal. When your mind is vital and you hardly feel any different than you did ten years ago—maybe a little slower on the tennis court, but in general pretty much the same—and here you begin to see marks of age, you feel as though your body is betraying you. In a culture that emphasizes youth, that's bound to be especially painful. But this unnecessary and outdated dread of aging is something our whole society is going to have to come to grips with, because we are living longer, and no matter how many times you have your face lifted, there are signs of aging that are inescapable. Maybe some of our powers will diminish, but that's something we have to be able to accept, just as we learned to accept some other parts of ourselves that we haven't necessarily adored. And in the long run, we shouldn't see it as a diminution of who we are as total human beings. *You* are a total person with many facets and experiences and options and abilities."

"And one part of the total me is that I'm the club's youngest grandmother?" Dottie tested the idea with a quizzical smile.

2. *"I'm seeing a whole new side of you."*

In our society, men are permitted and encouraged to be more nurturing and sentimental with their grandchildren than they were with their own children. A grandfather may feel free to cuddle the baby, play with the youngster in carefree, childish ways. His wife may say, "I never knew you had that in you!" Perhaps she feels warm and pleased and enjoys his new tenderness vicariously through the baby or through his increased demonstrativeness with her.

However, if she's feeling pushed out or less cared for by her mate, she may discredit his new way of being and say, "Can't you see you're making a fool of yourself when you play like that and get down to an infant's level?"

Perhaps she can't do what he's doing. Or perhaps she's reacting to the subtle implication that if he's going to be the nurturer and caretaker of this new baby, he's not going to be strong enough to protect *her*. Whenever you have a modification of role, it can arouse all sorts of concerns about being taken care of. Yet by understanding the source of your anxiety, you often can discard many unrealistic fears.

3. *"They don't respect us."*

To a degree, grandparents undergo a role reversal with their son or daughter, and their son- or daughter-in-law. The younger couple are at the height of their strength and youth, parents in their own right. The grandparents may experience a lessening of power and control, and this loss can also arouse feelings and concerns about being taken care of. A man may think, "My wife was such a strong woman. Look at her now, trying to please her daughter, letting herself be bossed so she can be with our grandchild." A woman may think, "How can he let our son talk to him that way, without respect?"

Rather than allow the situation to make them see each other as diminished, it's far better for the grandparents to discuss what's happening, agree that the younger generation must do things as they see fit, and that differences don't have to indicate disrespect. Above all, the grandparents can reestablish their own strengths and capabilities vis-a-vis each other.

How You May Be Using the Grandchildren

1. *"They're our whole life."*

An excessive preoccupation with the grandchildren can be an attempt to refill the empty nest. It can serve to maintain distance between partners who need to be distanced, and also camouflage problems within the marriage. Just as focusing on your own children may once have enabled you and your spouse to avoid closeness and a real examination of your marital relationship, so now your grandchildren may provide a common interest that diverts your time, attention and energy away from the two of you.

If the younger couple are immature and want this kind of help and supervision, your involvement may have positive aspects all around. Yet it does tend to keep the young parents dependent, and in the long run, conflicts almost inevitably arise. The younger cou-

ple usually start resenting their dependency and/or your in-
terference, and demand the right to raise their children as *they*
choose. Meanwhile, you're apt to fight not only with them but also
with each other over how to deal with them, what they should be
doing, how the grandchildren should be raised, and so forth. Typically, you'll tend to repeat the same pattern of battling that you
followed while rearing your own children. The result splits the two
generations and the two grandparents.

If your involvement includes giving financial aid to the
younger family, then the situation is even more complex. You have
a heightened sense of power, control and contact. You feel more
important, more needed. But the young couple are apt to resent
control imposed via the pursestrings. Furthermore, you'll now have
the money issue to deal with between the two of you. "How much
should we give? What should it be used for? What strings should
we attach to the gift? Who gets to give the goodies?" Each grandparent may want to give (and to receive the ensuing response), but
neither may be able to tolerate the other making a unilateral gift.
So you find grandparents sneaking money and presents to the
younger people, and a full-fledged battle for power and love may
develop. Whatever the effect on the children, the result for the
grandparents again is totally divisive.

For everyone's well-being, the grandparents must stop
focusing on and using their children and grandchildren to meet
their own needs. They should look outward toward the larger world
and see what possibilities exist there to challenge and fulfill them,
so that they *can* relinquish control and let their children live their
own lives, make their own mistakes. I really believe that even if you
see your child/parent doing something you think is very wrong,
unless it's terribly dangerous or disastrous, you must not step in.
Don't tell your children how to raise their kids, no matter how
much wiser or more experienced you are. They need the opportunity to explore for themselves and to *be* parents and solve their own
problems.

2. *"Who's taking care of me?"*

More often than not, only *one* grandparent—usually the
grandmother—becomes tremendously involved with the grandchild. Her association may be by choice, serving among other
things to separate her from her husband. It can also result from
practical need. The grandchildren's own mother may have to work;
the young couple may not be able to afford to hire outside help; so
the grandmother takes over as nurturer, babysitter, caretaker and
mentor. But whatever the reasons behind her involvement, her husband may resent it deeply because he feels that her services and

affection are being diverted from him. She's never around. It may be great for her to be out helping the kids, but where does he come in?

Usually there are ways in which a grandfather can be included in his wife's activities. Sometimes he can literally be brought along; otherwise he can share by hearing about experiences and plans. But when this is not working and the grandfather continues to resent his wife's absence, I think the wife has to become aware of all the implications of her actions. Unless she's prepared to take the consequences, she'd better not put her children first, because at another time, they won't put her first. If her marriage is to remain viable, her primary relationship must be with her husband. This may seem like a hard line to take, especially if there's a real need for the grandmother's help with the grandchildren, but young couples *are* resourceful; they have ways of solving problems for themselves when necessary; and most of them would prefer struggling in this manner to assuming the major responsibility for a grandmother who devotes herself to them at the expense of her marriage.

3. *"The baby loves* me."

Vying for a grandchild's love, or trying to show your partner that you can be the better, preferred grandparent really says more about you than about the baby or your mate. "Just watch how the baby looks at me when I come into the room, and see—he's scared of you, look at his face!" If this is the kind of thing you're saying or thinking, you have to question what's going on inside you that makes you compete for and need that extra helping of love. Are you trying to replenish your starved shell through love received from the grandchild? Will that work? Has outside love ever filled you sufficiently? It's more likely that you need to do things that make you feel good and warm and loving toward yourself. I don't mean you shouldn't also want your grandchild to love you, but not as a solution to your emptiness. It's better for everyone if you all feel that both grandparents are equally important and that there's plenty of space and love for everyone.

Sometimes it does happen that a child is temporarily drawn toward one grandparent to the comparative exclusion of the other. Chances are that the situation will alter as the child develops. Or the next child coming into the family may vastly prefer the other grandparent. Nevertheless, at the time, it seems like a blow for the less favored grandparent. If you see that happening, it's helpful and unifying to give your spouse extra affection and to remind him or her that people change and children develop through many different stages.

How the Children May Be Using You

1. *"Who do you think is right?"*

Grandparents are often called on to mediate in the relations between the younger couple, or between that couple and their children. Under some circumstances, the grandparents can provide a valuable sounding board, present new possibilities and be of significant help. A great deal depends on their skill and the complex relationship between individuals and couples. However, requests for advice or mediation can be manipulative, attempts to curry favor or line up allies in a power struggle. (They can also be appealing ego trips for the grandparents!)

I think that if you're in a position of intervening with the young couple, it would be wise to assess the results of your efforts realistically. If you find *yourselves* drawn into fights, or if one of you becomes resentful because only the other is asked to mediate, then you have to consider whether you want to impose this strain on your own relationship. At the same time, what is actually being accomplished for the young couple? If communication there is poor and the need for intercession seems recurrent, it would probably be best for them to get professional counseling before their problems become more serious.

2. *"Other grandparents are always there. How come you're not?"*

Sometimes your own children resent your not being more available. Particularly if they've been dependent on you and haven't grown sufficiently in their own right, they may resent the fact that you have your life and are not totally involved with the grandchildren, there to delight in every bit of progress and to crow over every single performance that the little one gives at school. You may have to deal with sharp feelings of guilt that are evoked—but are absolutely unnecessary!

You can live an active, fulfilling life and love your grandchildren but not feel that your world revolves around them. You may also be among the many youthful grandmothers who were homebound for a large part of their lives and are just entering or returning to the marketplace or school. *There is a whole different world of grandmothering today, and some younger people aren't prepared for it!* If you explain to them that this is your chance to fulfill your own potential, your time for great enrichment and personal development, they may willingly revise their expectations. But sometimes it takes a tougher approach. One grandmother who was being alternately begged and scolded by her daughter finally said, "You know, I wasn't consulted before you decided to make me a grandmother, and I didn't expect to be. But now I don't want to feel guilty for being a businesswoman, any more than you want to feel guilty for making me a grandmother!"

Occasionally a woman gets pressure from her husband to "be a real grandmother and give up this idea of working." If he doesn't want her to grow more independent and enlarge her world, he may use the grandchild as a means of keeping her at home, saying things like, "You're off teaching and taking care of other people's problems and look, your own grandchild is being cared for by strangers." As we discussed in an earlier chapter about wives going to work, the real issue that needs exploring is why a husband feels threatened by this, and how a wife might reassure him, or share her feelings, and try to make the change as comfortable as possible for him.

Special Situations

Grandparenting can become especially touchy in reconstituted families when divorce and remarriage have resulted in stepgrandchildren. Many of the issues raised in the discussion about remarriage—such as allowing time for love, trust and understanding to develop—apply to all members of the new family, including the grandparents.

Another very complex situation develops when the grandchildren and one or both of their parents must move in with the grandparents. Great understanding, delicacy and care are required, along with a total redefinition of the structure of the household. Areas of responsibility and authority must be specified and a new way of living devised.

Although my purpose has been to explore potential difficulties that grandparents may have to confront, I don't want to ignore the special relationship that they often enjoy with the youngsters. Grandparents who are open with the grandchildren, sharing stories about their past and the family's background, helping the young people understand what it means to grow older, giving them an outside viewpoint and source of acceptance and approval, an outside ear, will have their own lives enriched. Such grandparents and grandchildren can find in their relationship a quality of love that is unique.

25. Retirement

In our society, retirement almost always creates certain difficulties which can put a strain on a marriage. Mandatory retirement is especially corrosive since it essentially takes away an individual's sense of control over what's happening to him. This is bound to arouse grave feelings of anxiety and resentment, coming at a time when one is beginning to feel increasingly helpless because of diminishing strength and energy and perhaps poor health.

In a culture where work is so related to one's sense of well-being and self-esteem, the deprivation of it naturally constitutes a blow. "I'm no longer needed. I'm not earning a living. I'm not useful. What good am I to anyone?" A person is now apt to be doing things that he considered trivial in the past. Our work ethic tends to make us look down on many aspects of life, including hobbies and pastimes that can be rewarding, fun and fulfilling. We're taught that they lack value or significance because they're not work-oriented. For some people, there's almost a shame attached to not working. "How can I waste my time this way? *How do I justify my existence?*"

A final negative factor enters the picture when retirement causes financial problems. A couple may have to make additional adjustment in their life-style. There can be real hardships and limitations. There may also be a pervasive anxiety about how they're going to get by, and whether they'll end up destitute and a burden to someone.

In a recent Harris poll eighty-six percent of the population of the United States was against mandatory retirement. But even when retirement is by choice, or even if people have made active preparations and are looking forward to it, there is still a crucial period of adjustment to a new way of living and being.

With retirement, a fundamental role **change** takes place. In our society it's still usually the husband who stops working. If he's no longer the top salesman, head of a department or respected doctor or lawyer, if he no longer has quotas and schedules to meet or meaningful business decisions to make, then his view of himself is bound to undergo a revision. Remember, the masculine image is one of being in control, being aggressive and having a certain status concerning work. When a man loses all of that and must then enter his wife's domain, his feelings of anxiety and castration are bound to be exacerbated. There has to be a time of very active and accurate redefinition of roles by both partners, a time of conscious rebalancing.

It's hard to say how one spouse will feel about the other after the rebalancing. A lot of buried feelings may be released. And since a retired couple are thrown upon each other, usually without children or anybody else, all their feelings tend to be worked through within the marital relationship.

I knew a couple who acted out an absolutely devastating power struggle over the bridge table. They came into therapy because they were just tearing each other to pieces in this "play" situation. The wife was cold and controlling, he was a hysteric, and the card table was their battleground. She'd say, "That was really stupid. How on earth could you lead with that. Don't you ever *think* before you play a card?"

"For God's sake, what are you talking about? If you'd given me some indication of what the hell you had in your hand. . . ."

"Listen, if you don't know my bidding by this time, you're obviously hopeless. I don't know how you ever ran a business."

This was a bright businessman who really wasn't ready to stop working. He'd made a lot of money and had used his work both as a release and a support. His home life had always come second. When he retired and was available, his wife let out her compulsive need to control by belittling him, constantly picking on him, berating him, and leaving him practically no space in which to live. This wasn't a new situation, but it became more crucial because he couldn't escape to an office.

The couple's relative social isolation heightened their struggles. Aside from a regular bridge game once a week, they had few contacts outside their marriage. The husband's former associations had been largely business ones. Therefore all the nurturing they were going to get had to come from within the marital interaction. That can be an overwhelming burden for even a strong and mutually supportive relationship.

The tendency for some people to become socially isolated is

one of the dangers of the retirement stage. People need to find others they can relate to, participate in group activities that are interesting and rewarding for them. The Association of Retired People is one large organization that offers its members all kinds of help and support, including special insurance policies, seminars, trips and a variety of other activities. Just identifying with the group gives people the kind of support system which is so important.

People vary in their attitudes after retirement. Some are so devastated that they lose interest in living. They feel the most important aspect of their lives has been taken away. They miss their friends and contacts from work. Their financial situation may make it impossible for them to continue living as they did before. In response, they undergo a total withdrawal, inactivity and depression.

Other couples can genuinely enjoy the fact that they can collect a pension and have the time for some of the things they've always wanted to do. This is especially possible if they're physically active and their relationship is a good one. One couple I know retired to Florida and is having a fantastic time. She's a former teacher, and he was in a union which gives him a pension. These people have had a cut in income and have moved to unfamiliar surroundings partly for financial reasons. Yet rather than dwell on what they don't have, they are constantly finding or creating new opportunities. They are both wonderfully adjusted to each other and have found a totally new life together. The wife started a little theatre group, the husband created a newsletter for their community and they're both taking cooking classes together. While this presupposes an inherent vitality, the support and reinforcement they give each other is equally important.

I haven't had many cases of marital therapy for older people, but I do remember one couple in particular. They were both in their eighties when they came to me. The husband could not understand what was happening to his wife. He was absolutely appalled by the fact that she would accuse him of being interested in other women. He said, "She *knows* that I've never looked at another woman. Why is she doing this to me? What does she want?"

Well, it was the wife's way of reengaging herself with her husband in a much more dynamic manner. Seeing him as a sexual partner was very important to her. This meant that she herself was having sexual feelings but didn't know how to cope or what to do with them. The three of us had to talk about sex and come to the understanding that it was fine for them, and they didn't have to ignore their desires just because they were in their eighties. I always think of this couple because just their coming to a marital therapist indicated how much they wanted to be engaged and involved, participating in the whole life process.

PART 7:
Serious Losses and Illnesses

26. Alcoholism and Gambling

There are an estimated ten million alcoholics in this country. The number of women alcoholics is rising sharply. There are between six and eight million compulsive gamblers. While these two addictions have different causes, their similarities are most significant for our consideration here.

Any marriage that has a compulsive drinker or gambler is in a state of crisis at best and going rapidly downhill. All of the trust and support that we've said are so vital between husband and wife are out of the picture. Everything within the marriage takes second place to the liquor or the game. The lives of both spouses, and sometimes the children as well, become ruled by the problem, filled with lies, fear, denial, shame, guilt, and often stealing and financial ruin. The addict will do anything to get the price of the booze or the bet. The gambler gambles away the family money. If the alcoholic is the wage earner, he drinks away the money and isn't able to earn enough to support his wife and children. Sexually, the marriage inevitably deteriorates. The alcoholic often loses interest in sex or suffers sexual dysfunction; male hormones are damaged by alcohol. When a gambler is married to the horses or his betting, his interest in women always comes second and is likely to involve companions other than his wife. Finally, while both these sicknesses can be treated, a true alcoholic or compulsive gambler can rarely be helped by a spouse or marital counselor alone. The addicted person desperately needs the support of either Alcoholics Anonymous or Gamblers Anonymous. This is a fact I try to make clear when I'm dealing with anyone whose husband or wife is caught in either of these self-destructive patterns.

Frequently the spouse of an addict feels somehow responsible for what is happening. I've seen people endure humiliation and even physical abuse in the attempt to help a partner break the habit. But the effort is a futile, frustrating experience. If you're in such a situation, you must understand something about the drives behind the addiction, your role in relation to the addict, and the options that are available to you.

Alcoholism

Alcoholism usually stems from a terrible lack of self-esteem. Various factors can be involved—guilt, inadequacy, helplessness, the inability to cope. But the pervasive element is the negative sense of who and what one is. With this disastrously low self-esteem comes the need to escape and use alcohol to blot out a reality that's all too overwhelming.

Part of the alcoholic escape includes a need to deny the drinking problem, both to himself and to others. The alcoholic may block out conscious recognition of how much liquor he's consuming. If necessary, he sneaks drinks, keeps bottles hidden in available places, chews mints, uses mouthwash, lies about why appointments weren't kept and work wasn't accomplished.

When confronted, the alcoholic typically continues the denial, and the spouse often accepts it time and again. Most of us don't want to believe our partner is lying to us or has a serious problem. For personal reasons, we go through our denial avoiding that terrible word "alcoholic." We may wait for and/or demand an acknowledgment. "I know you're lying to me. Why won't you admit you're drinking? I want to help you."

One of the best things that can happen is for both partners to recognize and accept the truth. Then they can go together for help, to Alcoholics Anonymous or Al-Anon, which works with the families of alcoholics. But acknowledging the problem is tough and often unbearable to the alcoholic's already fragile self-esteem.

If you're married to an alcoholic and you understand the need for denial, it can lessen your frustration and resentment about the constant lies. If you realize that the problem stems from within the addict, there's a lot less guilt. If you know what a self-destructive pattern alcoholism is, it may give you the strength to risk your partner's anger, overcome the denial and say in a loving way, "You need help that I can't give you. I wish I could, but I don't know what to do. You have a drinking problem and you have to go to Alcoholics Anonymous. I'm more than ready to go with you, to give you every kind of support I can, but I won't stand by any longer and watch you destroy yourself. I won't continue living with you in this way." Then, if your partner still refuses, you should go to Al-

Anon alone. They will give specific and concrete help.

One of the facts that has been demonstrated over and over is that alcoholism in marriage is always a *folie a deux*. There are always two people involved, and one is unconsciously helping the other to remain an alcoholic. This collusion isn't deliberate or malicious. You probably believe you're helping, but you are unwittingly feeding into the addict's pattern. Your scorn or pity may be just what he needs to perpetuate his feelings that lead him to drink. You may plead, complain, glare, reason or angrily lash out when your partner takes a drink; you may force him into secret drinking; you may shut your eyes to the situation; but the fact is that you're still there, maintaining an interaction which is resulting in your partner's continuing to drink. You're in collusion in the sense that you are not doing everything in your power to end the alcoholic pattern. As long as you insist on trying to solve the problem alone, as long as you continue to tolerate, live with, succor and support the alcoholic in any way except that which is recommended by professionals such as Al-Anon, then you are in some degree of collusion with the addict.

Perhaps the unconscious reason for this collusion is that you are afraid to separate; you may need the security of the marriage, and therefore continue with this minimal relationship rather than face the prospect of being alone. You may also unconsciously feel superior to the alcoholic spouse and more in control. There may be the fear of incurring the alcoholic's anger and even long-term hatred. "How can I call him an alcoholic? How can I say I'll leave him if he doesn't go to A.A.? Suppose he goes. He'll end up hating me for what I've done."

The risk is there, no question about it. A great deal depends on how the alcoholic develops during the recovery process. Ideally, he will gain a certain amount of self-esteem, be able to forgive himself, relieve his guilt about the past and therefore be accepting of you, too. He may be ready to have a different, positive relationship with you. But there are no guarantees. You must decide whether to take the risk or to allow this person to remain an alcoholic and keep what little you have within the relationship for as long as you can have it.

One cause for the reluctance to say, "You must get help or I will divorce you," may be a fear of the alcoholic's response to the ultimatum. "He'll go into a room and drink himself to death if I really walk out. At least while I'm here he's going to eat one or two meals a day."

Sometimes the alcoholic's reaction to an ultimatum is self-destructive in an immediate sense. That's a horror and a risk each spouse has to face. Nobody else can tell you what to do. I have said to someone facing that decision, "Ultimately the only real hope for the alcoholic is to confront the situation. If you don't take action because you fear your ultimatum may mean risking another person's life, you are still in collusion with a self-destructive habit that's going to eventually end up killing the alcoholic. It may be cirrhosis of the liver, throat cancer or an accident. No one can predict what will happen or how long it will take—nor what the damage will be to you and your children. In the end, doing everything in your power to see that an alcoholic gets professional help offers at least the possibility of improvement. Otherwise there's really no hope. It's just a question of seeing somebody deteriorate—and that may be the ultimate horror."

Gambling

The compulsive gambler is usually living the dream of winning out over other men in a male's world. (Historically gambling hasn't held very much attraction for women, although it's difficult to say what's going to happen as women become more aggressive and competitive in all areas.) In fact, the world of gambling is almost always a world of men. The fantasy isn't to beat Lady Luck but to outsmart and beat the other guys—perhaps with the help of the Lady or with the incentive that you then win the Lady.

Clearly the compulsive gambler isn't *really* competing in the man's world. He's playing out a fantasy, and there's a magical element to it. Usually his self-esteem is low, but he has a wish to increase it and feels he can do so by winning a bundle and showing everybody. In a sense he's more optimistic than the alcoholic, who tends to be more depressive and to anesthetize himself, blocking out the world rather than trying for the gold ring.

If a gambler wins, he gets the reward of feeling like a big shot. He makes a killing and everybody says how smart and lucky he is. They aggrandize him. Because of these exhilarating moments, gambling can be even more addictive than alcohol. Somebody with a hunger for recognition and importance can have all his omnipotent fantasies gratified immediately. The crowds gather round and watch him, point him out to others. Even if he hasn't done anything else in his entire life, he is now the star of the show. In contrast, the alcoholic never gets to be the star and usually doesn't even know the show is on. He may be the focus of attention for a moment, but quickly turns into a buffoon. Thus in terms of immediate reward, the compulsive gambler has one advantage. In the longer run, however, the gambler is equally self-destructive. He can't stop when he's winning. If he makes a big score, he winds up giving it right back to "them." He usually ends up broke, in debt or even eventually in prison. There is nothing he won't do to get the money that will give him his chance to make the killing that's always just about to come his way.

A compulsive gambler has his own style of denying what's happening and viewing it as something other than a destructive pattern. "You go to the track and it's exciting, it's a whole different atmosphere; there's clean, fresh air!" or "I'm doing it for you and the kids. Remember last year when I came home with that big bundle? Didn't you feel good? You felt great. We celebrated, remember? Well, it's going to happen again." Often the gambler reacts with irritation at being "misunderstood." "Look, what I do is no different from what all those big industries do. They all take gambles. Some make their Edsel cars, but then they hit it big because the money's out there just waiting." At other moments, the gambler feels distraught at what he's doing to the people he loves. He vows to stop. But typically he thinks, "I'll never get out of debt unless I gamble. I've got to do it."

Gamblers Anonymous is the best source of help for compulsive gamblers, and Gam-Anon offers the support, advice and aid that the family requires.

27. Illness or Injury of Spouse

In recent years I've seen more and more people who must learn to cope with the shock of serious illness or injury to their partner because today people are not only living longer but also surviving incidents that once might have been fatal.

The difficulties couples face are often financial and logistical as well as emotional. The stress of constantly struggling with daily problems and emergencies related to major illness should not be underrated. But the emotional upheaval can be confusing or shattering and takes a greater toll. The sick partner is bound to feel, "I'm no longer the person I was." The other partner senses, "My spouse is suddenly different and it's changing my whole life."

When someone is incapacitated by a heart attack, cancer, stroke or major injury, for example, it immediately places him in a position of extreme dependency. After he comes home from the hospital, the other partner may have to feed and bathe him, tend to the bedpan or help him to the toilet, and generally do everything to take care of his bodily needs and emotional well-being. Frequently the dependent person is terribly ashamed of being "reduced" to this position. Strong men and women are apt to feel mortified, devastated and full of self-contempt because they've always placed such a high value upon independence.

Furthermore, there's generally the fear that if one's dependency needs are allowed to come to the fore, they may disclose some dependency *wishes*. This, however, would be so unacceptable that it has to be denied and masked. So a common reaction is, "Stay away from me. I can do it myself." Even when a person is about to fall on the floor in making some effort, he won't permit anybody to come near him. Although on one level he may desperately want and need the help, he may be terrified that if he gets it or allows his desire for it to emerge, he'll actually *become* a baby forever and never again to do anything for himself.

The dynamic here is a very difficult one: how much to give and how much not to give. I think you have to allow the spouse to dictate how much he can or cannot take. It helps to try to be casual about it, to be supportive and helpful, but not to infantalize.

Suppose somebody says, "You don't have to take me to the bathroom," but you're afraid that person will fall and hurt himself. There's no harm in saying, "Sure, you probably can do it, but maybe you're still a little shaky. Why don't I just stay near you? You can reach out and I'll be there if you want me." In this manner, you're giving the other person room. You're not insisting on your way or totally accepting his evaluation. You're just staying close enough, making yourself available and saving him from feeling terribly alone.

In contrast to people who are anxious about their dependency needs, there are those who cling desperately and constantly to the partner. This is devastating to the partner, who after a while finds himself just wanting to throw off the burden. Again, the question is how much to give. The partner can say, "I do want to take care of you, but let's see how much we can do together to help you become more independent." Try to aid in the development of independence, knowing that it's not going to be easy because of the tremendous fear. Imagine what it must be like to have had a stroke. You have to relearn how to walk. You feel weak and frightened when you see that your feet don't go the way you want.

Finding out as much as you can about the illness and then helping to educate the sick one can help both people. It's reassuring to the invalid to know that he's not suffering rare and ominous symptoms, but that such things do happen with this condition. Learning about the illness enables the well partner to understand what's occurring and participate in the progress.

Often people are hesitant to "bother the doctor with a lot of questions," or they feel embarrassed to ask certain things like when they might resume having sexual relations, how often, and will it be safe? They push the subject aside and deny that they have any desires. That's about as destructive as anything they can do because it reinforces the sense of despair, helplessness and uselessness. If you have questions, ask your doctor and stay with the subject until you feel satisfied.

In some instances, a patient wants to talk about the possibility of death. It's vital for him to have someone to talk to. The partner who says, "Oh, come on now, don't be morbid," is denying both the patient's feelings and probably his own as well. In the face of serious illness, thoughts of death are natural for both spouses.

Rejecting the subject shuts off the sick person and isolates him with his fears and feelings. It also excludes any possibility of valid reassurance and perhaps leaves him burdened with the things he wants said and/or done.

One effect of a serious illness or injury is a change in the power structure between spouses. The dependent person doesn't get to make the major decisions. This adds to his devastating feeling of worthlessness, which can become a conviction that "I'm a total burden and I'd be better off dead." Sometimes the partner feels, "Yes, you would be. And I'd be better off if you were dead."

It's crucial to understand that people *do* have these negative feelings. If you realize this, you can say to the ill person, "It's natural that you feel badly. It's hard to be dependent. But it doesn't wipe out the person you are." And when you're feeling guilty because you're thinking that you can't stand all this for another minute, you can also reassure *yourself* that your feelings aren't horrible, but natural and human.

One of the most helpful attitudes that anyone dealing with a dependent person can develop is to continually think in terms of, "Let's see how much I can help this individual participate in the decision-making process, how we can involve him and aid him in achieving a better sense of self, control and worth."

In view of all that's happening, the "well" partner has to anticipate having many different, sometimes conflicting feelings. There's the sense of being bereft, of having lost what the other partner brought to the marriage. Often a person feels angry, confused and put-upon. "Why did this happen to us? I'm feeling strong and eager to have a life of my own, but I have this burden." At the same time, there may be a fear of what will happen if the patient actually dies and the partner *is* left alone. Almost inevitably there's resentment at having to handle everything. The "well" person may also suddenly feel helpless and panicked.

People really need as much support as they can get from family, friends and community, including organizations which offer various kinds of services. It's desirable and healthy to feel free both to accept help when it's offered and to ask for it when it's available. None of us is so strong and autonomous that he doesn't need others. You might tell a friend, "You know, it would really be great if you could come over one afternoon or evening this week. I know that Martin would love to spend some time with you. He's feeling low. For him to have a companion, an outside face, just a change from me, would be wonderful and I'd really value that." Chances are that the person being asked will feel good about being wanted and needed.

28. Ill or Handicapped Child

Except for the pain and despair of having one's child die, the anguish that parents feel when something is seriously wrong, either mentally or physically, with their youngster is probably the most devastating emotion anyone can suffer.

The parents' identification with the child as an extension of themselves, together with the old shibboleth about the sins of the parents being visited upon the children, is bound to evoke extreme reactions and feelings. Guilt is almost universal. Parents of a baby born with a congenital problem will frequently ask me, "What did we do wrong? Maybe it's because we had too much sex during pregnancy. Could that have endangered the child?" A mother may remember a medication she took, a minor accident or strenuous activity she engaged in while she was pregnant. Even the ancient, magical beliefs are suggested—"I saw a handicapped person on the street and I was making fun. . . ."

Our natural instinct is to seek reasons, causes and scapegoats, rather than accept our helplessness in the face of certain kinds of natural accidents. Along with self-castigation comes the blaming of someone else, usually the spouse. "It must be in your family. It certainly doesn't come from my side. There's nothing like this in our history."

Sometimes such feelings are unspoken, sometimes even unconscious, but their effect is certain to be felt. Imagine carrying within you a deep sense of guilt over something you or your partner "must have done" to cause this tragedy. How can you live healthfully, lovingly or honestly with yourself or anyone else when destructive emotions are gnawing at you?

If the child's illness is long-term, or if there's little or no hope for improvement or recovery, it's natural and almost inevitable that there will be times when the parents only want relief. They want to be free of this burden, even if it means the death of the child. However, that normal reaction can cause its own devastating feelings of guilt and denial.

For people who haven't been through this, it's impossible to realize what it means to acknowledge all these emotions in yourself, much less share them with your spouse. There may be such strong denial, anger or shame, such sadness and pain that silence seems preferable to words which only remind you of the anguish. Yet it's always better to let the feelings come out. Unless a couple come to terms with their emotions, the effect on them and the family is sure to be highly divisive. They must talk through and share their feelings, face what is happening and consider the implications for themselves and the whole family unit. If this opening up doesn't seem to be taking place, I think that seeking some kind of professional counseling is warranted. The parents need to be able to reinforce and support each other, to draw together in a stronger, closer relationship which can enable them to deal with whatever situation they're confronting.

The following experience is related by a patient I'll call Rita.

When our daughter Penny was about a year old, Al and I noticed she was having a very difficult time walking and keeping her balance. But she was such a good and sweet child, so bright and happy, we just dismissed it. At one and a half, she was walking, but she seemed to be constantly off balance, and she fell all the time. I really began to worry, and I questioned her pediatrician. He said there was nothing wrong. Some children just take longer to walk steadily than others.

Then, shortly before her second birthday, I went into her room one morning and found her sitting up pulling at her wrist. There was a tight rubber band around it. She must have taken it out of her hair the day before and I didn't notice it in the crib. I pulled it off and saw a deep, red mark circling her left wrist. When I looked at her other arm, I panicked. The left wrist, where the rubber band had been, was swollen to twice the size of the right. I immediately brought her to the doctor, but oddly he seemed to be paying more attention to her right arm. Finally he told me that her left arm wasn't swollen; her right arm hadn't grown. I was so stunned I couldn't even comprehend what he was saying. He looked at her legs, then gave me the name of a specialist to see.

Then came tests and trips to clinics. That went on for weeks. My husband Al had to work, so I took Penny and our four-year-old son Ricky, and we'd wait at the clinics for hours with the carriage, the bottles, diapers, food and everything. The final test was for Penny's nerves, and Al came with me for that one. They told me it would be painful for Penny because it required inserting needles up and down her arm so they could record the nerve strength and response. They said they couldn't sedate her because that would also sedate the nerves, but they'd give her a tranquilizer to make her sleepy.

I carried Penny into the room with this huge machine. She started to scream and wouldn't let me go. She was pulling me down onto the table with her. I pushed her away and ran out of the room. I told Al he had to go inside with her. I couldn't do it, but I couldn't stand the thought of her being in there alone with the machine and strangers and all that pain. I sat outside the door and listened to her scream for almost an hour. Then it stopped. They brought her out asleep. I asked the technician about the results and she said it didn't look good.

I wanted to take Penny and run home from this place so full of pain—just to be with her and love her. I hated them and I didn't believe anything they said. I was furious that they put her through this torture. I was also furious with Al and hated him for allowing them to do it. Somewhere within me, I'd always felt it must be his fault. Penny looked like him. There must be a connection in his family or something. I then recalled a scene from a couple of years ago. I remembered standing on a subway platform commenting that Al's sister should try to improve her walking because it was so pigeon-toed. I was pregnant with Penny at the time, and just as I said it, I thought to myself, "I shouldn't be talking like this; I could have a child that walks like that."

At the hospital they asked us when we wanted to come back to get the results of the test. I knew they were going to be bad. Everyone there seemed so negative, hopeless and overly sympathetic that I knew they couldn't or wouldn't tell us anything hopeful. I decided we should go on vacation first and take the news when we returned. I wanted to take Penny away and show her something of the world. I knew they were going to tell me she was going to die.

I never expressed any of my feelings to Al or anyone else because if I'd said them, I would have fallen apart. Al had been very quiet all along, and I'd taken care of the appointments and everything. I had to have some control over something because I knew I couldn't control what was happening to my daughter. On vacation, Al and I didn't talk about Penny except in terms of the here and now. Nothing about the future. It wasn't that we were angry, but there seemed to be nothing to say except sad things—so better that we said nothing.

When we returned from vacation, we went back to the hospital. Dr. Krauss took us in the physical therapy room. There, amidst ramps, exercise bicycles and all sorts of equipment, she told us that Penny had spinal atrophy, a progressive disorder of the spine. Al and I were stunned. I knew it would be bad news, but I couldn't believe it now that I was actually hearing it. I wanted to be alone. I didn't want Al to know. I wanted to protect him. I also felt that if everyone knew, then I couldn't tell myself it wasn't true. Al just became more quiet and never discussed anything with me. We had a silent agreement to remain silent. Looking back, my heart still aches for all those years we spent in silence because the situation was too painful to talk about.

Dr. Kraus wanted me to bring Penny back for one more test, a muscle biopsy. I refused. I had had enough of that hospital, and I knew that they would only tell me bad things. If it was spinal atrophy, there was nothing they could do about it anyway. I hated them and vowed never to bring Penny back. I would love her and treat her as naturally and normally as possible. I still had hope that she wouldn't die. But if she did, at least she would have as normal a childhood as possible. I wouldn't allow her to be treated as an invalid with people feeling sorry for her. She was too happy and bright to have all that taken away and replaced by sadness, fear and hopelessness. I wouldn't let the doctors with their tests, their machines and their cold verdicts condemn us all to a life of helplessness and shame.

A few days later, I realized that Al was talking to people about Penny. He called his boss and I heard him crying on the telephone. I was shocked and embarrassed. How could he tell a stranger and cry? How could he let someone know that he couldn't handle it, that we couldn't survive? I was furious. How could he act as if there was no hope? I wouldn't allow it. Suddenly I realized that the reason I hadn't wanted him to know the test results was that I felt he couldn't handle the whole thing, and he'd treat Penny differently if he knew. He'd be weak.

I saw my task as one of keeping the family functioning as normally as possible and showing Al how to accept a situation and live as normally as he could. He was very depressed. I was, too, but I put my mind to organizing and taking care of things. I decided we had to move. We had to buy a house with a porch and a large back yard so Penny could at least sit outside, watch other children playing, and have a safe place for herself. I let her older brother play with her and just explained that Penny couldn't do some things the same way he did, that she had a weak arm and leg. Ricky would get angry and resentful at times when he felt she was getting special treatment or that he had more chores than she, but actually he kind of understood. His friends would ask him what was wrong with his sister, how come she walked funny? It would break my heart, but he would say that just as some people wear glasses or braces on their teeth, Penny had a problem, but it wasn't so terrible. I told the same thing to Penny and her friends. It's funny that I could discuss all this very openly with the children, but not with Al. It just seemed so sad that it should happen to us that I could never really discuss it with him or any other adult.

After almost another year, Rita took Penny for a muscle biopsy. This time the doctors said they didn't think she had spinal atrophy, but rather one of the muscular dystrophies. The disease was in remission but the prognosis was for a slow, progressive deterioration at an uncertain time in the future.

Soon afterward, Rita and Al separated. Rita came to see me, and later I started seeing Al as well. What had divided this couple was directly related to the impact of their child's illness and their inability to share what was going on within each of them.

Rita coped with Penny's illness by denying what was happening or going to happen, which meant not talking to Al or any other adult about it and by taking complete charge of their lives in whatever ways she could. Unfortunately her major mechanisms of control and denial didn't allow Al to come into the process and participate. The effect was to exclude any mutual support system between them. This would place a tremendous strain on any relationship, but it was especially destructive here because of Al's personality. He needed to share his grief and anxiety and to try to find support and consolation. He couldn't take Rita's denying their tragedy any more than she could tolerate his sharing it. They had two such different ways of coping with a terribly difficult situation that it prevented them from supporting one another and surviving as a couple.

There are many subtleties within a relationship. What gradually began to emerge under counseling was the fact that the very things that had originally divided this couple might also reinforce and bring them back together. They each needed elements that the other could offer. In many ways they complemented one another, as was demonstrated by Al's being able to go into the diagnosis room with Penny when Rita couldn't. And Rita wasn't able to continue being on her own. I felt that with better understanding of their own and each other's needs and strengths, there was a reasonable possibility that they would reestablish their marriage.

Mental Retardation

The problems faced by parents of seriously ill or handicapped children are always highly individual, yet there are certain common elements in most cases. Despite our "enlightened" approach, mental retardation still seems to bring with it a special sense of shame. With a physical handicap or malfunction, you might say, "Oh God, why did this happen to me and my baby? Am I being punished for something?" But the absolute shame that's evoked by all the negative, belittling words like stupid, dummy, idiot, loony, etc. is not there. With mental retardation, there seems to be a crushing shame—"Look what's showing up in our family . . . somebody who's inept, who isn't up to snuff, who'll never make it or be a whole person." In a competitive society like ours, a mental handicap is regarded as the ultimate shame, disaster and defeat.

Parents with a retarded baby may have a terrible time accepting the idea that their child is deficient in this way. The strength of their feelings is related to their own need to be perfect human beings. Particularly if they're both intelligent, striving, upwardly mobile people, the fact that their product could be anything less than perfect is a tremendous blow. It takes a great deal of adjusting and maturing before they can see the child as someone separate who still needs help to develop as fully as he or she is able.

Gradually, we are learning to accept and deal with the "special" members of our population. There are six million Americans who suffer some degree of retardation, ranging from mild to profound. Organizations exist to help the families of the mentally and physically handicapped. And today we have genetic counseling and diagnostic techniques that make pre-natal recognition of many problems possible. Still, when parents do have an impaired or seriously ill child, their emotional resources are put to a crucial test.

Usually the parents must decide whether to retain or institutionalize the child. The idea of placing your youngster in an institution can lead to agonizing self-doubts. "What kind of person am I? What kind of parents put their child away? Are we doing the right thing?" Siblings may also feel guilt at their own wish to be free of this burden or embarrassment. Furthermore, they could be frightened at the idea that a parent *can* send a child away. It takes a huge effort to be open, loving and supportive with all the members of the family in order to make this decision and then accept it as being truly in the best interests of the whole family.

Today, there is a greater tendency to try and keep the child in the household. Parents must be able to be honest about their own temperament and ability to cope with this. Not everybody can do it. For a parent of normal or above normal IQ, dealing with a mentally retarded child can be emotionally frustrating in terms of the need for constant physical attention and patience. Depending on the severity of the retardation, there may be little responsiveness from the youngster. Sometimes the parents simply cannot accept the child's inability to perform at his normal developmental level and prefer instead to see the child as being deliberately helpless or trying to outsmart the adult. "If you really wanted to, you could do this. You're just not trying, you're just doing that to get me mad." Reducing a tragic reality to a power struggle is a disaster for everyone involved.

As the child gets older, the retarded adolescent may start acting out his or her sexuality, and parents often need counseling in order to cope with that. There's also difficulty in dealing with and fear in facing an adolescent's anger or destructiveness.

There's no denying the importance of financial means in easing some of the burdens of caring for a handicapped child. If you can afford it, you can get household help to give you more time and some relief, and you can have your home physically reconstructed to aid the impaired youngster. You can also afford to select the best possible institutional care for the child, if that's your decision, and then have a nurse or other qualified assistance in your household when you bring the child home for visits.

What's most important in making this kind of decision is to acknowledge your true feelings. It's always much better to confront reality than to live under intolerable pressures for the rest of your life. It's certainly acceptable to say, "This isn't possible for me. Even though I know that ultimately it might be better for the child if he stays at home, I cannot in good conscience do that to myself, my husband and our other children. I'm not good at taking care of helpless children. The frustration and burden would be so enormous that I couldn't cope with it."

I worked with a couple whose son had a degenerative disease of the central nervous system. There were two older daughters in the family who were normal. The couple kept the boy at home, but they experienced such agony watching this boy deteriorate, seeing the lack of motor skills and nervous ability, that it had a profoundly adverse effect upon the whole family. The mother felt she had to devote all her time to the sick child, and as a result, the other children grew up with feelings of resentment and anger. They felt neglected and also guilty for their anger with the situation. And the mother, a creative person who had always worked out of her home, was absolutely distraught. The total impact on the family was extremely destructive.

On the other hand, there are some families who can accept a handicapped child within the household. They seem to mobilize all their care and supportiveness, growing stronger and closer in every way. They seem to share a problem and a goal, which unifies them and gives them a special sense of purpose, commitment and accomplishment. The decision to keep the child at home is the right one for them.

29. Death of a Child

The death of a child is probably the most devastating experience that any parent can have. Fortunately most of us don't face this tragedy in a lifetime, but for those who do, it is both a personal catastrophe and a momentous crisis within the marriage. I don't think the impact can ever be anticipated, and it's not possible to try to deal with the subject thoroughly in a relatively brief chapter within this book. However, it may be helpful to point out in a general way what emotions arise and what the effects are apt to be on a marriage. Perhaps I can reassure parents that however terrible or hopeless their feelings are, they are not alone in having them. Others have had the experience, survived and gone forward with their lives. One national Chicago-based organization, the National Sudden Infant Death Syndrome Foundation (SIDSF), has been formed by parents who have lost children to help others to cope with their loss. There are other groups that offer help, as well as some literature on this subject (see appendix). Almost all parents facing this situation will benefit from some personal professional counseling, even if it's of short duration. Perhaps the following thoughts will enable people to begin to recognize the profound struggle they're engaged in and feel that there is no need to face an overwhelming tragedy alone when help is available.

Because a child is so vulnerable, so precious, and so much a part of you, and because you have responsibility for the child, you experience more intense feelings over your child's death than over the loss of any other person in your life. Even a miscarriage can be a terrible blow, especially if you had difficulty conceiving, or if the pregnancy was far enough along so you'd developed some relationship with the fetus. Unfortunately, well-meaning people often try to play down the miscarriage in a misguided attempt to help a woman or couple get over it more easily. But with miscarriage as with any loss, the crucial thing is to talk through and share whatever feelings you're experiencing—self-blame, punishment, fear, despair—no matter how irrational they seem. You may find some reassurance in knowing that you can try again.

A couple's feelings following the death of a child may stay alive for years, and the mourning is torturous. One couple came to me two years after the accidental death of their four-year old, an only child, saying quietly, "We can't seem to begin to live again. We've been talking about divorce as the only way to even have a chance to start over. When we look at each other, all we see is the child we lost and the pain we still feel."

Parents can often be marvelously supportive of each other during this crisis. But what happens all too frequently is that each tends to hold the grief in himself, to feel unconscious guilt, or to unconsciously blame the other. The tragedy becomes divisive.

Grief is the emotion that Freud called "the work of mourning"—that is, the process by which you eventually let go of or disengage yourself from the dead love object, and gradually transfer your interest and emotional energy to the living world. Until this happens, until the mourning is over and the transfer has been made, you have little emotional capacity for anyone or anything else. You have little interest in the real world because in many ways you are still "with" your lost one.

In order for the separation to take place, you have to settle your relationship with your dead child. This may mean coming to terms with intense feelings of denial, rage, impotence, fear, anguish, self-accusation and recrimination.

To some degree, everyone keeps thinking, "Maybe I should have done this . . . suppose he had done that." Some questioning and doubting can't be avoided. In cases of sudden infant death syndrome, the searching for explanations, the feelings of impotence and the sense that you don't know how to protect against the next time are particularly excruciating. But if you *continue* to focus on the questions and doubts, your life is arrested because you are bound by emotional ties to the past.

Some of the most difficult emotions to bring out and deal with have to do with your own "bad" feelings toward your child. You may be outraged at him or her: "How dare you do this to me? If you'd been more careful, done what I told you to, or taken better cae of yourself, I wouldn't be going through all of this, wanting to die myself. . ."

Part of your reaction can be a defense against your possible ill thoughts toward the dead child. There's *always* some part of us that's ambivalent toward someone we have known intimately, no matter how much we adored him. We all have feelings of hostility and resentment along with the love and delight. The negative feelings, however, are enough to trigger a defensive reaction of terrible pain. "I couldn't have felt this way about the son I adored so much. I couldn't have been wishing for anything bad ever to happen to him. It was really his father who urged him to go swimming that day. . ." The need to blame is often a defense against our own "shameful" feelings. Yet our bad wishes, whatever they might have been, didn't magically hurt the child any more than our loving could save him.

Some couples face problems that arise from the special relationship of one of them to the child. If one parent has formed an unusually close attachment, the other may feel as though he never had a chance, and that's another divisive emotion. There may be great anger: "You never let me get close to Mary. You just kept her all to yourself and now she's gone. Now I'll never . . . ." The resentment as well as the reasons for the one-sided relationship have to be explored and confronted.

Occasionally the child or the child's illness has been the matrix that kept the marriage together. If the youngster had a degenerative disease, the parents may not have had the time or the emotional energy to think about inadequacies within their own relationship. Everything has been subsumed by the preoccupation with the child. The youngster's death then leaves a void. "What else do we have to be concerned about together? What else are we sharing?" Especially if it's an only child, the loss can cause the marriage to fall apart. One spouse may also turn his attention to caring for the partner in a way that infantalizes him and makes him a substitute child to take the place of the one who died.

The death of a brother or sister has a great impact on the siblings in the family. They have to deal not only with a sense of loss, loneliness and abandonment, but also with their feelings of guilt about ill wishes they've had toward the dead one. There are always these secret wishes, particularly between two children of the same sex. A younger brother wishes to dethrone the older, or an older sibling wishes the younger had never come along, threatening to displace him. Frequently when one child dies, the other feels he has to take over the attributes of the lost sibling in order to make up for his death wishes about him. The living child feels he has to be both children to the parents; in this way the dead child won't really be dead—he survives within the living one. This is a burden which can eventually destroy a young person.

Even though the parents are devastated, they need to pool

their resources, seek outside counseling if necessary, and help any surviving children accept the death and feel needed, wanted and loved in their own right.

PART 8: Seeking Professional Help

30. Selecting a Therapist

People generally go to a therapist or marriage counselor because they're in some kind of pain. The feeling that there is something so deeply disturbing, unpleasant or frightening within the marital relationship that you can't tolerate or cope with it is what triggers most people to seek help. Sometimes there's a sudden sense of panic. You may wake up during the night with an anxiety attack, palpitations, a feeling of peril. You may have a sense of being unable to reach your partner. "I can't get through to him. No matter how many times I say something, it doesn't have any impact. It seems as though he doesn't hear me or want to understand my feelings. Is there something wrong with me? Am I not saying it in the right way? Or is there truly something happening between us that we aren't facing?" Feelings of pain, deep distress, panic or isolation are signals for help, and it is probaby needed as soon as possible.

Sometimes couples go for therapy with limited or specific goals. There may be a particular problem they're facing or a difficult decision to be worked through—about a major job change, whether to have a baby or almost any of the crisis points we've discussed. In these cases short-term, focused counseling can be effective. A couple may be having trouble talking to each other directly. Perhaps their discussions spin off into arguments they can't handle. Therapy can offer help in communication and in understanding the overall interaction.

It's wise to become alert to certain common signs that indicate some sort of stress or distress. Any of the following symptoms suggest the need to stand back and examine what's really taking place:

—ongoing fatigue that doesn't seem to have any physiological causes;

253

  —a feeling of weight on your shoulders, or the sense that you're about to cry and don't know why;

  —a new physical ailment (backache, headache, digestive problem, etc.), or one that has been judged by a physician as not "serious;"

  —the need for drugs, liquor or medication (even aspirin) in order to help you make it through the day;

  —sexual disinterest or dysfunctioning;

  —a change in behavior such as quarreling if you tended not to quarrel before, or silence if you tended to be quarrelsome;

  —a change in appetite;

  —a change in sleeping habits.

  For many people, seeking professional help is tantamount to admitting failure and acknowledging a shameful flaw or weakness. Our cultural emphasis on independence and ability, plus the shame we attach to mental problems, seem to influence the way we view emotional difficulties. Nobody expects a man with a broken leg to bend over and set it. But many people still believe that when it comes to emotional injuries, we should somehow be able to pull ourselves together, take control and straighten things out. After all, if it's *our* problem, why do we have to run to somebody else to solve it? If there are no stitches being taken, no cast applied, no medication prescribed, and all we're getting are some insights or helpful words, why aren't we competent enough to supply those for ourselves?

  In the first place the problem doesn't simply come from within us. It usually stems from needs we had long ago that weren't adequately met, conflicts that weren't resolved. Furthermore, the problem doesn't present itself plainly the way a broken leg does. It comes in all sorts of extraordinary disguises. Finally, many people *could* help themselves if they had the training. And to a degree, professional therapy does supply some of that skill and ability. Sometimes the wisest, strongest and most truly independent action we can take is to recognize our need and decide to go for help before our marriage is in a state of dysfunction. A person doesn't have to suffer alone. Help is available for those who want it.

  The optimal way of getting marital therapy is for both husband and wife to acknowledge the need and enter the venture together. Frequently, however, one spouse refuses or is reluctant to take part in the analysis and may be extremely negative when his partner wants to go alone. The marital problems which have existed to this point then recede and the key issue of disagreement often becomes the therapy itself. Now the therapy has become the greatest threat to the one spouse because of what he fears it will "do." Sometimes the partner can approach it in those terms. A wife might say, "Gee, what's the big deal about analysis? What makes you react so strongly, as though it's threatening to you in some way?"

"Listen, you're always running for help instead of doing what you can on your own. You want to be an artist, but you don't do the projects assigned for your course. You don't spend any time drawing. Then you're upset and unhappy with your whole life, including our marriage. You just need to settle down and work at what you want to do."

"Don't you think that if I could, I would? Why do you think I'm having so much trouble doing it? It seems as though I'm repeating a pattern, and I don't want to do that anymore. That's why I need to get some help."

"So now you're going to run to an analyst, like a little child going to a parent to hold your hand. That's typical of the childish way you behave."

This wife is apt to believe that this is exactly what she's doing. But if I could prompt her, I'd suggest that she reply, "Actually, that's not the way analysis works, and I don't believe my therapist would permit me to be a foolish little girl seeking help. I think my analyst would help me to become more autonomous. That's one of my goals."

If a spouse feels that his control is going to be questioned and wrested from his hands, and if he needs to exercise that kind of control he'll naturally resist therapy and try to prevent his partner from entering it. He may make all kinds of devastating remarks, including ones belittling the therapist. In such circumstances, I try hard to engage the reluctant spouse and have him come in. Once he's in, I can usually deal with whatever is underneath his manifest behavior. Many times one partner will tell me that the spouse will never agree to join even one session, but in my experience, there are almost always ways of overcoming this resistance.

One of the fears people may have about therapy is that it, in and of itself, will be the thing that tips the marriage and brings it to an end. That's a risk, and it does sometimes happen. But if the marriage was that precarious, chances are it would have ended eventually on its own. By seeking help, you at least have a chance for evolving a more dynamic relationship if the potential is there.

If a person feels terribly frightened at the possibility of "losing" a marriage, it may be helpful to question what other kinds of losses he may fear. In other words, "Am I making a true evaluation of the precariousness of my marriage, or am I really afraid of change and loss, afraid that if I take any step in my own behalf, I'm going to evoke rage, anger and rejection?" Sometimes this approach can give a different perspective to the situation.

It's possible that part of the anxiety about therapy stems from a feeling that you'll be changed, and as a result, you may start to see things you didn't see previously. "What if I feel that I can't remain in this marriage, that I have to leave it?" The realization that you're going to have a lot of the responsibility for deciding either to break up or try to maintain the marriage can be frightening and difficult to bear. Yet the therapy itself may give you some of the needed strength.

Selecting a therapist involves both personal and professional considerations. There is the question of the therapist's "fit" with you. How does this person strike you? How comfortable are you with her/him? Do you feel she has a sense of her own automony? Can you trust her? Does she respect you? Sometimes you can ask whoever gave you the therapist's name to tell you a little about her: where does she come from, what's she like, why do you recommend her in particular, and what does she charge? The final basis for making a choice is your own comfort and ability to relate to her. It's not going to help if you sit with somebody and can't bring yourself to open your mouth for weeks. That's especially true in marital therapy, where the participation is usually more active and vigorous than in individual psychoanalysis or psychotherapy, where there can be long pauses in which people make few comments and the treatment is over a longer period of time.

If you're not sure about the first therapist you meet, you can shop around a little. And you can ask for credentials and qualifications, which brings us to the other crucial consideration in selecting a therapist.

Most of the people doing marital therapy were trained to treat individuals. Marriage counseling, as it was originally called, is a new field. For a long time, it was largely in the hands of ministers and religious advisers because they were the ones couples traditionally turned to for advice, yet they really weren't trained to deal with most marital problems. Social workers treated the whole family, but didn't focus on the marriage. The situation became more critical after World War II, when great numbers of returning veterans entered young marriages and had babies while still trying to finish school. Many found themselves in difficulty, and there was a sudden need, especially noticeable on campuses around the country, for some kind of marital therapy. But at that time, the only professional people available even at the intellectual and teaching centers were psychiatrists and psychologists trained to work with individuals. However, starting in the mid-forties, the new profession of marital therapy began to develop. There was a lot of resistance from individual therapists who kept saying, "How can you possibly work with two people at once? Clearly these problems stem from intrapsychic needs and conflicts. . . ." There was little sophistication in terms of understanding marital interaction.

When I got my doctorate in Education at Columbia University in 1962, it was in the field of the family, and we had to struggle to get practical training as marital therapists. I went beyond that and got training as an individual therapist and then as a group therapist. Today, more and more colleges are offering courses in marital therapy, and I believe there will soon be a greater number of graduate degrees in this profession. At present, people take what training is offered, then seek additional practical experience by working under the supervision of marital therapists at various agencies and institutions.

Frankly, dealing with couples is very hard. I don't believe that it's possible for an individual therapist to do justice to the treatment of a couple. My own prejudice is that the therapist absolutely needs both individual and marital training. When you work with a husband and wife, you have to maintain a position of neutrality and be able to truly empathize with each. Therefore you need to understand what's going on within each spouse and be able to support him or her, raise the proper questions and see where this person may have run into trouble and why. This is the province of the individual therapist. At the same time, you need to be able to focus on the interaction between the two people, observe their impact upon one another and upon yourself. (Among the many emotions that are thrown at you is rage, which is less threatening on a one-to-one basis, but in a "gang war" can be alarming.) You need to understand why these two people selected each other in the first place, what made their marriage mesh for a while, and then what happened to disenchant the couple or create disequilibrium within the relationship.

Clearly, I think it's crucial for people seeking marriage counseling to find someone who has been trained both as an individual and a marital therapist. Today almost all therapists have had some individual training, so the key question to ask is, "Have you had special training in marital therapy?" Often the answer will be, "Well, I haven't had specific marital training, but I've been a therapist. . . ." I don't believe that's sufficient.

The standards for my field of marital therapy have been set by the American Association for Marriage and Family Therapy. In order to become a member of our organization, one has to meet very rigorous requirements. (They differ slightly from state to state, and there are presently eight states that have licensing and certification laws for marriage counselors.) The A.A.M.F.T. has lists of thousands of specially trained marital therapists, and it's one source where you can either check on an individual therapist's qualifications or else obtain some other names. The organization has headquarters at: 924 West Ninth Street, Upland, Ca. 91786. There are other societies and clinics where similar information is available.

I think the most common attitude of people coming for marriage counseling is that it's going to change the spouse. "I'm going to this therapist with you because she's going to tell you that you're wrong. She'll make you see the light." The therapist has to help people gain an awareness of the roles each one is playing in the interaction.

Sometimes there's a hidden agenda to dissolve the marriage. One spouse has already made the decision to end the relationship and is coming in with the hope that the therapist will aid him by saying, "Of course, it's clear that the two of you can't live together." In trying to bring out the couple's reasons for coming to therapy, I can usually recognize any such intent. I simply bring it out into the open. "There's nothing wrong with wanting to dissolve a marriage, but if that's why you're coming, let's make sure we know it."

Couples often have magical expectations and imagine that the therapist in a short period of time will reverse the whole trend of their relationship and enable them to go home with a great marriage. Such expectations of instant change are unrealistic.

People also come in with certain fears. They may be afraid that this unknown person will force them to talk about delicate issues before they're ready. A great deal depends on the therapist's ease at opening up crucial areas, and his or her sensitivity about not ripping away defenses prematurely. Building a relationship with the patient is vital. People have to learn that they can develop a trust in the therapist, and this may take a long time. The patient needs the opportunity to open up if he wants to, or to say, "I'm having trouble talking about that, I'm uncomfortable discussing something so personal." Just sharing the difficulty can be helpful.

As a therapist, I see partners both together and separately to give each one a chance to say things he may not feel free to say in front of the spouse. Marriage is the most intimate relationship in the world, but there are times when one doesn't want to expose oneself that fully in front of a mate. Gradually, therapy can help the partners to be more open when it's appropriate, when it isn't devastating to one of them.

It's not unusual for people to be anxious about revealing certain things to the therapist. "How can I say that? What will she think of me? I can't tell *anyone* certain things because they'll be shocked, and I'll seem like a terrible person." The part of us that doesn't want to be rejected and hurt warns us to cover up what we see as our worst faults. But a therapist doesn't judge in a moralistic sense. It's simply not part of our frame of reference. Furthermore, after a certain amount of experience, we're really pretty shockproof. We've heard just about everything. No matter what the situation is, we've been there and have empathized with what it must feel like.

What can couples realistically expect as a result of marital therapy?

Initially, there's the chance for ventilation—getting certain things out in the open and alleviating some of the anxiety. There's the opportunity for the couple to communicate more honestly in a "protected" environment, and ideally, to become able to communicate more effectively when they're alone together. A couple may learn how to fight fairly, make decisions more equitably, or generally relate to one another on a different level and in a more rewarding way.

They can realistically expect to recognize what problems exist within their marriage and gain insights into the causes by discovering where many of the difficulties have originated. They can begin to see both the strengths and weaknesses in themselves and their relationship. In the course of this book, we've seen that within each individual, there exists the child of the past whose feelings towards parents or siblings are transferred onto the spouse. It's this transference that often causes the greatest problems within the marriage. And it's usually responsible for our feeling that "it's all my partner's fault." By becoming aware of our tendency to project or displace onto our partner, and by learning other ways of responding to stress, one can begin to sort out what belongs to the spouse and what has been transferred from one's own past.

The couple can develop a view of marriage as an ongoing, dynamic process rather than a static situation. They can anticipate that the marriage will be different tomorrow, next month and next year; and they can learn ways of handling the changes and enhancing the good. Hopefully, they will continue to get closer to recognizing and realizing the potential that's inherent within each one of them and within their marriage as well.

Afterword

So many events, experiences and people prompted and helped me to write this book—the fact that nearly one out of two marriages is collapsing, for one, and my conviction that many of these can be redefined. One of the problems is the American concept of technological obsolescence: we think in terms of replacing the old with the new rather than trying to repair it—a tragic *marry-go-round*. I am deeply indebted to the hundreds of couples who have worked together with me to reinforce my belief that many marital problems can be creatively resolved.

More reinforcement has come from the thousands of phone calls we've received at Save A Marriage (SAM—a help-line for people in marital conflict) from every state in the Union—Hawaii to Alaska. Many callers have never spoken to a professional counselor before, and probably wouldn't if the call were not anonymous and free. Some of the most touching calls are from children, deeply troubled by their parents' discord and not knowing where to turn.

My own life experiences—motherhood, widowhood, divorce, remarriage—have, I nope, helped me to understand and empathize with the joys, sorrows, hopes and fears of people undergoing similar experiences. While some couples in marital distress do require professional help, there are many who don't, even though they might feel "help-less" in their crisis at the time. There *are* alternatives. And it's the intention of this book to point out and demonstrate fresh perspectives.

There are times when simply reaching out to a service like SAM—just the act of telephoning—is therapeutic in itself. Feedback from our callers verifies this, and I am indebted to them for giving me and my colleagues the opportunity to serve in this way, and to the many trained professionals who share their time and expertise by volunteering to "be there" to empathise, listen and advise. Their steadfast devotion throughout our many years of working and thinking, planning and agonizing has been, and continues to be, invaluable.

As do the "teletherapists" who receive calls at Save A Marriage, in my own work I try to listen through the symptoms to the dis-ease. The outcome invariably involves interaction in the family unit. When I began my studies twenty-five years ago, most schools of thought were concerned only with treating the individual—family therapy is relatively new. I was fortunate to have studied with professionals who had the foresight to believe symptoms can't be treated in siolation. In addition to my gratitude to those who have taught me—especially my main mentor, Dr. Bertram Pollens, whose staunch support, wisdom and analytic insights have helped me gain knowledge of the people I work with—I am thankful to those I've had the opportunity to teach. The precise questions and insights of my thousands of students and trainees at Columbia University, the American Institute for Psychotherapy and Psychoanalysis and the New School for Social Research helped to focus and crystallize thinking in the field of marital therapy.

A variety of analytic schools and techniques influenced me during my training as a psychoanalytic psychotherapist and as a marriage and sex counselor and family life educator. Although my first analysis was with a Horneyan, my basic theoretical underpinnings are Freudian. With increasing experience I find it most useful to think in terms of the developmental levels of the human being, so I am particularly indebted to the developmental-ego psychologists who have advanced Freud's thinking, and also to the object-relations theorists as well as the communications and systems theorists. Much analytical material has of necessity been omitted from this book to make it readily accessible to the nonprofessional. I trust this is in no way considered a disservice to the very profound analytic contributions of my colleagues and mentors.

In the course of writing this book with Barbara Lang Stern, I have not only grown to know and love her as a friend, but also have developed a deep appreciation of her professionalism in the field. My special thanks to Barbara, and to Dr. Pauline Friedman for her astute suggestions, to Evriah Bader, Barbara Bass and Kathleen Guerzon for their yeoman duty as research assistants, to Lucille Greene for her help and encouragement, and to Rosemary Rochester, whose skill and support were instrumental in bringing this book to completion.

Two very important people in my life also contributed to this book—Sam and JoAnn—my dearest friends. By sheer coincidence, SAM is my husband's name. Thank you, Sam, for your loving support. And thank you, JoAnn, dearly loved daughter, for your insights and constant affection.

L.J.S.

APPENDIX:
Guide to Suggested Reading

This list is by no means all inclusive. The books have been carefully chosen for their insights and accessibility to the nonprofessional. There are some gaps, simply because there are subjects no one has dealt with in depth. We hope the books outlined here will be helpful to those who wish to explore further.

Part 1: You, Your Partner and Your Marriage

Bernard, Jessie. *The Future of Marriage*. New York: Bantam Books, 1972. $2.25

Although men have traditionally resisted marriage and women have desired it, statistics compiled by the author show that men are generally happier with the conjugal life than women. The differing views of marriage held by the two sexes are described in detail. Varying types of marital arrangements are surveyed, including the egalitarian marriage, geriatric marriage, and "group" marriage. The author explores the future of marriage, possibly including childless marriages and ones contracted for a specific time, and how these new forms may coexist with traditional coupling.

Bobley, Roger, ed. *The Family Guide to Good Living*. Woodbury, N.Y.: Bobley Publishing Corp. 1973. $14.95

This book, which resembles a textbook in format, is composed of a set of basic and comprehensive articles on the family and its problems. Among the crucial topics covered: sexual adjustment, marital conflict resolution, drugs, alcoholism, depression, death, child-rearing. Research on these topics is interspersed within the text in an informative manner.

Brodey, Warren A., M.D. *Changing the Family*. New York: Clarkson N. Potter, Inc., 1968. $6.00

This book is highly theoretical and very personal at the same time. The author adopts a novelistic approach to convey some of his experiences with disturbed families in some sections of the text. In other chapters he describes the processes of communication within the family and the problems of the individual in the familial unit.

Mace, David and Vera. *How to Have a Happy Marriage*. New York: Abingdon Press, 1977. $6.95

In this cheerful but realistic text, the authors, experienced marital therapists, prescribe a self-help program for married couples. Over a period of six weeks, husband and wife spend a total of 24 hours working on exercises aimed at improving awareness of crucial problem areas: communication and conflict-resolution skills. It is emphasized that although conflict is an essential part of any relationship, surmounting obstacles can be the cornerstone of a permanent and meaningful union.

McCary, James Leslie. *Freedom and Growth in Marriage*. Santa Barbara: Hamilton Publishing Co., 1975. $10.95

An uncompromising look at the institution of marriage in order to assess its future viability. The author concludes that the survival of marriage is dependent upon its ability to foster creative development in the individual. Human sexuality, parenthood, and interpersonal relationships within the conjugal unit are discussed in light of the most recent psychological and sociological literature.

Ravich, Robert, M.D., and Wyden, Barbara. *Predictable Pairing*. New York: Peter Wyden, 1974. $8.95

Dr. Ravich has invented a game, called The Train Game, which he says can reveal more about a marital relationship in one hour than is commonly discernible after many hours of clinical observation. The game involves a pair of toy electric trains, with tracks and switches. A computer is used to read the couple's responses to the game. Dr. Ravich posits eight types of relationships possible in the marital liaison. All eight types are based on what he calls the Big Three, (the main types of relationships). The Big Three are Dominant/Submissive, Cooperative and Competitive relationships.

Sager, Clifford J., M.D. and Bernice Hunt. *Intimate Partners*. New York: McGraw-Hill, 1979. $8.95

When two people marry, each has a host of unexpressed needs and desires that he/she hopes will be fulfilled by the partner. These "unwritten contracts" may jeopardize the relationship when the spouse is unable to live up to his/her mate's prior expectations. Dr.

Sager reports on the use of the written contract in marital therapy, and reproduces several used in the course of therapy. The author presents his theoretical analysis of the marital bond, including behavioral profiles of different types of marital profiles and relationships.

Zerof, Herbert G. *Finding Intimacy, The Art of Happiness in Living Together.* New York: Random House, 1978. $8.95

The central theme is that unreasonable expectations and overly romantic ideals can frustrate the rewarding process of finding intimacy through living with another person. Intimacy can grow over time when two people build on their common interests and work at compromise. The importance of communication skills, acceptance of one's own needs as well as those of a mate, and developing a realistic attitude about sex are emphasized. At the end of each chapter, there is a quiz for readers to help them to determine how well their relationship fosters intimacy and growth.

Part 2: The Critical First Year

Ihara, Toni, and Warren, Ralph. *The Living Together Kit.* New York: Fawcett Crest, 1979. $2.50

A practical guide to the legal and financial problems involved in entering a marriage. Advice is given on such topics as taxes, bank loans, credit cards, buying a house and the laws governing sexual activity. The authors are lawyers by profession, and they try to supply the reader with all of the preliminary information necessary in setting up a household.

Kilgore, James E. *Try Marriage before Divorce.* Waco, Texas: Word Books, 1978. $5.95

Author Kilgore believes that many couples divorce before they have really had a chance to work creatively at developing a balanced and fulfilling relationship. By offering a realistic discussion of the possibilities of the conjugal life and a treatment of some of its inevitable obstacles, he hopes to encourage those who feel they can make their marriage more rewarding before they decide to terminate the alliance. A 30-day program for revitalizing and reshaping a troubled marriage is outlined, including both verbal and nonverbal exercises. The importance of conflict resolution and communication skills is tactfully stressed throughout the text.

MacCoby, Eleanor Emmons, and Jaclin, Carol Nagy. *The Psychology of Sex Differences.* Stanford, Calif.: Stanford University Press, 1975. $18.95

The authors present an impressively extensive review of the current psychological and sociological literature on the differences between males and females. Achievement, motivation, intellectual capacities, aggressiveness, sociability, genetic and hormonal factors, temperament and emotionality are among the factors that have been studied in light of the sex differences. Their findings explode myths, but there may actually be some differences between the sexes. Girls appear to be more verbal; boys seem to excel in spatial-visual and mathematical abilities and appear to be more aggressive. The authors argue that sex differences should not be reenforced by society, but that education should be geared precisely to helping each sex complement its own character by working against its weakness. Although the language of the text weighs heavily on the social sciences, it is accessible to the lay reader.

O'Brien, Patricia. *Staying Together—Marriages That Work.* New York: Pocket Books, 1977. $1.95
After interviewing dozens of married couples, the author selected six for intensive study. The couples all had successful marriages but differed in other ways. Some were celebrities, some "isolates," others are designated as "sensualists." The book is an artfully written text in which the author describes the dynamics of these successful marriages: a sense of shared history, the ability to respect individual differences, and the capacity to reject outside definitions or judgments of their relationship.

Viscott, David, M.D. *How to Live with Another Person.* New York: Pocket Books, 1977. $2.25
Dr. Viscott details the basics of attaining a relationship which is highly satisfactory to both partners, while emphasizing that it is impossible for any relationship to satisfy all of one's needs. Discussions are included on: how to set reasonable goals for the relationship; how to live by the agreements set between two people; how to recognize small problems which may grow and ultimately destroy the alliance. The necessity of starting out with a reasonable definition of a relationship and allowing further intimacy to grow from there is stressed. The capacity to have a good argument without becoming destructive is essential, as is the right to self-respect and privacy.

Part 3: The Impact of Children on Marriage

Bittman, Sam, and Zalk, Sue Rosenberg, Ph.D. *Expectant Fathers* New York: Ballantine Books, 1980. $6.95
Advice for the father-to-be, written by an instructor of prenatal and postnatal parenting classes and a practicing psychologist. They explore the emotions that confront a man during this time of up-

heaval, the decisions he must share with his wife, and such key issues as: sex during pregnancy—fears and fantasies, jealousy toward the unborn and newborn child, the role of parents and in-laws, preparation for the newborn and the changes a baby makes in marriage.

Brenton, Myron. *How to Survive Your Child's Rebellious Teens*. Philadelphia: J. B. Lippincott & Co., 1979. $8.95
Members of Families Anonymous (FA), an association of parents with difficult teenagers, repudiate traditional methods of working with the disturbed teenager. Without accepting the guilt for their offspring's problem, these parents try to examine their own attitudes. They focus their energies on changing the one aspect of the troubled home environment that they can control. If the child is truly unmanageable, they "release with love." The teenager is either asked to leave home, or it is made clear to him/her that the parents will no longer perform rescue missions to bail them out of trouble at school, court, etc. The important point is that the child is not rejected in the process; the parents simply refuse the subtle support of delinquent activity. Using these techniques, many families have been able to elicit more responsible behavior from their adolescents.

Feldman, Dr. Silvia. *Choices in Childbirth*. New York: Grosset & Dunlap, 1978. $7.95
Critics of traditional hospital methods of childbirth say it's a cold and cruel welcome into the world. Dr. Feldman advocates a natural approach which fully involves the family and creates a warmer environment for mother-child interaction. She stresses that different birthing strategies may be appropriate, depending upon the woman, and examines the pros and cons of these. Practical counsel is given on how to choose a doctor, hospital or non-hospital birth setting, and how to take advantage of community services for young mothers. Names and addresses of childbirth education groups and community service organizations are included.

Fraiberg, Dr. Selma. *Every Child's Birthright: In Defense of Mothering*. New York: Bantam Books, 1979. $2.50
Should mothers of young infants work? Do nurseries, hired help and day-care centers provide a child with enough emotional support? How does "substitute parenting" affect a child's future? Dr. Fraiberg explores these questions as she examines the intertwining relationships of children, mothers and society.

Heffner, Elaine. *Mothering*. New York: Anchor Press/Doubleday, 1980. $4.95

A plea for a new concept of motherhood, written by the co-director of the Nursery School Treatment Center at New York Hospital, Payne Whitney Clinic. Heffner takes into account the nurturing instinct of a woman and her important role in a child's development—without denying her own needs and her right to develop herself in ways other than motherhood.

Kappelman, Murray M. *Sex and the American Teenager.* New York: Reader's Digest Press, 1977. $8.95
An aid to parents in understanding the special problems of adolescent sexuality. The author stresses that young people should assume responsibility for their sexual lives and believes that by cultivating responsible attitudes, teenagers will be able to avoid extreme and destructive behavior. Chapters on teenage pregnancy, contraception, venereal disease, homosexuality and bisexuality help to prepare the parent for some of the typical crises which may develop.

Kelly, Gary F. *Learning about Sex, the Contemporary Guide for Young Adults.* Woodbury, N.Y.: Barrons Educational Series, Inc., 1976. $2.95
An introductory book for young adults about sex. Direct and informative with a clarity that the young adult can appreciate. Topics covered include: sharing sexual feelings, communicating about sex, marriage, problems with sex and basics of sexual development. The author offers the reader a non-judgmental treatment of this sensitive subject and encourages the reader to reflect on his/her own sexuality.

McGinnis, Dr. Thomas C., and Ayres, John U. *Open Family Living.* New York: Doubleday, 1976.
The closed family is one that is restrictive and authoritarian and does not foster trust and growth. In the open family, on the other hand, dissent within the family is dealt with through opening the lines of communication between members, and a trusting and supportive attitude prevails. Most families are somewhere between these two poles. The goal of open-family living is to help people relinquish the security of the closed life-style for the warmth and flexibility of the open one. The author attempts to foster a sense of compassion and respect for the coexistence of many different types of people within the familial unit.

Robertiello, Richard C. *Hold Them Very Close Then Let Them Go.* New York: The Dial Press, 1975. $7.95
A text on child-rearing, this attempts to present a balanced philosophy of parenthood, incorporating insights which have sur-

faced since the influential "Spock" manuals. Spock-reared children, the author feels, did develop the warmth and liberal outlook considered desirable at that time, without necessarily gaining realistic attitudes toward life and work. Many of the nitty-gritty issues of childraising are discussed, including thumb-sucking, access to TV, toys and comic books; relegations of responsibility within the household for household chores. Wider issues in infant and child development are also explored.

Part 4: Common Crises between Husband and Wife

Block, Joel D., Ph.D. *The Other Man, The Other Woman: Understanding and Coping with Extramarital Affairs*. New York: Grosset & Dunlap, 1978. $8.95
Extramarital affairs, the author believes, should not be prejudged as immoral but should be seen instead as something which may be either useful or destructive to the marital bond. Author Block examines the many different needs that can be fulfilled by an extramarital alliance and some of the possible consequences, both positive and negative, that an affair may have on a marriage. For the relationship straining under the burden of discovery of a partner's outside romantic interests, a chapter on seeking help is provided.

Bolles, Richard Nelson. *What Color Is Your Parachute?* Revised Edition. Berkeley, Calif.: Ten Speed Press, 1979. $$11.95 Hardbound; $5.95 Paper
Career counseling for anyone in the job market which avoids the usual formula approach. How to deal with rejection, how to search out unadvertised vacancies, how to choose the right career, and how to get expert help—the author deals comprehensively with these topics and many more. He particularly stresses the importance of clearly setting career aims and then pursuing those people and organizations that can help and avoiding those that cannot. An extensive resources section details places to get help.

Burger, Sarah Greene, and D'Erasmo, Martha. *Living in a Nursing Home: A Complete Guide for Residents, Their Families and Friends*. New York: Ballantine Books, 1979. $2.50
Two highly trained professionals show how life in a nursing home can be a full and dignified alternative for the elderly, and answer such questions as: how to evaluate and choose a nursing home; how to prepare for admission; how to comfort the elderly; legal rights of the resident and obligations of the family; physiological changes in the elderly; how to integrate family life into the nursing home. Included are a glossary of medical and health-care terms and a com-

plete listing of private, state and federal agencies.

Kaplan, Helen Singer, M.D., Ph.D. *The Illustrated Manual of Sex Therapy.* New York: Quadrangle, The New York Times Book Co., 1975. $14.95

This book combines an informed discussion of sex therapy with sensitive and evocative drawings illustrating sexual techniques. The approach is unexploitative and direct, and although sex therapy is discussed from a somewhat academic standpoint, it is easily readable. Six types of sexual dysfunctions are treated in detail, including the common disorders of premature ejaculation and frigidity. The specific erotic techniques used in the therapeutic treatment of these sexual problems are described and illustrated.

Masters, William H., M.D., and Johnson, Virginia E. *Human Sexual Response.* Boston: Little, Brown & Co., 1966. $17.50

Although *Human Sexual Response* does employ some medical terminology that might be difficult for the layman to understand, I would definitely recommend it. A classic in its field, it is informative, nonexploitive and comprehensive. Male and female geriatric sexuality and the use of the artificial vagina in women are two of the more controversial topics discussed. Also included are detailed descriptions of the male and female sexual response. A glossary defines defficult terms for the reader.

Milman, Donald S., and Goldman, George D., eds. *Man and Woman in Transition.* Dubuque, Iowa: Kendall Hunt Publishing Co., 1978. $18.95

The articles compiled in this book address many different aspects of the ways changes in American society and marriage are affecting the population. Several articles discuss the new sexual aspirations which developed as a result of the women's liberation movement. The role of marriage and divorce in the individual's search for identity is also covered.

Money, John. *Sex Errors of the Body.* Baltimore, Md.: Johns Hopkins University Press, 1968. $4.95

John Money, one of the top experts in the country on sex, has written an informative and compassionate book on sexual defects. Various defects, including fetal, hormonal, chromosomal, gonadal and internal and external organ abnormalities are described simply, with their causes and cures clearly delineated. The book is well illustrated with photographs that have a disturbing quality due to the nature of these abnormalities, but which could be very important to a reader wanting to verify the signs of a particular abnormality.

Schlayer, Mary Elizabeth, Ed.D.; Cooley, Marilyn H. *How to Be a Financially Secure Woman*. New York: Ballantine Books, 1979. $2.50

A management consultant and economist, Dr. Schlayer discusses all aspects of money matters. What should a wife in a shaky marriage know in advance to protect herself financially should the marriage break up? What should a wife know about her will, her husband's, and their insurance policies? What does a woman need to know to start a business? The author advises women on budgets, setting up a prenuptial agreement, investing, tax shelters and many other financial problems from the basic to the complex.

Shaevits, Marjorie Hansen and Morton H. *Making It Together: A Guide for the New Working Couple*. Boston: Houghton, Mifflin Co., 1980. $9.95

Psychologist Marjorie Hansen and Morton H. Shaevitz write about the problems faced by 30 million American "two-career" families. Problems such as child management, dealing with bosses when time or other conflicts arise, cleaning house and dealing with inflexible employers are discussed in detail. The importance of planning and setting long-range career goals for both mates is stressed. Although some problems (for example, sexual ones) may be exacerbated by the stresses placed on an alliance in which both spouses are employed full time, the author believes it is possible for the two-career household to offer a rich life, combining the independence provided by an outside career with the supportive and loving environment available in a happy home.

Shanor, Karen, Ph.D. *The Sexual Sensitivity of the American Male: The Shanor Study*. New York: Ballantine Books, 1979. $2.75

Dr. Shanor's nationwide report discloses the views of over 4,000 men of various ages and backgrounds on their sexual preferences, fantasies and attitudes. Among the many questions discussed are: how are men's sexual fantasies different from women's; do men ever fake orgasms; what do men like their partners to do; do men prefer younger women or partners who are older; how does the American male feel about women's new attitudes and sexual freedom?

Part 5: Remarriage

Goldstein, Freud and Solnit. *Beyond the Best Interests of the Child*. New York: The Free Press, 1973. $7.95

Two renowned psychologists and a legal expert argue that the final decision in a custody case should be based on an analysis of what will be the least destructive situation for the child, rather than on the presently used legal concept of the child's "best interests." This shift in emphasis would underscore that the child is already an injured party in these battles. If there is a conflict between the needs of the parent and those of the offspring the author believes the children's requirements that should receive first priority, for example, in cases where a child's emotional development may be enhanced by living in a foster home or in an environment away from the biological parents. The authors suggest that the child be granted status as a party to the custody case, including the right to retain counsel.

Krantzler, Mel. *Creative Divorce.* New York: Signet Books, The New American Library, Inc., 1975. $2.25

Divorce is a painful experience but it is an opportunity for personal growth if the accompanying fears, guilt and sense of failure are coped with creatively. Remarriage or the possibility of new commitments must be based on a willingness to face these feelings. As the author states, "to say good-bye is to say hello," and divorcees may well succeed in working through interpersonal problems if, after a period of mourning and adjustment, they use their past experiences to help prevent old problems from recurring. Counselling, when necessary, should not be seen as a sign of failure, but an attempt to make the difference between a happy or unhappy remarriage.

Krantzler, Mel. *Learning to Love Again.* New York: Bantam Books, 1977. $2.25

Author Krantzler enumerates "the stages of learning to love again" and discusses each in detail. It is natural to remember the pain of a marital break, but a creative commitment can develop if an individual tries to grow beyond that stage. The problem of stepchildren, possible legal difficulties and subtle expectations brought to the new marriage from past experiences are dealt with.

Reingold, Carol Berman. *How to Be Happy If You Marry Again.* New York: Perennial Library, 1976. $1.75

People who remarry may have a more realistic attitude than first-timers, says the author. However, there are many unique problems that accompany remarriages. These include stepchildren who must be adjusted to ex-spouses who "won't let go," and worries about finding a peer group acceptable to both partners. The author tackles these problems with clarity. A section on the varying life-styles available to remarrieds, with material from interviews with remarried couples, provides the reader with first-hand information.

Part 6: Mid-Life & the Later Years

Clay, Vidal S. *Women: Menopause & Middle Age.* Pittsburgh, Pa.: Know, Inc., 1977. $5.00
A matter-of-fact text on menopause written from a feminist point of view. The physical, psychological and social sides of menopause are rigorously reviewed, with little sympathy for the cultural biases about the employability and emotional viability of the middle-aged woman. The author discusses the dangers of estrogen replacement therapy, a form of treatment for menopause which may induce cancer, as well as nonmedical approaches to the problems of the menopausal woman.

Higler, Homer R. *Overcoming Executive Mid-life Crises.* New York: John Wiley & Sons, 1978. $11.95
In this text on the mid-life crisis, the author distinguishes between internal symptoms, such as depression and anxiety, and external symptoms, such as alcohol abuse and failure on the job. He places a great deal of emphasis on preventing the mid-life crisis with careful forethought and, if necessary, professional help. The problems of those in top management positions are discussed and treated with compassion.

Luce, Gay Gaer, Ph.D. *Your Second Life: Vitality and Growth in Middle and Later Years from the Experiences of the Sage Program.* New York: Delacorte Press/Seymour Lawrence, 1980. $10.95
SAGE is an acronym for Senior Actualization and Growth Explorations. Co-founder of their program, Luce's book is based on revelations about old age discovered in the SAGE groups. Attitudes about longevity, self-image, intimacy and sexuality in later life, dreams, sleep, healing and death are explored. The second half of the book is devoted to exercises and techniques to restore and maintain a full sense of vitality: relaxation, autogenic training, limbering exercises, the uses of art and music, nutrition awareness and meditation.

Rose, Louisa, ed. *The Menopause Book.* New York: Hawthorn Books, Inc., 1977. $12.50
Eight women doctors explore menopause. Included are articles on the emotional, sexual and physiological consequences of menopause and discussions of the risks involved in estrogen therapy and hysterectomy. A record of seven interviews with menopausal women provides an interesting view of the many different ways women see this important event in female development. An extensive "Resources" section provides names and addresses of

groups offering services to the middle-aged woman.

Saul, Shura. *Aging: An Album of People Growing Old*. New York: John Wiley & Sons, Inc., 1974. $6.50

In this "Album," basic descriptions of the plight of the elderly are interspersed with a variety of literary comments on the topic. Vignettes, short stories, poems and letters are used to illustrate the dilemmas of the aged from an intimate standpoint. Sociological and psychological material is used to counterpoint the individualistic approach with a realistic assessment of the deficiencies in society's attitude and facilities for those who have passed the prime of life. The myths about the uniform sexual sterility of the aged, the clichés about their inferior mental capacity and productivity and other stereotypes are debunked by the author. This book has a solid, humanistic approach and could easily be read by youngsters troubled by the aging or death of a relative.

Weideger, Paula. *Menstruation & Menopause*. New York: Delta, 1977. $4.95

A review of the cultural, biological and psychological ramifications of the menstrual cycle. A feminist viewpoint prevails in the cultural analysis and the author draws extensively on psychological and archeological research to document the reasons for her concern that needless societal taboos prevent women from adopting a healthy attitude toward their ovulatory cycle. Although most of the basic physiological and psychological facts are presented, the majority of the text is devoted to social and anthropological issues.

Part 7: Serious Losses and Illnesses

Brown, S. L., and Moersch, M. S., eds. *Parents on the Team*. Ann Arbor, Mich.: Univ. of Mich. Press, 1978. $8.95 or $5.95

Articles dealing with the lifelong responsibility of parents of handicapped children. The problems which are addressed include issues of the rights of handicapped people as well as their impact upon parents and other family members. Suggestions are offered to help to make daily living easier for parents and child.

Ewing, J. A., and Rouse, B. A., eds. *Drinking: Alcohol in American Society—Issues and Current Research*. Chicago: Nelson-Hall, 1978. $19.95 in cloth, $8.95 paper

A book of 18 essays which deal with the major causes and impact of alcoholism. Topics include a history of alcoholic beverages; social, personal and medical problems encountered among teenagers, college students and other adults; as well as implications for social policy.

Fulton, Robert; Markusen, Eric; Owen, Greg; and Scheiber, Jane L. *Death and Dying: Challenge and Change*. Reading, Mass: Addison-Wesley, 1979. Paperback $5.95, hardcover $12.00

A collection of articles and poems dealing with all aspects of death and grief: death and the child, funeral customs, widowhood, the dying patient. Originally designed to expand the general public's understanding of the problems of death in contemporary society.

LeShan, Eda. *Learning to Say Good-by*. New York: Avon Books, 1978. $2.95

In a matter-of-fact way, the author addresses the child who is trying to cope with the stark reality of a parent's death. It is emphasized that grief is a natural reaction, shared by all human beings. Recovery is also important, and the author tries to help prepare the child to say "good-bye" and carry on with life. An unusually sensitive, clearly written book, valuable for adults as well as children.

Murray, J. B., and Murray, E. *And Say What He Is: The Life of a Special Child*. Cambridge, Mass.: M.I.T. Press, 1979. $.95

This is the story of a retarded child and his parents' attempts to search for and connect with his basic human qualities. Told through narrative, diary entries and letters.

Rudolph, M. *Should the Children Know? Encounters with Death in the Lives of Children*. New York: Schocken, 1978. $8.95

Anecdotes of a nursery school teacher's attempt to help young children and their parents come to grips with the death of a young classmate. The experiences described include the death of animals as well as the death of family members.

Sudden Infant Death Syndrome Foundation, 310 South Michigan Avenue, Chicago, Ill. 60604.

Offers free leaflets and reprints, as well as some films which are available on a loan basis. While these fine materials are geared to SIDS, their content often is helpful to parents who have lost children through other causes. This is one of the few sources of literature addressed to the family members who survive the death of a child or sibling.

Travis, Georgia. *Chronic Illness in Children*. Stanford, Calif.: Stanford University Press, 1976. $19.50

The trauma of chronic illness in a child can have wide-ranging psycho-social effects for an entire family. *Chronic Illness in Children* comprehensively reviews the etiology, development, treatment and bio-psycho-social implications of a wide range of diseases, varying from asthma, to spinal bifida and spinal cord injury. Especially useful because the author discusses the psychological problems which may accompany childhood illness.

Part 8: Seeking Professional Help

Koch, Joanne and Lew. *The Marriage Savers*. New York: Coward, McCann and Geohegan, Inc., 1976. $8.95

A consumer advocate approach for the couple who have decided to see a marriage counselor. Short synopses of the prevailing philosophies of marriage counseling are presented in order to help the couple choose the type of therapy they will undergo. The intricate details of how to eliminate harmful or underqualified therapists, what to expect in sex clinics, and how to locate a therapist are unsentimentally discussed. For those who feel that their marriages simply need fresh sources of energy, a chapter on "Alternatives to a Dull Marriage" may be helpful. The names and addresses of marital counseling and social service agencies accompany the text.

Kovel, Joel, M.D. *A Complete Guide to Therapy: From Psychoanalysis to Behavior Modification*. New York: Pantheon Books, Inc., 1976. $10.00

This "consumer's guide" to therapy is a valuable review of the predominant forms of therapy being practiced today. These include: bioenergetics, sex therapy, marital therapy and Freudian analysis. At the end of each chapter describing one of the therapeutic approaches currently available, a section entitled, "Practical Synopsis," synthesizes for the reader some of the practical considerations which might enter into the decision to pursue that form of therapy.

Mishara, Brian L., Ph.D., and Patterson, Robert D, M.D. *Consumer's Handbook of Mental Health, How to Find, Select and Use Help*. New York: The New American Library, 1977. $2.25.

A comprehensive text discussing mental health care today. Detailed information is given on a wide range of topics, including group, couple and family therapy, drug addiction, suicide, and sexual problems. However, the authors use a "consumer's advocate approach" when dealing with these sensitive issues. They also present an abundance of material on the choice and evaluation of therapists which should be reviewed by those seeking help. Problems in psychotherapeutic relationships are discussed, including sexual attractions and personality conflicts between patient and therapist.